Big Data and Decision-Making

EMERALD STUDIES IN POLITICS AND TECHNOLOGY

Series Editors: Anna Visvizi and Miltiadis D. Lytras

This series focuses broadly on the intersection of politics and technology. Its objective is to identify and explore the critical junctions where politics and information and communication technology (ICT) intersect to showcase the opportunities, raise awareness, and preempt impending risks for our societies.

The series has a broad scope and addresses a variety of topics, including but not limited to the following: cyber-intelligence; government analytics; user-generated data and its impact on human society; technology in healthcare and public services; quantitative measures in political discourse; public engagement with politics through technology for example, blogs and social media; freedom of the internet; text mining; e-participation in politics and digital diplomacy; international trade on the ICT market; information security risks; political communication in online social networks; big data; e-government and e-democracy; digital activism; ICT in developing nations; digital media; smart cities; disruptive effects of technology in politics; internet governance; citizen journalism; the politics of migration and ICT; and the European Union and ICT.

Interested in publishing in this series? Please contact Anna Visvizi and Miltiadis D. Lytras, avisvizi@acg.edu and mlytras@acg.edu.

Big Data and Decision-Making: Applications and Uses in the Public and Private Sector

EDITED BY

ANNA VISVIZI

SGH Warsaw School of Economics, Poland & The American College of Greece, Greece

ORLANDO TROISI

University of Salerno, Italy

AND

MARA GRIMALDI

University of Salerno, Italy

emerald PUBLISHING

United Kingdom – North America – Japan – India – Malaysia – China

Emerald Publishing Limited
Howard House, Wagon Lane, Bingley BD16 1WA, UK

First edition 2023

British Library Cataloguing in Publication Data
A catalogue record for this book is available from the British Library

ISBN: 978-1-80382-552-6 (Print)
ISBN: 978-1-80382-551-9 (Online)
ISBN: 978-1-80382-553-3 (Epub)

Printed and bound by CPI Group (UK) Ltd, Croydon, CR0 4YY

ISOQAR certified
Management System,
awarded to Emerald
for adherence to
Environmental
standard
ISO 14001:2004.

ISOQAR
REGISTERED
Certificate Number 1985
ISO 14001

INVESTOR IN PEOPLE

Contents

List of Figures

List of Tables

About the Contributors

Otmane Azeroual is a Senior Researcher and Project Manager at the German Centre for Higher Education Research and Science Studies and Assistant Professor in the Digital Business and Data Science course at the European University of Applied Sciences. He did his PhD in Engineering Informatics at Otto von Guericke University in Magdeburg and is an expert in the fields of databases and information systems and artificial intelligence.

Antonio Botti is a Full Professor of Management, Department of Management and Innovation Systems, University of Salerno, Italy, Affiliate Research Fellow, Ipag Business School, Paris. He is a member of various editorial committees of Italian and international academic journals. Recently, his research activity has focused on entrepreneurship and issues related to performance evaluation.

Vilma Çekani is a PhD student in Big Data Management at the Department of Business Sciences – Management and Innovation Systems of the University of Salerno. Currently, her main fields of interest are business intelligence, management, and marketing.

Mario D'Arco is a Research Fellow at the University of Sannio, Italy. He graduated in Semiotic at the University of Bologna and has a PhD in Marketing and Communication. His main research interests are linked to marketing, consumer behavior, and branding.

Artjoms Daskevics is a first year master student at University of Latvia, Faculty of Computing. He holds a bachelor degree in Computer Science, with the bachelor thesis devoted to the database security, developed under Assistant Prof. Nikiforova's supervision.

Benedetta Esposito is a PhD student in Big Data Management in the Department of Management and Innovation Systems at the University of Salerno. Her research is mainly focused on corporate social responsibility, sustainability, and circular economy in the agri-food sector.

Mara Grimaldi is a Research Fellow at the University of Salerno, Department of Business Science, Management and Innovation Systems. Her main areas of interest are: services marketing and management, information and knowledge management, and strategic innovation management.

Gianluca Maria Guazzo is a PhD student in Big Data Management at the Department of Business Sciences – Management and Innovation Systems of the University of Salerno. At present, his main fields of interest concern big data and its implications, marketing, and consumer behavior.

Xhimi Hysa is a Professor of Management and Dean of the Faculty of Management, Environment, and Urban Planning, at POLIS University. His research profile is interdisciplinary, ranging from systems theory to social business and sustainability, service science, and group dynamics.

Anne-Mari Järvenpää is a Senior Lecturer at Häme University of Applied Sciences, Finland, Department of Information and Communication Technology, Bioeconomy.

Jari Jussila is Director of HAMK Design Factory at Häme University of Applied Sciences, Finland.

Joana Kostaqi is a freelance Social Media Marketer. She is a business graduate from EPOKA University. Her research interests are mainly focused on digital marketing, data protection, and privacy. She is also an entrepreneur, running a family business.

Iivari Kunttu holds a PhD in Information Technology (2005), PhD in Economics (2017), and MA in Education (2020). Currently, he is the Leading Research Scientist in Häme University of Applied Sciences, Finland. His current research interests include R&D and innovation management, data analysis, business development, and digital services.

Giulia Leoni, PhD in Management and Law – Curriculum Business and Administration, Department of Management, Polytechnic University of Marche (Ancona). Her research interests include performance measurement and management systems, accounting and accountability in public administration, inter-municipal cooperation, and amalgamation processes.

Francesca Loia is a Research Fellow at the Department of Economics, Management and Institutions – University of Naples "Federico II." She is the author of many international scientific publications. She served as Visiting Scholar at Deree College – The American College of Greece, Faculty of Management Information Systems – MIS.

Ruslana Lutsiv is a PhD student at the Department of International Economic Relations, West Ukrainian National University, Ternopil, Ukraine.

Gennaro Maione, PhD, is a Researcher of Business Administration, Department of Economics and Statistics, University of Salerno, Fisciano, Italy. His research interests include environmental accounting, accountability, and digital technology.

Ornella Malandrino is a Full Professor of Commodity Science at the University of Salerno, where she teaches and conducts research on quality, sustainability, and corporate social responsibility. She is the Inter-departmental Observatory Director for Gender Studies and Equal Opportunities at the University of Salerno.

Radosław Malik, PhD, is an Assistant Professor of SGH Warsaw School of Economics, Institute of International Studies, International Political Economy Department. He is an Initiator of the SGH Young Scientist program workshop series. His research interests include offshoring and outsourcing, the labor market, megatrends, innovation in services, and science mapping analysis.

Luca Mazzara is an Associate Professor in Business Administration and Accounting Studies, Business and Public Institutions Economics – Department of Management, University of Bologna (Forlì Campus). He is the Director of the Master in City Management, University of Bologna (Forlì Campus). His research interests include performance measurement and management systems, territorial governance process and tools, inter-municipal cooperation and amalgamation processes, and internal control systems in public administration.

Antonietta Megaro, PhD in Management and Information Technology, Curriculum Marketing, at the University of Salerno (Italy) – Department of Business Sciences, Management and Innovation Systems. She graduated in Accounting at Sapienza University of Rome. Her main research interests focus on service research and systems theory.

Antonella Monda, PhD, is a member of the LISA Lab (Laboratory in Innovative Entrepreneurship and Academic Spin-offs), University of Salerno, Italy. Her research interests include technology and innovation across fields and issues.

Anastasija Nikiforova is a Researcher (PhD in Comp. Sc.), whose research interests include data management with a particular focus on data quality, open government data, Smart City, Society 5.0, sustainable development, internet of things (IoT) human-computer interaction (HCI) and digitization. She is an Assistant Professor of Information Systems at University of Tartu (Institute of Computer Science), a part of European Open Science Cloud Task Force "FAIR Metrics and Data Quality," a Visiting Researcher at Delft University of Technology, and an expert of the Latvian Council of Sciences.

Katarzyna Rybkowska is a PhD student at the SGH Warsaw School of Economics in Field Management and Quality Sciences. Her research interests are focused on agile project management, digitalization, and e-business.

Maria Rosaria Sessa has a PhD in Management and Information Technology and Research Fellow in Commodity Science in the Department of Management and Innovation Systems at the University of Salerno, where she teaches quality management and control of tourist service. Her research mainly focuses on developing quality and environmental management systems, corporate social responsibility, environmental assessment tools, and competence certification.

Daniela Sica has a PhD in Commodity Science and is a Lecturer in Quality Management and Control of Tourist Service in the Department of Management and Innovation Systems at the University of Salerno. Her research interests mainly focus on the sustainable production process, quality management systems, and corporate social responsibility.

Olena Sokhatska is a Full Professor of Department of International Economic Relations, West Ukrainian National University, Ternopil, Ukraine.

Orlando Troisi is Associate Professor in Business Management at the Department of Business Science – Management and Innovation Systems, University of Salerno. His main research interests focus on service research and, in particular, value co-creation, public management, and governance. He is author of numerous papers published in national and international journals.

Anna Visvizi, PhD (dr hab.) is Associate Professor at SGH Warsaw School of Economics & Visiting Professor at Effat University, KSA. An economist and political scientist, she is an experienced editor and researcher, as well as political consultant with extensive experience in academia, think-tank and government sectors in Europe, including the OECD. Her expertise covers issues pertinent to the intersection of politics, economics and ICT.

Editors' Preface

Very few topics remain as opaque and unclear to the broader public today as "big data". Similarly, as artificial intelligence, big data has turned into a buzzword of our times, frequently deployed absolutely uncritically as a veil usurping to be an explanation. Against this backdrop, the rationale behind this book was to offer a simple, but not simplistic, insight into the realm of big data, its application, and implications. The selections of chapters included in this book will guide the reader through diverse fields and domains of big data's use and application, including public policy, the business sector, including managerial practices, as well as smart cities' growth and management. This book is by no means exhaustive. Rather, it recognizes the value of the debate unfolding in the literature. By so doing it seeks to add to the debate in a manner that may be useful to researchers, practitioners, as well as to those of us who are also involved in teaching. The idea here is that all frequently topics pertaining to big data constitute either a part of papers too sophisticated for an average student to comprehend, or form a part of overly simplified, even if fancy, magazine content. And yet, it is mandatory that similarly as in our research, also in our teaching we go beyond what the curriculum defines as needed.

This book is a tribute to teamwork in that it would not be possible without the Publisher, especially the Commissioning Editor, Ms Iram [ir-rum] Satti who embraced the idea of the book and skillfully guided us through the initial reviews and the subsequent production process. We would also like thank the reviewers and the contributing authors. We remain grateful to the entire production team, who were consequential in the stages of the cover design, proofs, etc. In brief, a great number of people, forming a virtual team, collaborated to have this book delivered. We, the Editors, can only hope that this book will be of use to the broader audience.

We dedicate this book to fellow researchers, who – similarly as we do – seek to find a balance between the idealistic urge to explore and conduct research, the necessity to make ends meet by delivering on the teaching load, and private life.

The Editors: Anna Visvizi, Orlando Troisi
and Mara Grimaldi

Chapter 1

Big data and Decision-making: How Big Data Is Relevant Across Fields and Domains

Anna Visvizi, Orlando Troisi and Mara Grimaldi

Abstract

Big data is a buzzword of our times, and yet the awareness of what big data is, how it permeates our daily lives, and how it is applied either in the policy-making process or in the business sector remains relatively low. From a different perspective, while specialists, that is, practitioners and researchers, dealing with the technical facets of big data successfully uncover new features, new domains, and new opportunities related to big data, there is a need of evaluating and examining these findings through the lens of social sciences and management. This chapter offers an insight into key issues and developments that shape the broad and multi-directional big data debate. To this end, the content of the book is elaborated and the key findings are highlighted. In this way, this chapter serves as a very useful guide into the question of how big data is applied across issues and domains and how it is valid and relevant to all of us today.

Keywords: Big data; policymaking; strategy; business; public policy; society

1. Introduction

Big data is a buzzword of our times, and yet the awareness of what big data is, how it permeates our daily lives, and how it is applied either in the policy-making process or in the business sector remains relatively low. From a different

Big Data and Decision-Making: Applications and Uses in the Public and Private Sector, 1–11

Published under exclusive licence by Emerald Publishing Limited
doi:10.1108/978-1-80382-551-920231001

perspective, while specialists, that is, practitioners and researchers, dealing with the technical facets of big data successfully uncover new features, new domains, and new opportunities related to big data, there is a need of evaluating and examining these findings through the lens of social sciences and management (Visvizi et al., 2020). The challenge is that respective research communities, on the one hand, the computer science community, and on the other hand, social scientists and students of management, remain divided. It is thus important that connections, or bridges, are built that will allow these communities to enter a dialogue and seek synergies between their respective research agendas. This book responds to this plea by looking explicitly at the question of how big data is applied across issues and domains and how it is valid and relevant to all of us today.

This book derives from the understanding that big data and the supporting ecosystem of technologies, including blockchain and smart contracts, artificial intelligence (AI) and machine learning, internet of things (IoT), etc., and applications have a dramatic impact on the decision-making process (Corvello et al., 2021; Provost & Fawcett, 2013; Visvizi, 2022) across issues and domains, including politics, policies, and the business sector (Loebbecke & Picot, 2015; Visvizi & Bodziany, 2021). At the same time, the very nature of big data, a term originating in the computer science discourse, remains opaque to research communities more closely associated with social sciences and management. And yet, it is in the fields of research that these communities are engaged with that the impact of big data is pervasive (Chen et al., 2012; Wamba et al., 2015) and, hence, requires in-depth exploration. In other words, it is imperative to build bridges between the computer science-driven debate on big data and research taking place in social sciences and management (Visvizi et al., 2022). This book dwells on this multifaceted issue.

The objective of this book is to examine in which ways, that is, through which mechanisms and to what end, big data influences contemporary societies, and especially the processes of decision-making, strategy setting, and overall performance in such domains as politics, specific policy fields, and the business sector. The chapters included in this book have been divided into three parts. The chapters included in Part 1 seek to conceptualize big data and its value added for the society, including the big questions of privacy, safety, and security of big data and intra-municipality relations. In Part 2 through a careful analysis of selected case studies, including healthcare (Botti & Monda, 2020), hospitality, tourism (Li et al., 2018), and agri-food policy, an overview of big data and its application is offered. In Part 3, the focus of the discussion is directed at the business sector and the connection between big data and the efficiency of the decision-making process is discussed. Respective findings are examined critically.

The value added for this book is threefold, that is, first and foremost, this book queries the applied aspect of big data. For anyone who always knew big data as an abstract term, this book will be an eye-opener. In this way, this book may encourage new research in the field of social science on big data (Grimmer, 2015), its application, and related opportunities and caveats. Second, this book focuses on the question of how big data is integrated in the fabric of (public and private) institutions and organizations and how its value can be exploited. Third, this book offers a critical appraisal of lessons learnt until now in the process of harnessing the promise inherent in big data.

2. The Structure of the Book and the Methodological Approach Adopted

The book has been divided into three parts dealing with diverse aspects of big data and its value added for the decision-making process and policymaking (Höchtl et al., 2016), in general. Part 1 contains chapters (Chapters 2–5) that deal with exploring the concepts and meaning attached to big data. By doing so, the chapters included in this part also highlight the value added of big data and the relevance of big data-driven approaches in today's world (Troisi, et al., 2020). Part 2 (Chapters 6–9) elaborates on diverse ways in which big data is applied across issues, domains, and policy fields. In this way, the topics discussed in this part of the book revolve around big data and its uses in healthcare (Dash et al., 2019), the agri-food sector, hospitality, and circular economy (CE). Part 3 (Chapters 10–13) deals with business and policy-making processes that are empowered by big data. The following topics are discussed: big data, CE, and the small- and medium-sized (SMEs) sector; smart organizations and big data, including the local government, cities, and smart cities.

The discussion throughout the book is embellished by references to case studies focusing on selected policy fields, for example, safety and security, healthcare, tourism, etc. Detailed and methodologically sound reviews of literature add to the depth of the discussion. The content of the book is inter- and multi-disciplinary, because to address the complex set of questions defining the objective of the book, a variety of insights originating in diverse fields of social sciences, including politics and international relations, as well as public policy, business and management, and at times computer science are employed. In other words, the discussion in this volume builds bridges across disciplines to navigate complex challenges that require multi-disciplinary approaches and methods. Indeed, the chapters included in this volume employ an array of conceptual approaches and methodological tools, always in line with the precepts of good science. Qualitative and quantitative research methods are applied. These are embedded in a variety of conceptual frameworks originating in social sciences, managerial research, and other.

3. Detailed Content of the Book

The discussion in the book opens with a discussion (Chapter 2) on the key concepts defining the broader debate on big data, on the caveats and on the challenges that beset the debate and the application of big data. To this end, the authors, Anna Visvizi, Orlando Troisi, and Mara Grimaldi, argue that the possibility to collect and analyze unprecedented quantities of data pertaining not only to the operation of private and public sectors, but also to the lives of individuals, bears the potential to employ the data as invaluable source of information, and possibly knowledge. The latter, in turn, may lead to innovation (Trabucchi & Buganza,

2018), and innovation-led sustainable growth and development of our societies (Dubey et al., 2019; Etzion & Aragon-Correa, 2016). Inasmuch as the promise inherent in – what tends to be termed – big data is huge, so are also the caveats related to the prospect of exploiting the benefits of big data. In this chapter, it is argued that four challenges beset the possibility of effective and efficient use of big data today. These include: a substantial degree of ignorance as to what big data actually is; the challenge of obtaining quality data; the challenge of the utilization of big data in the decision-making process; and, finally, the twin ethical and legal challenge pertaining to the acquisition and the use of big data. It is also argued that the awareness of the existence of these caveats enables a critical insight into the promise big data brings about for our societies today.

In Chapter 3, Giulia Leoni, Gennaro Maione, and Luca Mazzara, discuss performance measurement and management systems (PMMS) in the inter-municipal cooperation context by considering the development of new capabilities required to exploit the digital governance potentialities in which data integration is essential (Andrejevic, 2014). The analysis relied on the advent of digital governance, the Italian public informative systems reform, as well as on local governments renewals through the Union of Municipalities (UMs) – one of the most widespread structured forms of inter-municipal cooperation – based on the sustainability of local service delivery. Through a review of the literature and the conceptual outcomes resulting from the analysis of the dynamic capabilities theory applied to digital governance, this chapter aims at suggesting a useful contribution for an effective improvement of PMMS in the public sector networks, with the consequent improvement of resilience in policy management. Thus, the broad information required by the UMs and the complexity of its administration together with the constraints regarding the need to share a common vision and strategy, plan objectives, targets, measurement, and evaluation processes are considered. In particular, three propositions have been developed as guidelines for achieving coordination, coherence, and integration of measuring and managing performances in public networks. This evidence will offer insights allowing scholars and practitioners a practical understanding on whether and how dynamic capabilities – applied to digital governance – address PMMS challenges within an inter-municipal cooperative context.

In Chapter 4, the authors, Xhimi Hysa, Mario D'Arco, and Joana Kostaqi explore the question of the misuse of personal data in times of big data analytics. Specifically, this chapter explores young individuals' attitude toward protection of personal data. Specifically, the discussion focuses on the General Data Protection Regulation (GDPR) and the introduction of a property right over personal data. To this end, a total of 10 in-depth interviews were conducted with both Albanian and Italian college students. Transcribed data from the interviews were analyzed through thematic analysis. Four main themes emerged from the interviews: (i) distrust toward the way personal data are used online, (ii) no change in behavior after the introduction of GDPR, (iii) limited knowledge regarding terms and conditions of websites, and (iv) individual desire for more control over his/her data. In light of the research findings, the present contribution highlights that, despite the GDPR enhances individuals' data protection and rights, there is an intention–behavior gap that has been labeled by extant literature as a "privacy paradox" (Jain et al., 2016). Furthermore, findings reveal that treating personal data as a property right has pros and cons.

Chapter 5, by Anastasija Nikiforova, Artjoms Daskevics, and Otmane Azeroual, offers a detailed insight into NoSQL security, with the key question addressed being: can my data-driven decision-making be affected from outside? As the authors stress, today, there are billions of interconnected devices forming Cyber-Physical Systems, IoT, and Industrial Internet of Things (IIoT) ecosystems. With an increasing number of devices and systems in use, amount, and the value of data, the risks of security breaches increase. One of these risks is posed by open data sources, by which are meant databases, which are not properly protected (Kitchin, 2014; Nikiforova, 2021). These poorly protected databases are accessible to external actors, which poses a serious risk to the data holder and the results of data-related activities such as analysis, forecasting, monitoring, decision-making, policy development, and the whole contemporary society. This chapter aims at examining the state of the security of open data databases representing both relational databases and NoSQL, with a particular focus on a later category.

In Chapter 6, Gianluca Maria Guazzo and Vilma Çekani investigate how big data influences the diffusion of knowledge in firms and how it influences the firm's innovation process. The chapter identifies gaps that exist in the current literature on the topic. This study is conducted by using a qualitative methodology. PRISMA methodology is used to carry out a systematic literature review. The results shown in this study indicate the positive influence that technology has on knowledge sharing and innovation and on the other hand how good management of knowledge can benefit SMEs. The limitation of this study is related to the methodology, whereas it is considered that a quantitative methodology can be incorporated into the other research resources. The chapter's aim is to fill a gap in the current literature and to be a new starting point for scholars and managers. Through this work, managers can better understand how to improve the innovation process through knowledge sharing in their organizations. The originality of the present study represents a first step in understanding the mechanisms of knowledge sharing within firms, how it supports the innovation process, and what role big data plays in this context.

In the context of the debate on the healthcare sector, Chapter 7, by Antonietta Megaro, addresses the question of transparency in AI-supported systems. The objective of this chapter is to offer an understanding of the role AI plays in value co-creation in healthcare service. It is argued that AI, as an operant resource, can stimulate a completely patient-centered, adaptive and resilient healthcare system, and governance models in healthcare based on data-driven decision-making, ensuring faster choices, more timely diagnoses, and more personalized treatment paths. However, the full implementation of AI in healthcare is inhibited by some frictions, mainly related to the risk that the AI black box may generate an inadequate automatic decision, also due to the quality of data used, often partial and unstructured, given the reluctance to share them by patients concerned by privacy threats. The co-design (multi-part and multi-level) of a predictive decision model based on the functional transparency of the AI algorithm, would allow for augmented decision as result of an effective human–machine interaction. Healthcare actors could thus make decisions using the information detected by the software (based on clear cause-and-effect correlations and modifiable variables in case of mistakes), integrated with their professional knowledge. This would also help to strengthen the patient's perception of the decision's reliability and accuracy and the safety of the tool (factors that can affect his/her trust). AI may be considered as a driver for value co-creation in healthcare, thanks to transparency. It would allow the promotion of collaborative behaviors between involved actors by generating new institutions and new resource integration practices among them.

In Chapter 8, authored by Antonio Botti and Antonella Monda, big data's impact on tourism and entrepreneurship is examined. As the authors stress, the progressive increase in the size of the data present in datasets, the so-called big data, provides researchers with the opportunity to extract a greater amount of useful information in many sectors, especially for the tourism industry. This chapter demonstrates that sustainable tourism (ST) may be favored by using big data and a data-driven approach. Furthermore, as ST appears in line with a new type of responsible entrepreneurship, called Humane Entrepreneurship (HumEnt), this chapter investigates the link between ST and HumEnt and the impact of big data and data-oriented approaches on ST and HumEnt. The chapter analyzes these relationships using a qualitative approach and applying the case study technique. Findings show the advantages of the data-driven approach to tourism and entrepreneurship.

The authors of Chapter 9, Benedetta Esposito, Ornella Malandrino, Maria Rosaria Sessa, and Daniela Sica, explore the use of big data and digital technologies in context of the agri-food sector. It is argued that the improvement of the agri-food supply chain sustainability plays a pivotal role in the planet's survival and in overcoming climate disasters. Digital technologies that support the collection of Big Data produced along the agri-food supply chain emerge as powerful tools to accelerate the ecological transition of the sector. Digital technologies can support the implementation of circular business models by sharing data across the supply chain, monitoring in real-time the materials flow, automatizing some agricultural practices, and improving the decision-making through the development of decision support systems (Curry, 2016). Despite the relevance of these arguments, there is a lack of shared frameworks and guidelines for the effective development of a "data-driven circular economy" in the agri-food supply chain. In this scenario, the present study examines how scholars investigate data-oriented strategies to accelerate the ecological transition and the adoption of CE models in the agri-food sector. To this end, a systematic literature review was performed. Twenty-nine papers were selected following a rigorous sampling process. Both bibliometric and descriptive results are provided in the first part of the paper. According to the analytical framework developed, the selected papers were examined through the lens of the "reduce, reuse, and recycle" (3R) paradigm. Moreover, an additional R was retrieved from the systematic review (i.e., redesign), broadening the analytical perspective. The results indicate that scholars have predominantly provided theoretical contributions concerning the role of digital technologies and big data for the agri-food circular transition from a macro perspective. The findings are useful for policymakers and managers, who can promote and implement the big data-oriented approach to facilitate the circular transition. Limitations and future research directions are also provided.

Chapter 10, by Radosław Malik and Katarzyna Rybkowska, employs the Science Mapping method to explore how the intersection of big data and the business process has been explored in the literature. Specifically, this chapter uses multiple research methods, including quantitative science-mapping analysis (SciMat) and a qualitative literature review, to provide insight into the academic debate unfolding at the intersection of big data and business processes. SciMat analysis based on keyword co-occurrence enabled identifying 12 of the most productive research themes, as reflected in a poll of 301 articles about big data and business processes. The three most important themes are: firm performance, Industry 4.0, and innovation. The traditional literature review on firm performance indicated that big data analytics positively influence business process performance and have a beneficial impact on a firm's performance, that is, the role of big data is viewed as critical in the context of Industry 4.0 because it enhances productivity and improves business processes. The benefits of big data analytics can be achieved only if the organizational obstacles related to planning, workforce attitude, and alignment with strategy are overcome. Moreover, big data is perceived as a significant source of innovation in an organization and can be conceptualized with the use of a resources-based view of the firm. Big data analytics positively influence business processes, which is strengthened by adequate implementation and openness to innovation.

In Chapter 11, by Anne-Mari Järvenpää, Jari Jussila, and Iivari Kunttu, the barriers and practical challenges for data-driven decision-making in CE SMEs are explored. It is argued that the CE model is seen as an alternative model to the linear economy models, which seem to be reaching their physical limits. The CE business model aims to reuse materials and decrease the need for virgin materials. This requires the implementation of a reverse supply chain, close collaboration between actors, as well as well-organized logistics. For this reason, the CE companies have typically high demand for digitalized processes and the utilization of data on both operational and business development dimensions. Also, the utilization of big data collected from the companies' business environment can provide new opportunities for business development in CE. Even though utilization of data collected from the business environment and operations enables data-driven approaches for various decision-making functions in companies, many companies still struggle to figure out how to use analytics to take advantage of their data. In the SMEs, the managers are facing difficulties with ever-increasing amounts of data and sophisticated analytics. Indeed, prior research identified several kinds of barriers to the effective utilization of data in SMEs. Still, research on data-driven decision-making remains scarce in CE context. This paper presents a case study consisting of seven cases, all representing SMEs operating in the field of CE in Finland. In the case study, the barriers, and challenges for data-driven decision-making in CE SMEs are investigated. Based on the case study results, the paper proposes that utilization of data, lack of resources, lack of capabilities, and regulation are the main barriers to data-driven decision-making in CE SMEs.

Chapter 12, is authored by Francesca Loia. The key line of the argument is that the growing turbulence of the external environment has progressively led to the necessity by organizations of exploiting new opportunities (Troise et al., 2022). The new digital environment has led to the development and adoption of innovative approaches; also in the urban context which has always been characterized by different, interconnected, and dynamic dimensions. Urban governance models have been enhanced by smart technologies, which act as enablers of advanced services and foster connections between citizens, public and private organizations, and decision-makers. In this context, the objective of this chapter is to examine the role of data-driven approaches in the urban context during the chaotic and high variable circumstances related to the diffusion of the Covid-19 (Polese et al., 2022). Thanks to the adoption of the co-evolutionary perspective, a cycle in urban governance decision-making approach based on digital technologies is depicted and its contribution for managing the ongoing Covid-19 is traced. The results of the analysis highlight how the data-driven approach supports urban decision-making and shed light on the co-evolutionary perspective as a heuristic device to map the interactions settled in the networks between local governments, data-driven technologies, and citizens. In this sense, the study offers interesting insights, potentially capable of generating useful implications for both researchers and professionals in the public sector.

The discussion in the book closes with a chapter that showcases how big data may be useful in modeling and building a smart city. Chapter 13, authored by Olena Sokhatska and Ruslana Lutsiv, offers an in-depth insight into factors and processes necessary for a smart city development. In particular, the authors underline that the cities of the twenty-first century are becoming independent actors on the international scene. Due to decentralization, cities gradually gain more power to independently identify their policies, strategies and related priorities, as well as ways of their implementation. As a result, several initiatives can be implemented at the city level at a much faster pace and more efficiently than ever before. The United Nations' (UN) "Transforming our world: the 2030 Agenda for Sustainable Development" focuses on issues related to sustainable development. In relation to cities, it aims to make them "inclusive, safe, resilient and sustainable." This chapter investigates the conceptual foundations of the term smart sustainable cities and summarizes strategies that have been undertaken in cities, as a means of making them smart and sustainable. Against this backdrop, by focusing on Ukraine, an implementation algorithm based on selected examples drawn from Europe is proposed. Sadly, as the story accompanying this chapter proves, big data, algorithms, and the will to promote growth and development alone are not sufficient in a world where recourse to violence and breaches of international treaties are met with impunity. Note that the chapter was written shortly before the Russian invasion in Ukraine and hailed the prospects and strategies of developing smart cities in Ukraine. Subsequently, the chapter was edited in the hope that smart cities will be a possibility in a free Ukraine soon.

4. By Means of Conclusion

The objective of this book was to showcase big data as an important artifact of today's world, and therefore also a major variable that influences all facets and dimensions of the business sector, politics, management, and administration, as well as our private lives. The idea underlying the book was to make big data, seen as a concept and a part of our daily life, understandable to all those who may not have technical background and yet would like to know what the term denotes, how to conceive of its impact on our society and what to expect from it. In this view, the content of the book will be of great value to undergraduate and graduate students as well as scholars and practitioners, who would like to grasp the essence of big data and grapple with its impact on their domains of professional engagement.

The variety of contributions included in the book will help researchers, managers, and policymakers understand how opportunities resulting from the strategic use of big data can be effectively exploited by redesigning business models (Troisi et al., 2021), refocusing strategies and redefining stakeholders' engagement in the decision-making of private and public organizations. In this way, this book addresses the need to investigate the strategic role of (big and small) data as the key enabler of business and innovation opportunities, resilience, and growth. Finally, one of the big questions this book addresses is that of whether (big) data can be strategically incorporated into corporate orientation, business models, and strategies. An important thread of the discussion that weaves through the chapters included in this book is that of how (big) data can be efficiently included in the decision-making process at the local, regional, and national levels, thereby contributing to the development of sustainable and resilient practices in the domains of politics, society, and economy.

References

Andrejevic, M. (2014). Big data, big questions| the big data divide. *International Journal of Communication*, *8*, 17. Retrieved from https://ijoc.org/index.php/ijoc/article/view/2161

Botti, A., & Monda, A. (2020). Sustainable value co-creation and digital health: The case of Trentino eHealth ecosystem. *Sustainability*, *12*(13), 5263.

Chen, H., Chiang, R. H., & Storey, V. C. (2012). Business intelligence and analytics: From big data to big impact. *MIS Quarterly*, *36*(4), 1165–1188.

Corvello, V., De Carolis, M., Verteramo, S., & Steiber, A. (2021). The digital transformation of entrepreneurial work. *International Journal of Entrepreneurial Behavior & Research*, *28*(5), 1167–1183.

Curry, E. (2016). The big data value chain: Definitions, concepts, and theoretical approaches. In *New horizons for a data-driven economy* (pp. 29–37). Cham: Springer.

Dash, S., Shakyawar, S. K., Sharma, M., & Kaushik, S. (2019). Big data in healthcare: Management, analysis and future prospects. *Journal of Big Data*, *6*(1), 1–25.

Dubey, R., Gunasekaran, A., Childe, S. J., Papadopoulos, T., Luo, Z., Wamba, S. F., & Roubaud, D. (2019). Can big data and predictive analytics improve social and environmental sustainability?. *Technological Forecasting and Social Change*, *144*, 534–545.

Etzion, D., & Aragon-Correa, J. A. (2016). Big data, management, and sustainability: Strategic opportunities ahead. *Organization & Environment*, *29*(2), 147–155.

Grimmer, J. (2015). We are all social scientists now: How big data, machine learning, and causal inference work together. *PS: Political Science & Politics*, *48*(1), 80–83.

Höchtl, J., Parycek, P., & Schöllhammer, R. (2016). Big data in the policy cycle: Policy decision making in the digital era. *Journal of Organizational Computing and Electronic Commerce*, *26*(1–2), 147–169.

Jain, P., Gyanchandani, M., & Khare, N. (2016). Big data privacy: A technological perspective and review. *Journal of Big Data*, *3*(1), 1–25.

Kitchin, R. (2014). *The data revolution: Big data, open data, data infrastructures and their consequences*. Sage.

Li, J., Xu, L., Tang, L., Wang, S., & Li, L. (2018). Big data in tourism research: A literature review. *Tourism Management*, *68*, 301–323.

Loebbecke, C., & Picot, A. (2015). Reflections on societal and business model transformation arising from digitization and big data analytics: A research agenda. *The Journal of Strategic Information Systems*, *24*(3), 149–157.

Nikiforova, A. (2021). Smarter open government data for society 5.0: Are your open data smart enough?. *Sensors*, *21*(15), 5204.

Polese, F., Botti, A., & Monda, A. (2022). Value co-creation and data-driven orientation: Reflections on restaurant management practices during COVID-19 in Italy. *Transforming Government: People, Process and Policy*, *16*(2), 172–184.

Provost, F., & Fawcett, T. (2013). Data science and its relationship to big data and data-driven decision making. *Big Data*, *1*(1), 51–59.

Trabucchi, D., & Buganza, T. (2018). Data-driven innovation: Switching the perspective on big data. *European Journal of Innovation Management*, *22*(1), 23–40.

Troise, C., Corvello, V., Ghobadian, A., & O'Regan, N. (2022). How can SMEs successfully navigate VUCA environment: The role of agility in the digital transformation era. *Technological Forecasting and Social Change*, *174*, 121227.

Troisi, O., Grimaldi, M., & Loia, F. (2021). Redesigning business models for data-driven innovation: A three-layered framework. In A. Visvizi, M. D. Lytras & N. R. Aljohani (Eds.), *The international research & innovation forum* (pp. 421–435). Cham: Springer. https://doi.org/10.1007/978-3-030-62066-0_32

Troisi, O., Maione, G., Grimaldi, M., & Loia, F. (2020). Growth hacking: Insights on data-driven decision-making from three firms. *Industrial Marketing Management*, *90*, 538–557.

Visvizi, A. (2022). Artificial intelligence (AI) and sustainable development goals (SDGs): Exploring the impact of AI on politics and society. *Sustainability*, *14*, 1730. https://doi.org/10.3390/su14031730

Visvizi, A., Bodziany, M. (Eds.). (2021). *Artificial intelligence and its contexts. Security, business and governance*. Springer. https://doi.org/10.1007/978-3-030-88972-2

Visvizi, A., Lytras, M.D. & Aljohani, N. (2020). Big data research for politics: Human centric big data research for policy making, politics, governance and democracy. *Journal of Ambient Intelligence and Humanized Computing*, *12*(4), 4303–4304. https://doi.org/10.1007/s12652-021-03171-3

Visvizi, A., Troisi, O., Grimaldi, M., & Loia, F. (2022). Think human, act digital: Activating data-driven orientation in innovative start-ups. *European Journal of Innovation Management*, *25*(6), 452–478. https://doi.org/10.1108/EJIM-04-2021-0206

Wamba, S. F., Akter, S., Edwards, A., Chopin, G., & Gnanzou, D. (2015). How 'big data' can make big impact: Findings from a systematic review and a longitudinal case study. *International Journal of Production Economics*, *165*, 234–246.

Part 1

Conceptualizing Big Data, Its Value Added and Relevance in the Modern World

Chapter 2

Mapping and Conceptualizing Big Data and Its Value Across Issues and Domains

Anna Visvizi, Orlando Troisi and Mara Grimaldi

Abstract

In today's world, the possibility to collect and analyze unprecedented quantities of data pertaining not only to the operation of private and public sectors, but also to the lives of individuals, bears the potential to employ the data as invaluable source of information, and possibly knowledge. The latter, in turn, may lead to innovation, and innovation-led sustainable growth and development of our societies. Inasmuch as the promise inherent in – what tends to be termed – big data is huge, so are also the caveats related to the prospect of exploiting the benefits of big data. In this chapter, it is argued that four challenges beset the possibility of effective and efficient use of big data today. These include: a substantial degree of ignorance as to what big data actually is; the challenge of obtaining quality data; the challenge of the utilization of big data in the decision-making process; and, finally, the twin ethical and legal challenge pertaining to the acquisition and the use of big data. It is also argued that the awareness of the existence of these caveats enables a critical insight into the promise big data brings about for our societies today. This chapter dwells on these issues.

Keywords: Small data; big data; data-driven decision-making; data analytics; business; politics; society

1. Introduction

The possibility to collect and analyze unprecedented quantities of data pertaining not only to the operation of private and public sectors, but also to the lives

Big Data and Decision-Making: Applications and Uses in the Public and Private Sector, 15–25

Published under exclusive licence by Emerald Publishing Limited
doi:10.1108/978-1-80382-551-920231002

of individuals, bears the potential to employ these data as invaluable sources of information, and possibly knowledge. The latter may foster innovation, and innovation-led sustainable growth and development of our societies. Inasmuch as the promise inherent in big data is huge, so are also the caveats related to the prospect of exploiting the benefits of big data. In this chapter, it is argued that four challenges beset the possibility of effective and efficient use of big data today. These include: a substantial degree of ignorance as to what big data actually is; the challenge of obtaining quality data; the challenge of the utilization of big data in the decision-making process; and, finally, the twin ethical and legal challenge pertaining to the acquisition and the use of big data. This chapter dwells on these issues.

Even if the "volume" seems to be one of the key features of big data, the adjective "big" can be misleading, since small data sets can also be large. Making sense of big data implies that large data set should be skimmed to extract relevant information and insightful and actionable results. Hence, in the discussion on big data, it is equally important to talk about small data. Viewed in this way, big data may be seen as a set of relatively neutral artifacts, as a commodity of great value, and consequently also as an asset, a source of information, to be deployed strategically. While several definitions of big data exist in the literature (Gandomi & Haider, 2015), it is useful to define them by reference to five integrated criteria, including volume, velocity, variety, veracity, and value (Diebold, 2012; Laney, 2001; Song & Zhu, 2017). In other words, for a given set of data to be referred to as big data, it should be of a certain size, it should have been accumulated quickly, have a heterogeneous nature (structured or unstructured), be reliable, and be a bearer of useful meaning. Given – related to advances in sophisticated information and communication technology (ICT) – the possibility to collect and analyze data today, there is a tendency in the literature and in the popular debate (Kitchin & Lauriault, 2015) to focus on big data, and specifically on their volume, velocity, and variability. In this context, the salience of small data (Kitchin, 2015; Lindstrom, 2016; Miller, 2014) tends to be undermined, as if volume was the key value inherent in data and data sets. Clearly it is not the case.

In contrast to big data, small data are of limited volume, their collection is non-continuous, their variety is limited, and the corresponding data sets are generated to answer very specific questions (Kitchin & Lauriault, 2015, p. 463). A good, even if counterintuitive, example of small data is that of census data sets. These have high volume even if they lack velocity, variety, and flexibility (Kitchin & Lauriault, 2015). In general, small data sets may feature some of the characteristics specific to big data. Conversely, each large data set, to become usable, that is, to serve as a source of information, has to be "skimmed," to obtain a sample, and then possibly insightful and actionable results on a narrow set of variables. In this sense, even big data and big data sets, if they are to serve as a source of information, and knowledge, and thus inform strategy- and/or policy-making process, will be seen as a small data at some point. "Small," in this case, is not a descriptor of quantity, but rather an indication of the narrower scope of the focus.

There is a growing understanding, both in the literature and among the practitioners, that the integration of small and big data is the most proper solution to achieve an efficient use of data for the sake of the economy and the society.

Aggregating different sets of small data into big data can improve the knowledge about different kinds of phenomena. Even if in the first attempts to define the difference between big data and small data and to state the autonomy of small data literature (Kitchin & Lauriault, 2015) hypothesized that small data must converge into big data sets, it can be said that it is through a wise and smart collection and analysis of big data that small data can be generated to extract value. Indeed, small data can connect people with timely and meaningful insights derived from big data, organized, and visually arranged to be accessible, understandable, and actionable for everyday tasks. If it is true that data are useful only if managers, employees, policymakers, users, and citizens can do something with it in everyday jobs, then small data can be considered as a means to extract usefulness and value from big data (Pollock, 2013) and not anymore as hardly useful and poor data. The possibility to turn big data sets into actionable small data can offer advantages not only to data analysts and organizations but also to end-users. The great opportunities offered from the integration of small data and big data can be the great accessibility, availability, understandability, and actionability of the insights extracted even for the users of products and public services.

Even if collecting large amount of data from different sources with an unexpected velocity and often at low cost can seem an attractive source of utility, it is also true that knowledge can advance only if data can address some limited research questions, if can be sub-divided into variables to conceptualize, and give sense to the information extracted to be turned into knowledge. Making sense of big data implies the creation and integration of small data packages, not building big data monoliths, by partitioning problems in a way that works across people and organizations, not through creating massive and centralized data sets. Distributed models and collaboration are the two key levers for a fruitful integration of small data and big data. The reminder of this chapter is structured as follows. Section 2 dwells on the challenge of obtaining quality data. Section 3 elaborates on challenges that beset the exploitation of big data in the decision-making process. Section 4 highlights issues located at the intersection of big data, society, and politics. Discussion (Section 4) and conclusions (Section 5) follow.

2. The Challenge of Obtaining Quality Data

The quality and integrity of information remains essential in the process of utilizing data. That is, for data to be useful, it must be reliable (Laney, 2001; Mayer-Schönberger & Cukier, 2013). Bad data are worse than no data (Renshaw, 2003). The simple data collection, while exploiting the best technologies available on the market, does not guarantee to have information and, above all, to extract knowledge. A datum is a coded representation of an entity, a transaction, and an event. The information is the result of a data analysis process, it often has meaning only for analysts. Knowledge is obtained when the extracted information is used and put into practice to make decisions and carry out actions.

Despite the great potential of data analysis, the variety, and heterogeneity of data collected around the world or across the business sector can compromise a proper exploitation of the information. In fact, not all the data gathered are collected based on the same methodology or the same formats (Frascati, 2015). Big data are usually derived from different sources and represent information from different sub-populations. To solve this issue, big data sets require sophisticated statistical techniques. However, the estimation of predictive models can run into some sources of error or accumulation of noise. In this way, some variables with substantial explanatory power risk being underestimated.

Hence, to address the abovementioned criticalities and ensure the proper transition from data into useful information for business processes by building knowledge to improve performance, the fifth "V" is crucial: the value. The methodologies employed to use data analytics are fundamental, through their proper selection and use a company to extract value or make more informed and timely decisions. The growing amount of data, which is gathered, selected, and analyzed through a vast set of technologies within today's ecosystems (from cloud computing systems to mobile devices to track and store customer information to machine learning) should be strategically managed to optimize business processes, overcome complexity, and mitigate the risk of transforming the advantages offered by ICT tools into threats (Chen et al., 2013; Gupta & George, 2016).

3. The Challenge of the Utilization of Big Data in the Decision-making Process

If, on the one hand, the multiplication of data sources for companies, institutions, and users seems to offer immeasurable benefits, then, on the other hand, strategies to manage data effectively, that is, to improve decision-making, should be identified. In this way, the potential of ICT can be fully exploited by preventing the risk of transforming technological opportunities into threats (Gandomi & Haider, 2015). Despite the recognized impact of the new technologies for data analysis (Gobble, 2013; Manyika et al., 2011; Yang et al., 2017), uncritical and devoid of strategy use of technological tools does not foster the attainment of innovation (Wamba et al., 2015). It is the way data are strategically managed and, ideally, turned into information and knowledge, that can trigger innovation. Therefore, it is imperative to understand not only how the new technologies for data analysis reshape businesses but also how they can redefine the decision-making processes of both organizations (Neslin et al., 2006) and consumers, who can exchange, co-create, and enrich the value extracted from data to turn it into actionable insights.

A proper exploitation of big data analysis can potentially generate substantial benefits by improving business functions, management, and by enhancing citizens' and users' participation into public life and policy-making. Indeed, one of the big questions that needs to be addressed in contemporary research is the strategic integration of data into corporate orientation, business models, strategies, and into the development of sustainable and resilient practices for ecosystem's well-being. Hence, the potential entailed by the smart application and the strategic and effective exploitation of data in different (economic, social, and political) contexts should be explored. The following paragraphs examines how organizations can make the best use of big data opportunities. That is, the question is how and to what extent big data plays a role in redesigning business models, refocusing strategies, and redefining stakeholders' engagement in private and public organizations.

The application of big data as a tool in private and public organizations cannot automatically guarantee the achievement of competitive advantage. As outlined earlier above, an efficient useful exploitation of big data can be influenced by numerous factors, such as data accessibility, availability, quality, heterogeneity (Frascati, 2015; Gupta & George, 2016), or data analysis' skills, management's attitude to and perception of data (Chen et al., 2013; Kearns & Sabherwal, 2007). While the huge amount of analytics available in contemporary market can have a significant impact on growth, organizations should learn the best ways to manage data, which can otherwise become an additional and useless expense.

Big data is not only an operational tool that can increase profits and competitive advantage, but it can redefine business and organizational orientation to redesign the entire process of business modeling and of creating value by obtaining economic and social well-being. There is the need to support data analysis with the adoption of a new culture grounded on data, new ways of capturing, sharing, and creating value (within and outside the organization), and to develop continuous improvement by reframing all the dimensions of business models.

For this reason, *data-driven decision-making* (DDDM, Brynjolfsson et al., 2011; LaValle et al., 2011) has been conceptualized in extant research to stress the necessity for a new orientation grounded on data collection as a driving force to revise business strategies to promote data as a strategic lever to undertake more effective decisions. Data-driven orientation can enable the complex transition from data collection to the extraction of information and, then, value or new value (Troisi et al., 2020). In this way, the data collected are translated potentially into insights, novelties, and innovative actions that can improve business processes and foster continuous learning. This complex process requires the active role of management in fostering an innovation-oriented culture and a careful data management based on a learning orientation aimed at turning data into relevant insights, effective decisions and, thus, innovative actions, processes, products, or services (Marsh et al., 2006; Xu et al., 2016). According to a process-based view, DDDM can revolutionize not only business models but also the way organizations interact with customers, transform how customers access useful data, and improve the relationship between organizations and users (Erl et al., 2016).

Big data analysis and the adoption of related analytics should be incorporated into the complex corporate decision-making process starting from the enhancement of the managerial intention to adopt big data analytics to the recruitment of specialized analysts and the development of an adequate infrastructure that supports the process technically. Therefore, the internalization of a data-oriented corporate culture should be disseminated at every organizational level. Through the lens of DDDM, big data can be defined as a disruptive and integrated set of tools and technologies that reformulates the orientation of private and public organizations and the way in which they create value with their stakeholders.

Hence, the possibilities and advantages deriving from the introduction of data-driven orientation in the business, managerial, political, and social sector, the key dimensions of application of big data identified above, should be explored. Examples from business sector suggest that data-driven orientation can help companies redefine their strategies according to a total data approach that introduces a new smart culture that can redesign the organizational structure, processes, and resources management by improving knowledge exchange and promoting the constant creation of new knowledge, by encouraging continuous improvement. Only through a culture grounded on data as a strategic asset, the cases described above implemented a technological infrastructure based on multiple touchpoints, IT and ICT tools (cloud computing systems, decision-support systems, fuzzy logic, and agile work system), and a set of analytics and tools in line with the strategic objectives (e.g., new product development, redefinition of business models, customer relationship management, etc.). The internalization of data-driven culture and the effective use of digital technologies can enhance knowledge exchange, increase know-how, by extracting new knowledge from raw data to draw insights and innovative ideas. The redefinition of information flow and knowledge exchange enable not only product innovation but also process and business model innovation thanks to the promotion of a proactive attitude which can lead to the constant renewal of value and foster the emergence of innovation over time.

4. Big Data, Society, and Politics

A data-driven orientation in public organizations and communities can be characterized by the promotion of diffused-bottom-up decision-making grounded on the willingness to engage people into public decisions and to promote their social inclusion. An integrated set of data-driven services provided by internet of things (IoT) devices based on artificial intelligence (AI)-based systems, cloud computing, machine learning, and sensors can estimate and prevent the negative implications of pandemic (Shorfuzzaman et al., 2021) and improve citizens' well-being despite the limitations posed by social distancing. The ability to create shared and integrated systems for data sharing and collection can significantly improve well-being and quality of life, by strengthening citizens' involvement in policy-making, and generate added value (Ciasullo et al., 2020; Lytras et al., 2021). Moreover, an integrated system of smart technologies can help the creation of a dynamic network of relationships among actors mediated through a series of mobile devices, application, and cloud computing systems. AI-based platforms can help companies and institutions gather data and realize deeper and smarter decision-making that analyze and predict object/human behavior changes.

Despite the all-encompassing impact of big data on the life of companies, the need to explore this phenomenon from multiple perspectives highlights how the implementation of a technological infrastructure based on data analytics, albeit composite, cannot automatically guarantee the achievement of the advantage. As shown in Fig. 2.1, in fact, a profitable exploitation of data can be influenced by numerous variables (Gupta & George, 2016) and at the same time needs to redefine not only the technological asset of the company, the managerial attitude, and entrepreneurial orientation (Chen et al., 2013; Kearns & Sabherwal, 2007) but

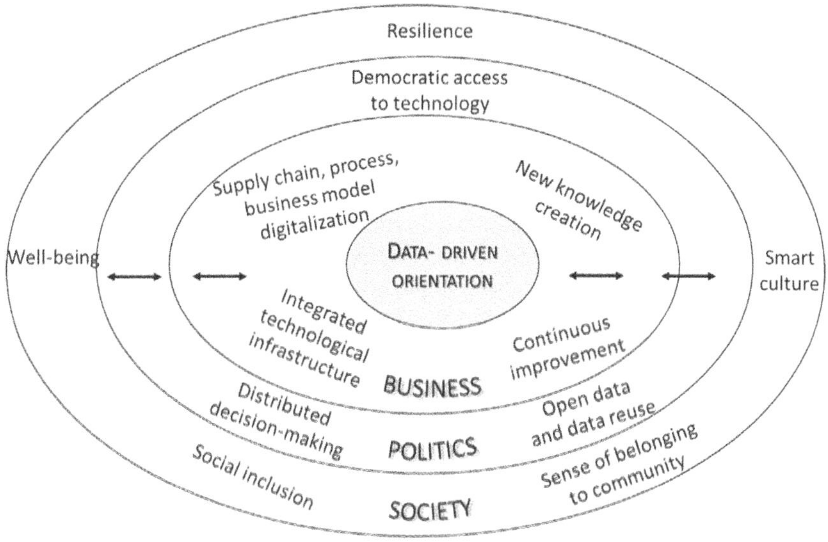

Fig. 2.1. The Key Outcomes of the Application of Data-driven Orientation in Business, Politics, and Society. *Source*: The authors.

also users' digital skills by enhancing their social inclusion and their involvement in public policy-making. Hence, a strategic approach to big data impact should be incorporated not only in business life but also in political and social life. The key outcomes that can be developed through data-driven orientation across business, political and social systems are depicted in Fig. 2.1.

In light of the integrated perspective introduced above (which takes into account the managerial, political, and social sides of big data), big data can be defined here as the pivot around which a disruptive and integrated set of technologies is arranged that reformulates: (1) business intelligence in information systems; (2) decision-making and policy-making in institutions and organizations; and (3) social inclusion and community's well-being. As for the business dimension, the introduction of big data in the life of companies thus has a disruptive impact, which leads to the reformulation of business processes and management processes, exerting an impact on decision-making in general and on marketing and management decisions (Loebbecke & Picot, 2015). For this reason, it is necessary to identify the different areas of application of big data and the different opportunities that these, if dropped to 360 degrees, offer to the management of the company, starting from the value chain up to the decision-making processes (so much of management and marketing) and strategies and the redefinition of business models.

Regarding the interface of politics and big data, highly interesting debate unfolds in the literature (Mureddu et al., 2020; Okuyucu & Yavuz, 2020; van Veenstra et al., 2021). Several topics are discussed. What needs to be stressed here is that big data, and the related emergence of a smart integrated systems, in the domain of public service delivery, information sharing, safety management, elections, etc. has a huge, still unrecognized, impact on citizens' behavior, the quality of the service, extent and quality of civic engagement, etc. In brief, big data and its intrusion into the realms of politics and of the political has the potential of redefining how we conceive of the political process and of the decision-making process. Ideally, if the first is driven by vested interests, emotion, and ideology, the latter – once separated from politicking – could greatly benefit from big data and its skillful utilization (Visvizi et al., 2020). Of course, very few benefits come without a price to pay. In this context, attention needs to be paid to questions of privacy and security of data (Boussios, 2021; Calzada & Almirall, 2020).

Finally, with regard to the social impact, big data plays a role vis-á-vis social inclusion and the ability of government to involve citizens in the use of technologies by removing social and economic imbalances in the access to infrastructure can enhance the general sense of belonging and the social trust in community (Grimmer, 2015). The changes triggered by the Covid-19 pandemic (Parry et al., 2021; Visvizi & Lytras, 2021) reframed the relational modalities and the interactional patterns among people and within/among societies. Diffused decision-making and the involvement of citizens in the co-design of new solutions can trigger the creation of new knowledge, new communication modes and practices, a new digital culture and, eventually, innovation. Therefore, it can be noticed that communication and collaboration are pivotal for inclusion and resilience (Troisi et al., 2022; Visvizi & del Hoyo, 2021).

5. By Means of Conclusion: Looking Ahead

Big data is but a part of the broader ecosystem of tools and technologies that defines what is termed as the 4th Industrial Revolution (Schwab, 2017). Despite the growing interest, on the part of academia and practitioners, in big data, studies that analyze how it is applied either in the policy-making process and or in the business sector remain relatively few. Considering that no one can "escape" big data today, it is imperative to nourish the understanding of what big data is and what kind of threats/opportunities it generates (Visvizi et al., 2020). From a different angle, even if big data may have a huge positive social, managerial, and political impact, the opportunity to consciously utilize big data enhanced decision-making, etc. remains accessible only to a handful of experts and practitioners (Andrejevic, 2014). Hence, to be capable of collecting and analyzing data equals to have power, to be advantageously positioned compared to those without such access, who are excluded from the process. Moreover, one of the most controversial issues relating to the use of big data is the ethical and legal challenge pertaining to the acquisition and the utilization of data: privacy, civic liberties, and unauthorized use of big data for malicious purposes. The collection of big data and the use of big data analytics can create some challenges related to confidentiality and privacy of users' data and susceptibility of service systems to software bugs, hardware glitches, and malicious cyberattacks. Computer science is working to deal with these issues and developing protocols to ensure data security and resistance to hacking. Personal data privacy and security is essential for the improvement of people's acceptance of technology and for the enhancement of citizens' awareness of the fine line between sharing and abusing private data to enhance their inclusion and make them become active contributors of community's quality of life. Thus, not only practitioners but also further studies should consider risks and threats involved in the creation and configuration of smart systems. Predictive modeling that helps address emergencies and surveillance systems that increase safety and security are crucial to ensure smart communities' and cities' well-being and sustainability. The different drivers that can enhance businesses', cities', and organizations' smartness should be identified to detect the key enablers of long-term well-being of citizens and to reduce the negative implications of disruptive technological changes.

References

Andrejevic, M. (2014). Big data, big questions: The big data divide. *International Journal of Communication*, *8*, 17.

Boussios, E. (2021). Because of Snowden? The three leakers and privacy issues in the cyber matrix. In A. Visvizi, O. Troisi, & K. Saeedi (Eds.), *Research and innovation forum 2021. RIIFORUM 2021. Springer proceedings in complexity*. Cham: Springer. https://doi.org/10.1007/978-3-030-84311-3_47

Brynjolfsson, E., Hitt, L.M., & Kim, H.H. (2011). Strength in Numbers: How Does Data-Driven Decisionmaking Affect Firm Performance? (April 22, 2011). Retrieved from https://ssrn.com/abstract=1819486

Calzada, I., & Almirall, E. (2020). Data ecosystems for protecting European citizens' digital rights. *Transforming Government: People, Process and Policy*, *14*(2), 133–147. https://doi.org/10.1108/TG-03-2020-0047

Chen, J., Chen, Y., Du, X., Li, C., Lu, J., Zhao, S., & Zhou, X. (2013). Big data challenge: A data management perspective. *Frontiers of Computer Science*, *7*(2), 157–164. https://doi.org/10.1007/s11704-013-3903-7

Ciasullo, M. V., Troisi, O., Grimaldi, M., & Leone, D. (2020). Multi-level governance for sustainable innovation in smart communities: An ecosystems approach. *International Entrepreneurship and Management Journal*, *16*(4), 1167–1195. http://dx.doi.org/10.1007/s11365-020-00641-6

Diebold, F. X. (2012). *On the origin (s) and development of the term 'big data'*. PIER Working Paper No. 12-037. https://doi.org/10.2139/ssrn.2152421

Erl, T., Khattak, W., & Buhler, P. (2016). *Big data fundamentals: Concepts, drivers & techniques*. Prentice Hall Press.

Frascati. (2015). Guidelines for collecting and reporting data on research and experimental development. http://www.oecd.org/sti/frascati-manual-2015-9789264239012-en.htm

Gandomi, A., & Haider, M. (2015). Beyond the hype: Big data concepts, methods, and analytics. *International Journal of Information Management*, *35*(2), 137–144.

Gobble, M. M. (2013). Big data: The next big thing in innovation. *Research-Technology Management*, *56*(1), 64–67.

Grimmer, J. (2015). We are all social scientists now: How big data, machine learning, and causal inference work together. *PS: Political Science & Politics*, *48*(1), 80–83.

Gupta, M., & George, J. F. (2016). Toward the development of a big data analytics capability. *Information & Management*, *53*(8), 1049–1064. https://doi.org/10.1016/j.im.2016.07.004

Kearns, G. S., & Sabherwal, R. (2007). Antecedents and consequences of information systems planning integration. *IEEE Transactions on Engineering Management*, *54*(4), 628–643.

Kitchin, R. (2015). The opportunities, challenges and risks of big data for official statistics. *Statistical Journal of the IAOS*, *31*(3), 471–481.

Kitchin, R., & Lauriault, T. P. (2015). Small data in the era of big data. *GeoJournal*, *80*(4), 463–475.

Laney, D. (2001). 3D data management: Controlling data volume, velocity and variety. META Group Research Note 6.

LaValle, S., Lesser, E., Shockley, R., Hopkins, M. S., & Kruschwitz, N. (2011). Big data, analytics and the path from insights to value. *MIT Sloan Management Review*, *52*(2), 21–32.

Lindstrom, M. (2016). *Small data: The tiny clues that uncover huge trends*. St. Martin's Press.

Loebbecke, C., & Picot, A. (2015). Reflections on societal and business model transformation arising from digitization and big data analytics: A research agenda. *The Journal of Strategic Information Systems*, *24*(3), 149–157. https://doi.org/10.1016/j.jsis.2015.08.002

Lytras, M. D., Visvizi, A., Chopdar, P. K., Sarirete, A., & Alhalabi, W. (2021). Information management in smart cities: Turning end users' views into multi-item scale development, validation, and policy-making recommendations. *International Journal of Information Management*, *56*, 102146. https://doi.org/10.1016/j.ijinfomgt.2020.102146

Manyika, J., Chui, M., Brown, B., Bughin, J., Dobbs, R., Roxburgh, C., & Byers, A. H. (2011). *Big data: The next frontier for innovation, competition, and productivity* (pp. 1–137). McKinsey Global Institute .

Marsh, J. A., Pane, J. F., & Hamilton, L. S. (2006). *Making sense of data-driven decision making in education: Evidence from recent RAND research* (pp. 1–16). Occasional Paper. Rand Corporation. https://doi.org/10.7249/OP170

Mayer-Schönberger, V., & Cukier, K. (2013). *Big data: A revolution that will transform how we live, work, and think*. Houghton Mifflin Harcourt.

Miller, S. (2014). Collaborative approaches needed to close the big data skills gap. *Journal of Organization design*, *3*(1), 26–30.

Mureddu, F., Schmeling, J., & Kanellou, E. (2020). Research challenges for the use of big data in policy-making. *Transforming Government: People, Process and Policy*, *14*(4), 593–604. https://doi.org/10.1108/TG-08-2019-0082

Neslin, S. A., Grewal, D., Leghorn, R., Shankar, V., Teerling, M. L., Thomas, J. S., & Verhoef, P. C. (2006). Challenges and opportunities in multichannel customer management. *Journal of Service Research*, *9*(2), 95–112.

Okuyucu, A., & Yavuz, N. (2020). Big data maturity models for the public sector: A review of state and organizational level models. *Transforming Government: People, Process and Policy*, *14*(4), 681–699. https://doi.org/10.1108/TG-09-2019-0085

Parry, L. J., Asenbaum, H., & Ercan, S. A. (2021). Democracy in flux: A systemic view on the impact of COVID-19. *Transforming Government: People, Process and Policy*, *15*(2), 197–205. https://doi.org/10.1108/TG-09-2020-0269

Pollock, R. (2013). Forget big data, small data is the real revolution. *The Guardian* [cited 31 January 2017]. http://www.theguardian.com/news/datablog/2013/apr/25/forget-big-data-small-data-revolution

Renshaw, A. A. (2003). Rescreening in cervical cytology for quality control. When bad data is worse than no data or what works, what doesn't, and why. *Clinics in Laboratory Medicine*, *23*(3), 695–708. doi:https://doi.org/10.1016/S0272-2712(03)00054-4

Schwab, K. (2017). *The fourth industrial revolution*. New York: Currency.

Shorfuzzaman, M., Hossain, M. S., & Alhamid, M. F. (2021). Towards the sustainable development of smart cities through mass video surveillance: A response to the COVID-19 pandemic. *Sustainable Cities and Society*, *64*, 102582.

Song, I. Y., & Zhu, Y. (2017). Big data and data science: Opportunities and challenges of iSchools. *Journal of Data and Information Science*, *2*(3), 1–18.

Troisi, O., Kashef, M., & Visvizi, A. (2022). Managing Safety and Security in the Smart City: Covid-19, Emergencies and Smart Surveillance. In A. Visvizi & O. Troisi (Eds.), *Managing Smart Cities* (pp. 73–88). Cham: Springer. https://doi.org/10.1007/978-3-030-93585-6_5

Troisi, O., Maione, G., Grimaldi, M., & Loia, F. (2020). Growth hacking: Insights on data-driven decision-making from three firms. *Industrial Marketing Management*, *90*, 538–557. https://doi.org/10.1016/j.indmarman.2019.08.005

van Veenstra, A. F., Grommé, F., & Djafari, S. (2021). The use of public sector data analytics in the Netherlands. *Transforming Government: People, Process and Policy*, *15*(4), 396–419. https://doi.org/10.1108/TG-09-2019-0095

Visvizi, A., & del Hoyo, R. P. (2021). Sustainable development goals (SDGs) in the smart city: A tool or an approach? (An introduction). In A. Visvizi & R. P. del Hoyo (Eds.), *Smart cities and the UN SDGs* (pp. 1–11). Elsevier. https://doi.org/10.1016/B978-0-323-85151-0.00001-4

Visvizi, A., & Lytras, M. D. (2021). Guest editorial. *Transforming Government: People, Process and Policy*, *15*(2), 193–196. https://doi.org/10.1108/TG-05-2021-315

Visvizi, A., Lytras, M. D., & Aljohani, N. (2020). Big data research for politics: Human centric big data research for policy making, politics, governance and democracy. *Journal of Ambient Intelligence and Humanized Computing*, *12*(4), 4303–4304. https://doi.org/10.1007/s12652-021-03171-3

Wamba, S. F., Akter, S., Edwards, A., Chopin, G., & Gnanzou, D. (2015). How 'big data' can make big impact: Findings from a systematic review and a longitudinal case study. *International Journal of Production Economics*, *165*, 234–246. https://doi.org/10.1016/j.ijpe.2014.12.031

Xu, Z., Frankwick, G. L., & Ramirez, E. (2016). Effects of big data analytics and traditional marketing analytics on new product success: A knowledge fusion perspective. *Journal of Business Research*, *69*(5), 1562–1566.

Yang, C., Huang, Q., Li, Z., Liu, K., & Hu, F. (2017). Big Data and cloud computing: Innovation opportunities and challenges. *International Journal of Digital Earth*, *10*(1), 13–53.

Chapter 3

Digital Governance for Addressing Performance Challenges Within Inter-municipalities

Giulia Leoni, Gennaro Maione and Luca Mazzara

Abstract

This chapter focuses on performance measurement and management systems (PMMS) in the inter-municipal cooperation context by considering the development of new capabilities required to exploit the digital governance potentialities in which data integration is essential. The analysis relied on the advent of digital governance, the Italian public informative systems reform, as well as on local governments (LG) renewals through the Union of Municipalities (UMs) – one of the most widespread structured forms of inter-municipal cooperation – based on the sustainability of local service delivery. Through a review of the literature and the conceptual outcomes resulting from the analysis of the dynamic capabilities (DCs) theory applied to digital governance, this chapter aims at suggesting a useful contribution for an effective improvement of PMMS in the public sector networks, with the consequent improvement of resilience in policy management. Thus, the broad information required by the UMs and the complexity of its administration together with the constraints regarding the need to share a common vision and strategy, plan objectives, targets, measurement, and evaluation processes are considered. In particular, three propositions have been developed as guidelines for achieving coordination, coherence, and integration of measuring and managing performances in public networks. This evidence will offer insights allowing scholars and practitioners a practical understanding of whether and how DCs – applied to digital governance – address PMMS challenges within an inter-municipal cooperative context.

Big Data and Decision-Making: Applications and Uses in the Public and Private Sector, 27–42

Published under exclusive licence by Emerald Publishing Limited
doi:10.1108/978-1-80382-551-920231003

Keywords: Digital governance; big data; performance measurement and management system; inter-municipal cooperative context; dynamic capabilities; municipalities

1. Introduction

Digital governance and LG networking have generated increasing attention in public management literature (i.e., Bertot et al., 2016; Dollery et al., 2020). Sub-national government cooperation rates increased among several countries, with particular emphasis on the cooperation among municipalities (Hulst & van Montfort, 2012). This situation may be represented by the shift of the "big paradigms." Since the 1980s, the shift from New Public Management (NPM) to New Public Governance (NPG) has focused on inter-dependent horizontal relationships, and thus governance structures, managerial, and accounting concepts have significantly changed. NPM promoted the outsourcing of both core and non-core services, such as information and communication technologies (ICT). However, this approach has shown a possible increase of transaction costs and an ineffective use of public resources, since public service providers tend to act opportunistically to serve their own interests (Hoffman et al., 2010; Le Grand, 1999) and often seem to be more focused on quantity than on quality (Almqvist, 2004; Le Grand, 1999). As a response, NPG transforms the make-or-buy decision as a means by which resources, information, and different competencies are shared to promote cooperation in the provision of services (Osborne, 2006). Therefore, there is a growing need for a more complete and innovative set of management and accounting systems to provide feedback for decision-making and for improving accountability (i.e., increasing reliance on big data). During these years there was a delegation of competencies from the state to the LGs – along with a broad set of data to administer it – where often the model adopted is based on the creation of stable cooperative relationships between institutions on the same scale with the aim to increase the capacity, efficacy, and efficiency in delivery of local public services. Namely, in past decades inter-municipal cooperation emerged throughout Europe (i.e., Finland, France, Spain, and the Netherlands), although there are remarkable differences in the way they are implemented (Bolgherini, 2011; Hulst & van Montfort, 2012). The UMs constitute one of the main structured forms of inter-municipal cooperation in Italy (Puntillo, 2017). However, PMMSs studies mainly investigate within the boundaries of organizations (i.e., municipalities), often without considering the need to adapt those systems to new contexts, despite their importance (Dekker, 2004), as Covid-19 has proved. Indeed, within the inter-organizational context, PMMSs are considered the most common approach used for network control, as they support monitoring, coordination, and trust between network actors (Bryson et al., 2006). The institutional adaptations toward the digital governance and the inter-organizational context requires the development of new capabilities able of creating inter-organizational coordination, coherence, and integration of PMMSs in an ongoing context of emergency and the need for resilience. Thus, the aim of this chapter is to understand the potentialities of digital governance through the DCs theory (Teece et al., 1997) to comprehend how to address PMMSs implementation issues in public networks (Agranoff & McGuire, 2001). The chapter proceeds as follows: the second section describes the DCs framework; subsequently, in the third section, the advent of digital governance and the performance management system within an inter-municipal context are exposed. Next, drawing on the DCs theory, propositions on dynamic digital governance for improving PMMSs within inter-municipal contexts are proposed: finally, conclusions follow.

2. DCs as a Conceptual Framework to Study

The phrase "dynamic capabilities," which today constitutes a widely debated framework in the social sciences, was first developed by Teece et al. (1990) in a working paper, published in a peer-reviewed version several years later (Teece et al., 1997). Unlike operational capabilities, DCs do not refer to the skills needed to carry out current operations but, on the contrary, they reflect the aptitude to generate a long-term competitive advantage, enabling organizations to survive (Ludwig & Pemberton, 2011) by stimulating the development of new competencies to cope with discontinuous changes of internal and external conditions (Alojairi et al., 2019). The underlying idea is that, when the environment evolves rapidly and unpredictably, organizations may achieve and maintain their competitive advantage through a constant development of resources (Teece et al., 1997) and routines (Eisenhardt & Martin, 2000), capable of ensuring a continuous adaptation. According to Teece et al. (1997), the concept of DCs summarizes in a single expression the two key elements for achieving competitive advantage: the term "dynamic" refers to the ability to renew competencies to be in tune with environmental changes and the term "capabilities" emphasizes the ability of strategic management to redefine and integrate resources and competencies with those held by other organizations (Vicari, 1995). The DCs can be qualified as emerging structures (Zollo & Winter, 2002) defined at a local level (Teece et al., 1997), rooted in organizational learning (Leonard-Barton, 1992), and designed to mitigate the problem of excessive rigidity generated by using ordinary capabilities (Easterby, Lyles, & Peteraf, 2009). However, over time, the concept of DCs has changed undergoing numerous interpretations, not always coincident (Ambrosini et al., 2009), as a result of the absence of a terminology capable of clarifying the various meanings with which the expression is used (Winter, 2003). To ensure ease of reading and to facilitate the understanding of the different meanings connected to the definitions of DCs, in Table 3.1, the most widely used conceptualizations in the literature are synthesized.

By considering the different meanings recognized to the concept of DCs, exegetical nuances emerge, recalling multiple interpretations within the same strand, with regard to effects, scope, observability, genesis, heterogeneity, and processes.

Regarding the consequences deriving from their exploitation, some academics believe that DCs affect the governance of lower order skills or routines (Collis, 1994; Zahra et al., 2006; Zollo & Winter, 2002; Zott, 2003), while for others

Table 3.1. DCs' Main Definitions

Author(s)	DCs' Definition
Teece et al. (1997)	DCs synthesize the firm's ability to integrate, build, and reconfigure internal and external competences to address rapidly changing environments. DCs thus reflect an organization's ability to achieve new and innovative forms of competitive advantage given path dependencies and market positions
Eisenhardt and Martin (2000)	DCs are linked to the firm's processes that use resources – specifically the processes to integrate, reconfigure, gain, and release resources – to match and even create market change. DCs thus are the organizational and strategic routines by which firms achieve new resource configurations as markets emerge, collide, split, evolve, and die
Zollo and Winter (2002)	DCs configure a learned and stable pattern of collective activity through which the organization systematically generates and modifies its operating routines in pursuit of improved effectiveness
Winter (2003)	DCs are capabilities that operate to extend, modify, or create ordinary capabilities
Zahra et al. (2006)	DCs consist of the abilities to reconfigure a firm's resources and routines in the manner envisioned and deemed appropriate by its principal decision-maker(s)
Teece (2007, p. 1319)	DCs can be disaggregated into the capacity (a) to sense and shape opportunities and threats, (b) to seize opportunities, and (c) to maintain competitiveness through enhancing, combining, protecting, and, when necessary, reconfiguring the business enterprise's intangible and tangible assets.
Pavlou and El Sawy (2011)	DCs reflect the ability to deploy superior new configurations of functional competencies by sensing the environment, generating new knowledge, coordinating activities and integrating resources
Schoemaker et al. (2018)	DCs enable firms to identify profitable configurations of competencies and assets, assemble, and orchestrate them, and then exploit them with an innovative and agile organization. DCs help identify new products and services, potentially opening new markets where rivals have not yet appeared. Each type is important in different ways. DCs are about doing the right things at the right time, based on new product (and process) development, unique managerial orchestration processes, a strong and change-oriented organizational culture, and a prescient assessment of the business environment and technological opportunities

Source: The authors.

the effects involve all resources (Helfat et al., 2009) and business management (Eisenhardt & Martin, 2000). Hence, whether some scholars consider DCs as high-level processes or routines (Eisenhardt & Martin, 2000; Winter, 2003; Zollo & Winter, 2002; Zott, 2003), others define them as capabilities that may be employed at any level (Helfat et al., 2009; Teece, 2007; Zahra et al., 2006). Moreover, whether some authors consider them as a typical expression of entrepreneurial activity (Newey & Zahra, 2009; Zahra et al., 2006), others claim that the dynamism of capabilities is mainly found in managerial activity (Helfat & Peteraf, 2003; Sirmon et al., 2011). With reference to observability, the idea that DCs are identifiable in any context and in any company regardless of the specific characteristics of the environment (Eisenhardt & Martin, 2000; Zahra et al., 2006; Zollo & Winter, 2002) is contrasted by those who believe that observability is conditional on the presence of highly dynamic contexts (Teece, 2007; Teece et al., 1997) or, on the contrary, relatively stable ones (Barreto, 2010). A further difference concerns the genesis: following an evolutionary perspective (Becker et al., 2005), some scholars attribute DCs to a specific learning process that, involving both the company actors and the production network (Rothaermel & Hess, 2007), leads to the institutionalization of a set of management solutions to the problem of renewing company competences (Zollo & Winter, 2002). According to this interpretation, the variation–selection–retention circuit of new solutions to management problems develops through their legitimization in the institutional context of the organization (DiMaggio & Powell, 1983): the development of DCs is understood as the result of trial and error, improvisation, and imitation. Therefore, DCs may also depend on random factors. Other authors (Zollo & Winter, 2002) take the opposite view, emphasizing the deliberate, bottom-up component of the learning process that leads to the formation of DCs. Following this approach, it is possible to distinguish a knowledge articulation phase – the result of collective comparison and evaluation – and a knowledge codification phase through which the knowledge produced is crystallized to be more easily transferred (Foss et al., 2012). A further perspective is provided by the emphasis on the role played by top management (Easterby-Smith et al., 2009), which is considered capable of providing the impetus to generate competences by imprinting its cognitive orientation, permeating every layer of the organization according to a top-down logic (Narayan et al., 2019). Another open aspect in the scholarly debate on DCs concerns their characteristic heterogeneity. In this regard, although most scholars believe in an essentially specific and unique nature, some assume that DCs have common and recognizable traits (Barreto, 2010). Finally, concerning the processes through which DCs may be exploited, although over time several conceptualizations have been proposed, none of them differ much from the prevailing orientation in the literature, which goes back to Teece et al.'s (1997) view, recognizing the presence of three inter-dependent stages (Casebeer et al., 2010; Coulon et al., 2020; de Oliveira & dos Santos Junior, 2018; Kalim & Arshad, 2018; Trivellato et al., 2021): resource coordination/integration (a static concept); learning (a dynamic concept); and asset reconfiguration (a transformational concept).

3. Theoretical Background

3.1. The Advent of Digital Governance

Over the last decade, the literature on the use of technologies in government has advanced from an e-government perspective to a digital transformation (Bertot et al., 2016), focused on institutional factors and the role that key actors play in outlining governance policies (Ciasullo & Troisi, 2017). Digitalization policies enable innovative forms of mediation and practices (Troisi et al., 2021; Visvizi et al., 2021) that represent a great opportunity to promote higher inclusion, efficiency, and effectiveness for service delivery in LGs, since digital transformation occurs during processes of institutional change where different actors have the chance to choose and make decisions (Visvizi et al., 2018; Visvizi & del Hoyo, 2021a, 2021b; Visvizi & Lytras, 2019). In this vein, modern digital public service platforms offer a new relationship standard between bureaucracy and society (O'Reilly, 2011), as well as the possibility of using data to transform policies, increase transparency, and promote open governments (Masoumi et al., 2021; West, 2004). Also, the pandemic seems to have given an impetus to the digitization of public services (Löfving et al., 2021), stimulating a "race" that in the last years the European and national institutions have been encouraging (European Commission, 2020a) to promote internet access, technology skills, and digital inclusion (European Commission, 2020b). The spread of Covid-19 has highlighted the importance of redesigning the relationship among citizens and public administration (Christensen & Lægreid, 2020), underlining the benefits deriving from increased digital culture in the processes of public services delivery and use. This effect is felt not only at the level of single LGs but also within inter-municipal contexts, where the existence of shared policies fosters a vision and an organic mission of governance (Juell-Skielse et al., 2017; Khisro et al., 2021). Technological infrastructures, telematic services, and digital culture are the pillars of a cooperative approach to the governance of inter-municipalities (Hoornbeek et al., 2016). In fact, implementing policies oriented toward digital governance makes possible to concretely support the networks of LGs – especially the small ones, often undersized in terms of personnel – which have competitive deficits in terms of intangible infrastructures, organizational resources, and IT skills (Benton, 2013; Troisi, 2016). Making investments for technological transformation, diffusion of digital culture, and resizing of the digital divide is fundamental for the territory and the well-being of the whole community (Ciasullo et al., 2020; Polese et al., 2018, 2021; Visvizi & Lytras, 2020). Digital governance embeds electronic delivery at the heart of the government model of inter-municipal contexts (Williamson, 2014), and includes activities such as digitizing interactions with citizens, new forms of automation using zero-touch technologies that do not require human intervention, and isocratic administration (self-government) (Margetts & Dunleavy, 2013). In this sense, through the promotion of technological training initiatives, digital governance makes possible to strengthen and support the innovation culture of municipalities and inter-municipal contexts (Dollery et al., 2020). Thus, it is important that all institutions, associations, and municipalities dialogue horizontally to adopt effective and timely measures capable of providing valid support to the inter-municipal context (Teles, 2016). However, especially within inter-municipal setting, the digital transformation of public services is neither linear nor ensured, since the availability of a technology does not mean that it is going to be employed (Fountain, 2004): institutional actors with decision-making powers over the process of digital transformation choose which services will be digitized (Filgueiras et al., 2019). In digital governance initiatives of municipalities networks, the main decisions require choices about the policy-making lifecycle and tools to be explored over a wide available range, since promoting engagement with citizens becomes strategically and operationally important (Panagiotopoulos et al., 2012).

3.2. Performance Management Systems Within an Inter-municipal Context

UM is the most widespread structured form of inter-municipal cooperation (Puntillo, 2017). To succeed, cooperation among municipalities requires clear governance, shared strategies, and trust. Moreover, a defined performance measurement system based on an informative infrastructure would also be required. The informative system allows generating a specific set of performance indicators useful to program targets related to strategic plans, to control final performance results, and to evaluate managers behaviors (Polese et al., 2017). The approach to PMMSs was introduced in Italy by the legislative decree 150/2009 (the so-called "Brunetta Reform") and subsequently developed by the legislative decree 174/2012 concerning the internal control system reform. Therefore, every public sector organization should measure, evaluate, and report their performance by producing different documents (performance measuring and evaluating system, performance plan, performance report, and so forth). Despite the innovative elements and pragmatic approach, the implementation of this reform by LGs, and their form of cooperation, has proved to be a big challenge. The 2008 Global Financial Crisis was the trigger for the debate on inter-municipal cooperation in the EU, where austerity policies were introduced, therefore reducing the transfer that municipalities have been receiving from the state (Pollitt & Bouckaert, 2017). This opens possibilities for a radical renewal of LGs that find themselves managing a series of problems that the decentralization has poured into the territories, often with few resources, pressed by stakeholders that have higher and higher expectations. The risk is that single municipalities, especially the small ones, might not be able to meet the standard level demands of local public services while reducing expenditure. To deal with these issues, central and regional governments are implementing inter-municipal cooperation tools, such as the UMs, with the aim to enhance efficiency and the quality of local policies and to meet the higher citizens' expectations. The UM may be considered as an inter-organizational network, characterized by high integration, and institutionalized level (Hulst & van Montfort, 2012). It is a voluntary second-grade election level order constituted by two or more municipalities that, through a formalized long-term cooperative relationship, may adopt a variety of solutions to provide services and implement public programs and policies. Specifically, juridically and economically autonomous organizations (partner municipality) draw up long-term deals to share resources (financial and non-financial, know-how, and political authority) for the joint exploitation of specific activities, with the aim to reach greater performance of particular services. For this reason, the critical engine for the whole network would be the ability to contribute to services and activity integration as well as the problem-solving capabilities needed to guarantee the achievement of higher performance. As pointed out by Crosby and Bryson (2005), cooperation operates more smoothly with effective leadership, which reduces the risk for the participants and shares responsibilities. It is important to highlight how these networks, as stable as they may be, are ever-changing since boundaries can adjust across time, depending on partner participation and withdrawal or depending on functions that can be enhanced or reduced. Thus, the UM dissolution may derive from the exit of an involved municipality that would block the interaction processes by withdrawing their resources. The replacement of these resources is not always possible and when it is, it might be costly and time consuming (Klijn & Koppenjan, 2000). This situation might be the result of a structural engineering process without the development of the proper capabilities needed for the achievement of a tight integration among LGs, a characteristic that would increase the success rate (Jacobsen & Kiland, 2017). In this case, one or more partners would feel that the inter-municipal cooperation does not fulfill its needs and might bypass the UMs that are starting to develop their own services, furthering their separate aims (Crosby & Bryson, 2005). The exploitation of economies of scale and the improvement of services provided are considered the main influencing factors for the establishment of inter-municipal cooperation. Nevertheless, through these associative processes, public administrations as agents may be controlled less by the citizenries (Ruggiero et al., 2012). Indeed, in LGs that are "closer to people," elections play the key role in shaping bureaucratic behaviors (Hong, 2017). However, when the inter-municipal context leads toward a second-level entity (as the UMs), there is a minor "legitimacy of entrance" (Ciapetti, 2014), as politicians do not face direct elections. But managers are more responsible for organization performance when public services are provided through networking. For such reasons, in this situation a greater emphasis is placed on the development of shared PMMSs, needed for a common vision and strategy, plan objectives, targets, measurements, and evaluation processes. However, most LGs still do not understand the value of PMMSs, especially for a multi-level system of performance analysis, such as that of the UMs. The criticisms are primarily based on the different cooperating partner organizations and cultures that also differentiate the PMMSs design and use, and that cannot address the broad scope of information required by the UMs. Indeed, the provision of sufficient information and necessary knowledge to allow proper decision-making becomes difficult without a well-articulated definition of performance information and indicators (Bleyen et al., 2017) capable of allowing interoperability among cooperating partners. Moreover, adverse effects in terms of low importance and consideration of PMMSs might derive from differences among partners (i.e., regarding size, there could be small municipalities with low human resources), especially whether the activity is politically disinterested (Barretta & Busco, 2011). This leads to measurement difficulties and limited availability of performance information to provide feedback for internal management and external accountability purposes. Managerial actions refer to the ability to detect environmental signals and understand the context in which inter-municipal (network) actors are operating, providing support for the decision-making, and motivation, which concerns the behavioral aspects related to PMMs (Hall, 2010). The use of performance measurement systems increases the level of communication, trust, commitment, and participation among networks, recognizing that these are key levers for the success of a network (Kaplan et al., 2010). Moreover, the literature recognizes the effects that PMMSs produces on partner behaviors and on the structure of their relationships: "governance as a set of coordinating and monitoring activities must occur in order for collaborations to survive" (Bryson et al., 2006, p. 49).

4. Dynamic Digital Governance for Improving Performance Management Systems in an Inter-municipal Context

Within the wider body of literature on public sector digitalization, an increasingly debated research strand focuses on the relevance of network collaboration since collaborative strategies emerge as more valuable than isolated approaches in dealing with problems and proposing solutions (Trivellato et al., 2021). In this regard, over the last decade, a renewed interest in collaborative innovation is orienting the ongoing scientific debate to stimulate contributions on digital governance of public sector networks (Gullmark, 2021, Luna-Reyes et al., 2020). Agranoff (2007) states that public sector networks (such as the UMs) may successfully cope with challenges by means of coordinated actions among LGs and other organizations, both public and private. In this vein, McGuire (2006) points out that a multi-organizational governance fosters public managers equipped with DCs in reaching objectives. In the inter-municipal context, digital governance takes on an even more decisive role since it allows dynamically managing multi-lateral relationships among LG agencies, and among governments, private companies, universities, and non-profits (Eggers & Singh, 2009). Hence, DCs applied to digital governance permit and facilitate the overcome of bureaucratic resistances typical of public sector organizations through the networking of LGs pursuing the same or compatible goal. Such a consideration allows highlighting both governance and managerial implications of this chapter. In fact, within the inter-municipal context, dynamic digital governance implies collaborative interactions aimed at triggering new ideas and their implementation by exchanging both hard and soft skills, resource coordination and integration, and the dissemination of innovative forms of sharing (Torfing, 2019). Being dynamic means that multi-actor digital governance enables the regeneration of competences and the exploitation of all the relevant resources in terms of knowledge, imagination, creativity, courage, transformative capacity, and political authority among the involved actors (Trivellato et al., 2021), such as municipalities. Thereby, the latter may keep on being relevant to changing environments and prompt to respond to the administered communities' needs and expectations. As concerns the theoretical implications arising from embracing and adapting the Teece et al.'s (1997) conceptual view, DCs applied to digital inter-municipal governance might be opportunely unbundled into three organizational levels: (1) sensing and shaping opportunities; (2) seizing opportunities; and (3) enhancing, combining, and reconfiguring the assets of both single LGs and the network as a whole. To sense and shape the emerging opportunities at both theoretical and practical level, inter-municipal networks shall steadily explore the chance to employ new digital technologies. Once an opportunity is picked out, a shared strategy must be outlined to achieve the common or compatible goal (or goals) pursued. Finally, a reconfiguration of systems, procedures, routine, structures, and know-how is needed to solve complex issues by adapting the inter-municipal network to the volatile environment where many LGs operate (Piening, 2013). Thus, dynamic digital governance increasingly takes shape as a critical success factor for public sector organizations (Salge & Vera, 2013) since governments are continuously asked to face up expectations concerning their responsiveness (Walker, 2014) and the effectiveness of the services supplied. With reference to the UMs and coherently to the developed framework based on the abovementioned DC theory, hereinafter, three sequential propositions are proposed:

P1. The employment of digital technologies may lead to a more efficient and effective network relationships (both internal and external).

P2. A shared strategy enhances the diagnostic analysis necessary to define priorities and solutions aimed at solving specific problems.

P3. The process of reconfiguration for adaptation of environmental changes requires the redesign or revision of performance measurement systems, internal procedures, and the establishment of common standards with regard to timing.

In light of what has been discussed so far, the use of the DCs framework applied to digital governance may prove useful in contributing to improve the inter-municipal networks outcomes and to foster the achievement of the objectives pursued. In this perspective, the application of DCs to digital governance may favor an improvement of PMMSs in the inter-municipal context, such as the UMs.

5. Concluding Remarks

This chapter focuses on the DC theory contextualized in a digital governance era as a lens to understand the possible influence on the issues in LG networking regarding PMMSs. The chapter contributes to the expanding literature on PMMSs and to the DC theory by focusing on the impact that the digital governance may have on PMMSs implementation on a multi-organizational dimension. The propositions proposed rely on relevant literature with the hope that future research will develop empirical evidence of inter-municipal cooperative experiences. Empirical works would offer valuable insights, allowing understanding whether DCs provide concrete support to digital governance in addressing performance management system challenges within inter-municipal cooperative contexts. In this regard, it is worth pointing out that some scholars (e.g., Wangel, 2010) affirm that the use of DCs theory may prove to be dangerously vague and tautological, theorizing only an indirect effect those capabilities on performance. This is also the limit of this chapter: whether on the one hand the DCs theory may prove useful for dealing with environmental changes, on the other, it is unclear how this result may be achieved (Wheeler, 2002). Such a criticality depends on the consideration according to which DCs often appear difficult to be identified and operationalized (Lawson & Samson, 2001). In this context, a data-driven orientation and its systematic interpretation may help to ensure the DCs application on PMMSs as the collaborative environment and joint management not only can prevent from inefficient bureaucratic provision, but also may lead to a sustainable performance in the long term. For this reason, new and deeper research on the subject is expected.

References

Agranoff, R. (2007). *Managing within networks: Adding value to public organizations*. Georgetown University Press. https://doi.org/10.1002/pam.20373

Agranoff, R., & McGuire, M. (2001). Big questions in public network management research. *Journal of Public Administration Research and Theory*, *11*(3), 295–326. https://doi.org/10.1093/oxfordjournals.jpart.a003504

Almqvist, R. M. (2004). *Icons of new public management: Four studies on competition, contracts and control* [Doctoral dissertation, Företagsekonomiska institutionen].

Alojairi, A., Akhtar, N., Ali, H. M., & Basiouni, A. F. (2019). Assessing Canadian business IT capabilities for online selling adoption: A net-enabled business innovation cycle (NEBIC) perspective. *Sustainability*, *11*(13), 3662. https://doi.org/10.3390/su11133662

Ambrosini, V., Bowman, C., & Collier, N. (2009). Dynamic capabilities: An exploration of how firms renew their resource base. *British Journal of Management*, *20*, S9–S24. https://doi.org/10.1111/j.1467-8551.2008.00610.x

Barretta, A., & Busco, C. (2011). Technologies of government in public sector's networks: In search of cooperation through management control innovations. *Management Accounting Research*, *22*(4), 211–219. https://doi.org/10.1016/j.mar.2011.10.002

Barreto, I. (2010). Dynamic capabilities: A review of past research and an agenda for the future. *Journal of Management*, *36*(1), 256–280. https://doi.org/10.1177/0149206309350776

Becker, M. C., Lazaric, N., Nelson, R. R., & Winter, S. G. (2005). Applying organizational routines in understanding organizational change. *Industrial and Corporate Change*, *14*(5), 775–791. https://doi.org/10.1016/10.1093/icc/dth071

Benton, J. E. (2013). Local government collaboration: Considerations, issues, and prospects. *State and Local Government Review*, *45*(4), 220–223. https://doi.org/10.1177/0160323X13515683

Bertot, J., Estevez, E., & Janowski, T. (2016). Universal and contextualized public services: Digital public service innovation framework. *Government information quarterly*, *33*(2), 211–222. https://doi.org/10.1016/j.giq.2016.05.004

Bleyen, P., Klimovský, D., Bouckaert, G., & Reichard, C. (2017). Linking budgeting to results? Evidence about performance budgets in European municipalities based on a comparative analytical model. *Public Management Review*, *19*(7), 932–953. https://doi.org/10.1080/14719037.2016.1243837

Bolgherini, S. (2011). *Local government and inter-municipal cooperation in Italy and Germany*. Inst. für Politikwiss.

Bryson, J. M., Crosby, B. C., & Stone, M. M. (2006). The design and implementation of cross-sector collaborations: Propositions from the literature. *Public Administration Review*, *66*, 4455. https://doi.org/10.1111/j.1540-6210.2006.00665.x

Casebeer, A., Reay, T., Dewald, J., & Pablo, A. (2010). Knowing through doing: Unleashing latent dynamic capabilities in the public sector. In K. Walshe, G. Harvey & P. Jas (Eds.), *Connecting knowledge and performance in public services: From knowing to doing* (pp. 251–257). Cambridge University Press. https://doi.org/10.1017/CBO9780511762000.013

Christensen, T., & Lægreid, P. (2020). Balancing governance capacity and legitimacy: How the Norwegian government handled the COVID-19 crisis as a high performer. *Public Administration Review*, *80*(5), 774–779. https://doi.org/10.1111/puar.13241

Ciapetti, L. (2014). Il territorio tra efficienza e sviluppo: la riforma delle Province e le politiche di area vasta. *Istituzioni del federalismo: rivista di studi giuridici e politici* (2), 251–283.

Ciasullo, M. V., & Troisi, O. (2017). *La visione relazionale dell'impresa: Un approccio per la Strategic Governance* (Vol. 68). G Giappichelli Editore.

Ciasullo, M. V., Troisi, O., Grimaldi, M., & Leone, D. (2020). Multi-level governance for sustainable innovation in smart communities: An ecosystems approach. *International Entrepreneurship and Management Journal*, *16*(4), 1167–1195. https://doi.org/10.1007/s11365-020-00641-6

Collis, D. J. (1994). Research note: How valuable are organizational capabilities?. *Strategic Management Journal*, *15*(S1), 143–152. https://doi.org/10.1002/smj.4250150910

Coulon, T., Templier, M., Bourdeau, S., Pascal, A., & Vieru, D. (2020). Open innovation in the public sector: A dynamic capabilities perspective and the role of information technology. Proceedings of the 53rd Hawaii International Conference on System Sciences, 5942–5951. https://doi.org/10.24251/HICSS.2020.728

Crosby, B. C., & Bryson, J. M. (2005). *Leadership for the common good: Tackling public problems in a shared-power world* (Vol. 264). John Wiley & Sons.

DiMaggio, P. J., & Powell, W. W. (1983). The iron cage revisited: Institutional isomorphism and collective rationality in organizational fields. *American Sociological Review*, *48*(2), 147–160.

de Oliveira, L. F., & dos Santos Junior, C. D. (2018, July). Open innovation in the public sector. In J. A. Morales, C. Gershenson, D. Braha, A. A. Minai & Y. Bar-Yam (Eds.), *International conference on complex systems* (pp. 458–466). Springer. https://doi.org/10.1007/978-3-319-96661-8_47

Dekker, H. C. (2004). Control of inter-organizational relationships: Evidence on appropriation concerns and coordination requirements. *Accounting, Organizations and Society*, *29*(1), 27–49. https://doi.org/10.1016/S0361-3682(02)00056-9

Dollery, B., Kitchen, H., McMillan, M., & Shah, A. (2020). Intermunicipal cooperation. In B. Dollery, H. Kitchen, M. McMillan & A. Shah (Eds.), *Local public, fiscal and financial governance* (pp. 257–285). Palgrave Macmillan.

Easterby-Smith, M., Lyles, M. A., & Peteraf, M. A. (2009). Dynamic capabilities: Current debates and future directions. *British Journal of Management*, *20*, S1–S8. https://doi.org/10.1111/j.1467-8551.2008.00609.x

Eggers, W. D., & Singh, S. K. (2009). *The public innovator's playbook: Nurturing bold ideas in government*. Ash Institute, Harvard Kennedy School.

Eisenhardt, K. M., & Martin, J. A. (2000). Dynamic capabilities: What are they?. *Strategic Management Journal*, *21*(10–11), 1105–1121. https://doi.org/10.1002/1097-0266(200010/11)21:10/11<1105::AID-SMJ133>3.0.CO;2-E

European Commission. (2020a). *Shaping Europe's digital future*. Digital Innovation Hubs (DIHs) in Europe. https://digital-strategy.ec.europa.eu/en/activities/edihs

European Commission. (2020b). *Smart villages*. European Network for Rural Development. https://enrd.ec.europa.eu/enrd-thematic-work/smart-and-competitive-ruralareas/smart-villages_en

Filgueiras, F., Flávio, C., & Palotti, P. (2019). Digital transformation and public service delivery in Brazil. *Latin American Policy*, *10*(2), 195–219. https://doi.org/10.1111/lamp.12169

Foss, N. J., Heimeriks, K. H., Winter, S. G., & Zollo, M. (2012). A Hegelian dialogue on the micro-foundations of organizational routines and capabilities. *European Management Review*, *9*(4), 173–197. https://doi.org/10.1111/emre.12001

Fountain, J. E. (2004). *Building the virtual state: Information technology and institutional change*. Brookings Institution Press.

Gullmark, P. (2021). Do all roads lead to innovativeness? A study of public sector organizations' innovation capabilities. *The American Review of Public Administration*, *51*(7), 509–525. https://doi.org/10.1177/02750740211010464

Hall, M. (2010). Accounting information and managerial work. *Accounting, Organizations and Society*, 35(3), 301–315. https://doi.org/10.1016/j.aos.2009.09.003

Helfat, C. E., Finkelstein, S., Mitchell, W., Peteraf, M., Singh, H., Teece, D., & Winter, S. G. (2009). *Dynamic capabilities: Understanding strategic change in organizations*. John Wiley & Sons.

Helfat, C. E., & Peteraf, M. A. (2003). The dynamic resource-based view: Capability lifecycles. *Strategic Management Journal*, *24*(10), 997–1010. https://doi.org/10.1002/smj.332

Hoffman, W. H., Neumann, K., & Speckbacher G. (2010). The effect of interorganizational trust on make-or-cooperate decisions: Disentangling opportunism-dependent and opportunism-independent effects of trust. *European Management Review*, *7*(2), 101–15. https://doi.org/10.1057/emr.2010.8

Hong, S. (2017). What are the areas of competence for central and local governments? Accountability mechanisms in multi-level governance. *Journal of Public Administration Research and Theory*, *27*(1), 120–134. https://doi.org/10.1093/jopart/muw048

Hoornbeek, J., Beechey, T., & Pascarella, T. (2016). Fostering local government collaboration: An empirical analysis of case studies in Ohio. *Journal of Urban Affairs*, *38*(2), 252–279. https://doi.org/10.1111/juaf.12204

Hulst, J. R., & van Montfort, A. J. (2012). Institutional features of inter-municipal cooperation: Cooperative arrangements and their national contexts. *Public Policy and Administration*, *27*(2), 121–144. https://doi.org/10.1177/0952076711403026

Jacobsen, D. I., & Kiland, C. (2017). Success with a bitter aftertaste: Success factors in inter-municipal cooperation. *Scandinavian Journal of Public Administration*, *21*(4), 53–76.

Juell-Skielse, G., Lönn, C. M., & Päivärinta, T. (2017). Modes of collaboration and expected benefits of inter-organizational E-government initiatives: A multi-case study. *Government Information Quarterly*, *34*(4), 578–590. https://doi.org/10.1016/j.giq.2017.10.008

Kalim, K., & Arshad, M. A. (2018). Towards high performance strategy: Context of Pakistan's public sector organisations. *International Journal of Public Sector Performance Management*, *4*(4), 498–515. https://doi.org/10.1504/IJPSPM.2018.095219

Kaplan, R. S., Norton, D. P., & Rugelsjoen, B. (2010). Managing alliances with the balanced scorecard. *Harvard Business Review*, *88*(1), 114–120.

Khisro, J., Lindroth, T., & Magnusson, J. (2021). Mechanisms of constraint: A clinical inquiry of digital infrastructuring in municipalities. *Transforming Government: People, Process and Policy*, *16*(1), 81–96. https://doi.org/10.1108/TG-01-2021-0014

Klijn, E. H., & Koppenjan, J. F. (2000). Public management and policy networks: Foundations of a network approach to governance. *Public Management an International Journal of Research and Theory*, *2*(2), 135–158. https://doi.org/10.1080/14719030000000007

Lawson, B., & Samson, D. (2001). Developing innovation capability in organisations: A dynamic capabilities approach. *International Journal of Innovation Management*, *5*(03), 377–400. https://doi.org/10.1142/S1363919601000427

Le Grand, J. (1999). Competition, cooperation, or control? Tales from the British National Health Service: In the battle between market competition and central control in Britain's health care system, control won. Will Labour's new version of the market prevail?. *Health Affairs*, *18*(3), 27–39. https://doi.org/10.1377/hlthaff.18.3.27

Leonard-Barton, D. (1992). Core capabilities and core rigidities: A paradox in managing new product development. *Strategic Management Journal*, *13*(S1), 111–125. https://doi.org/10.1002/smj.4250131009

Löfving, L., Kamuf, V., Heleniak, T., Weck, S., & Norlén, G. (2021). Can digitalization be a tool to overcome spatial injustice in sparsely populated regions? The cases of Digital Västerbotten (Sweden) and Smart Country Side (Germany). *European Planning Studies*, *29*(1), 1–18. https://doi.org/10.1080/09654313.2021.1928053

Ludwig, G., & Pemberton, J. (2011). A managerial perspective of dynamic capabilities in emerging markets: The case of the Russian steel industry. *Journal for East European Management Studies*, *16*(3), 215–236. http://www.jstor.org/stable/23281688

Luna-Reyes, L., Juiz, C., Gutierrez-Martinez, I., & Duhamel, F. B. (2020). Exploring the relationships between dynamic capabilities and IT governance: Implications for local governments. *Transforming Government: People, Process and Policy*, *14*(2), 149–169. https://doi.org/10.1108/TG-09-2019-0092

Margetts, H., & Dunleavy, P. (2013). The second wave of digital-era governance: A quasi-paradigm for government on the Web. *Philosophical Transactions of the Royal Society A: Mathematical, Physical and Engineering Sciences*, *371*(1987), 1–17. https://doi.org/10.1098/rsta.2012.0382

Masoumi, H., Farahani, B., & Shams Aliee, F. (2021). Systematic and ontology-based approach to interoperable cross-domain open government data services. *Transforming Government: People, Process and Policy*, *16*(1), 110–127. https://doi.org/10.1108/TG-08-2021-0132

McGuire, M. (2006). Collaborative public management: Assessing what we know and how we know it. *Public Administration Review*, *66*(s1), 33–43. https://doi.org/10.1111/j.1540-6210.2006.00664.x

Narayan, J. J., Gudergan, S., Pathak, R. D., & Singh, G. (2019). *Dynamic capabilities in public enterprises*. Springer Nature.

Newey, L. R., & Zahra, S. A. (2009). The evolving firm: How dynamic and operating capabilities interact to enable entrepreneurship. *British Journal of Management*, *20*(1), S81–S100. https://doi.org/10.1111/j.1467-8551.2008.00614.x

O'Reilly, T. (2011). Government as a Platform. *Innovations: Technology, Governance, Globalization*, *6*(1), 13–40. https://doi.org/10.1162/INOV_a_00056

Osborne, S. P. (2006). The new public governance? *Public Management Review*, *8*(3), 377–387. https://doi.org/10.1080/14719030600853022

Panagiotopoulos, P., Al-Debei, M. M., Fitzgerald, G., & Elliman, T. (2012). A business model perspective for ICTs in public engagement. *Government Information Quarterly*, *29*(2), 192–202. https://doi.org/10.1016/j.giq.2011.09.011

Pavlou, P. A., & El Sawy, O. A. (2011). Understanding the elusive black box of dynamic capabilities. *Decision Sciences*, *42*(1), 239–273. https://doi.org/10.1111/j.1540-5915.2010.00287.x

Piening, E. P. (2013). Dynamic capabilities in public organizations: A literature review and research agenda. *Public Management Review*, *15*(2), 209–245. https://doi.org/10.1080/14719037.2012.708358

Polese, F., Troisi, O., Carrubbo, L., & Grimaldi, M. (2018). An integrated framework toward public system governance: Insights from viable systems approach. In *Cross-sectoral relations in the delivery of public services*. Emerald Publishing Limited.

Polese, F., Troisi, O., Grimaldi, M., & Loia, F. (2021). Reinterpreting governance in smart cities: An ecosystem-based view. In A. Visvizi & M. Lytras (Eds.), *Smart cities and the un SDGs* (pp. 71–89). Elsevier.

Polese, F., Troisi, O., Torre, C., & Maione, G. (2017). Performance evaluation and measurement in public organizations: A systematic literature review. *International Journal of Business Administration*, *8*(1), 106–117. http://dx.doi.org/10.5430/ijba.v8n1p106

Pollitt, C., & Bouckaert, G. (2017). *Public management reform: A comparative analysis-into the age of austerity*. Oxford University Press.

Puntillo, P. (2017). Inter-municipal cooperation in service delivery and governance: Insights from Italy. *International Journal of Business Governance and Ethics*, *12*(3), 197–217.

Rothaermel, F. T., & Hess, A. M. (2007). Building Dynamic capabilities: Innovation driven by individual-, firm-, and network-level effects. *Organization Science*, *18*(6), 898–921. https://doi.org/10.1287/orsc.1070.0291

Ruggiero, P., Monfardini, P., & Mussari, R. (2012). Territorial boundaries as limits: A Foucauldian analysis of the agglomeration of municipalities. *International Journal of Public Administration*, *35*(7), 492–506. https://doi.org/10.1080/01900692.2012.661171

Salge, T. O., & Vera, A. (2013). Small steps that matter: incremental learning, slack resources and organizational performance. *British Journal of Management*, *24*(2), 156–173. https://doi.org/10.1111/j.1467-8551.2011.00793.x

Schoemaker, P. J., Heaton, S., & Teece, D. (2018). Innovation, dynamic capabilities, and leadership. *California Management Review*, *61*(1), 15–42. https://doi.org/10.1177%2F0008125618790246

Sirmon, D. G., Hitt, M. A., Ireland, R. D., & Gilbert, B. A. (2011). Resource orchestration to create competitive advantage: Breadth, depth, and life cycle effects. *Journal of Management*, *37*(5), 1390–1412. https://doi.org/10.1177%2F0149206310385695

Teece, D. J. (2007). Explicating dynamic capabilities: The nature and microfoundations of (sustainable) enterprise performance. *Strategic Management Journal*, *28*(13), 1319–1350. https://doi.org/10.1002/smj.640

Teece, D. J., Pisano, G., Shuen, A. (1990). *Firm capabilities, resources, and the concept of strategy* [Working Paper 90–8 ed.]. University of California, Berkeley, Center for Research on Management.

Teece, D. J., Pisano, G., & Shuen, A. (1997). Dynamic capabilities and strategic management. *Strategic Management Journal*, *18*(7), 509–533. https://doi.org/10.1002/(SICI)1097-0266(199708)18:7%3C509::AID-SMJ882%3E3.0.CO;2-Z

Teles, F. (2016). *Local governance and intermunicipal cooperation*. Springer.

Torfing, J. (2019). Collaborative innovation in the public sector: The argument. *Public Management Review*, *21*(1), 1–11. https://doi.org/10.1080/14719037.2018.1430248

Trivellato, B., Martini, M., & Cavenago, D. (2021). How do organizational capabilities sustain continuous innovation in a public setting? *The American Review of Public Administration*, *51*(1), 57–71. https://doi.org/10.1177%2F0275074020939263

Troisi, O. (2016). *Governance e Co-creazione di valore nella PA: Una rilettura in ottica Service-Dominant Logic* (Vol. 60). G Giappichelli Editore.

Troisi, O., Visvizi, A., & Grimaldi, M. (2021). The different shades of innovation emergence in smart service systems: The case of Italian cluster for aerospace technology. *Journal of Business & Industrial Marketing*. https://doi.org/10.1108/JBIM-02-2020-0091

Vicari, S. (1995). *Brand Equity. Il potenziale generativo della fiducia*. Egea.

Visvizi, A., & del Hoyo, R. P. (2021a). Sustainable development goals (SDGs) in the smart city: A tool or an approach? (An introduction). In A. Visvizi & R. Perez del Hoyo (Eds.), *Smart cities and the UN SDGs* (pp. 1–11). Elsevier.

Visvizi, A., & del Hoyo, R. P. (2021b). Transforming the city from within: SDGs and their transformative dynamics in the smart city (conclusions). In A. Visvizi & R. Perez del Hoyo (Eds.), *Smart cities and the UN SDGs* (pp. 253–257). Elsevier.

Visvizi, A., & Lytras, M. D. (Eds.). (2019). *Politics and technology in the post-truth era*. Emerald Publishing.

Visvizi, A., & Lytras, M. D. (2020). Government at risk: Between distributed risks and threats and effective policy-responses. *Transforming Government: People, Process and Policy*, *14*(3), 333–336. https://doi.org/10.1108/TG-06-2020-0137

Visvizi, A., Lytras, M. D., Damiani, E., & Mathkour, H. (2018). Policy making for smart cities: Innovation and social inclusive economic growth for sustainability. *Journal of Science and Technology Policy Management*, *9*(2), 126–133. https://doi.org/10.1108/JSTPM-07-2018-079

Visvizi, A., Troisi, O., Grimaldi, M., & Loia, F. (2021). Think human, act digital: Activating data-driven orientation in innovative start-ups. *European Journal of Innovation Management*, 25(6), 452–478. https://doi.org/10.1108/EJIM-04-2021-0206

Walker, R. M. (2014). Internal and external antecedents of process innovation: A review and extension. *Public Management Review*, *16*(1), 21–44. https://doi.org/10.1080/14719037.2013.771698

Wangcl, A. (2010). Dynamic capabilities: A review and research agenda. *International Journal of Management Reviews*, *9*(1), 31–51. https://doi.org/10.1111/j.1468-2370.2007.00201.x

West, D. M. (2004). E-government and the transformation of service delivery and citizen attitudes. *Public Administration Review*, *64*(1), 15–27. https://doi.org/10.1111/j.1540-6210.2004.00343.x

Wheeler, B. (2002). The net-enabled business innovation cycle: A dynamic capabilities theory for harnessing it to create customer value. *Information Systems Research*, *13*(2), 147–150. https://doi.org/10.1287/isre.13.2.125.89

Williamson, B. (2014). Knowing public services: Cross-sector intermediaries and algorithmic governance in public sector reform. *Public Policy and Administration*, *29*(4), 292–312. https://doi.org/10.1177%2F0952076714529139

Winter, S. G. (2003). Understanding dynamic capabilities. *Strategic Management Journal*, *24*(10), 991–995. https://doi.org/10.1002/smj.318

Zahra, S. A., Sapienza, H. J., & Davidsson, P. (2006). Entrepreneurship and dynamic capabilities: A review, model and research agenda. *Journal of Management Studies*, *43*(4), 917–955. https://doi.org/10.1111/j.1467-6486.2006.00616.x

Zollo, M., & Winter, S. G. (2002). Deliberate learning and the evolution of dynamic capabilities. *Organization Science*, *13*(3), 339–351. https://doi.org/10.1287/orsc.13.3.339.2780

Zott, C. (2003). Dynamic capabilities and the emergence of intraindustry differential firm performance: Insights from a simulation study. *Strategic Management Journal*, *24*(2), 97–125. https://doi.org/10.1002/smj.288

Chapter 4

Misuse of Personal Data: Exploring the Privacy Paradox in the Age of Big Data Analytics

Xhimi Hysa, Mario D'Arco and Joana Kostaqi

Abstract

This chapter explores young individuals' attitude toward protection of personal data. Specifically, the discussion focuses on the General Data Protection Regulation (GDPR) and the introduction of a property right over personal data. To this end, a total of 10 in-depth interviews were conducted with both Albanian and Italian college students. Transcribed data from the interviews were analyzed through thematic analysis. Four main themes emerged from the interviews: (i) distrust toward the way personal data are used online, (ii) no change in behavior after the introduction of GDPR, (iii) limited knowledge regarding terms and conditions of websites, and (iv) individual desire for more control over his/her data. In light of the research findings, the present contribution highlights that, despite the GDPR enhances individuals' data protection and rights, there is an intention–behavior gap that has been labeled in the literature as "privacy paradox." Furthermore, findings reveal that treating personal data as a property right has pros and cons.

Keywords: Data privacy; data protection; data-driven approach; ethics; data ownership; General Data Protection Regulation

1. Introduction

Personal information is at the core of "data-driven economy." By collecting and analyzing data, both companies and public institutions can extract new knowledge about human behavior and create new forms of value (Mayer-Schönberger &

Big Data and Decision-Making: Applications and Uses in the Public and Private Sector, 43–57

Published under exclusive licence by Emerald Publishing Limited
doi:10.1108/978-1-80382-551-920231004

Cukier, 2013). For example, companies use data to improve levels of customer insights and engagement, as well as to compile user profiles and make prediction about consumption patterns. Similarly, governments and political institutions employ data analytics to inform policy, make decisions, and change citizens' behaviors (Visvizi & Lytras, 2019).

This process of collecting, analyzing, and interpreting data is an essential component of data-driven decision-making approach (Lytras et al., 2020; Troisi et al., 2020; Troisi, Grimaldi, et al., 2021a; Troisi, Visvizi, et al., 2021b). However, despite its many advantages, the analysis of massive amounts of data from a variety of sources through algorithmic decision-making implicates several ethical challenges related to data surveillance (Zuboff, 2019), data ownership (Hummel et al., 2020), data privacy (Saura et al., 2021), and misuse or mishandling of personal information (Bauer et al., 2021).

In recent years, a series of events related to the misuse of individuals' personal information have captured the attention of the public opinion (Boussios, 2019, 2021). One of the most sensational is the Cambridge Analytica scandal (Wagner, 2021). Cambridge Analytica was accused to have acquired data on millions of the US Facebook users without their clear permission (Kumar & Kumar, 2021). Data were used to understand users' behavioral characteristics and probably to manipulate through advertising campaigns of the 2016 US presidential elections and the UK Brexit referendum (Duguid, 2021). Facebook admitted the Cambridge Analytica data breach only in 2018. However, as highlighted by Wagner (2021), this scandal represented more than a simple data breach, it is a privacy harm. A similar event has occurred in Albania where personal information of individuals has been stolen from E-Albania, an online platform created by the Albanian government to offer assistance in documentation delivery. The data of 910,000 citizens were allegedly collected by the Socialist Party and illegally used as a tool for its own political interests (Osservatorio Balcani e Caucaso Transeuropa, 2021).

Many people seem to ignore or downplay privacy risks (Rughiniş et al., 2021). This issue has been termed the "privacy paradox" (Gerber et al., 2018; Kayes & Iamnitchi, 2017), since individuals are aware of privacy troubles, but they do not take action. The "privacy paradox" characterizes especially the digital natives (Rughiniş et al., 2021), that is, the generational cohort born between 1997 and 2012 (Dimock, 2019). This generational cohort to be present on social media and to continue to use mobile apps gives away personal data without worrying about privacy.

According to Goddard (2017, p. 703),

> personal data is information that, directly or indirectly, can identify an individual, and specifically includes online identifiers such as IP addresses, cookies and digital fingerprinting, and location data that could identify individuals.

After the introduction of the GDPR, internet users have more control over their data (Goddard, 2017). However, studies regarding the GDPR revealed that individuals continue to exercise little power to limit the effect of cookies and online tracing (Becher & Benoliel, 2021; Urban et al., 2019). Therefore, the success of the GDPR is correlated to user's GDPR awareness and engagement (Rughiniş et al., 2021).

The ongoing debate about the effectiveness of the current legislative framework regarding data protection in the era of data economy is also characterized by another policy solution that considers data as a property right (Purtova, 2009; Stepanov, 2020). According to this proposal, individuals own their personal information and can decide to sell them to other actors.

Against this backdrop, this chapter attempts to explore the point of view of a small group of Albanian and Italian college students about the following issues: (i) awareness of the GDPR; (ii) actions to protect personal information online; and (iii) consideration about the introduction of a property right to protect personal data.

The argument in this chapter is organized as follows. First, the conceptual background regarding privacy issues is presented. Second, the methods adopted to collect and analyze data are illustrated. Third, the discussions, implications, and practical recommendations arising from the results are presented. Lastly, conclusions and suggestions for future studies are put forth.

2. The Conceptual Background

2.1. Privacy Paradox

In the present day, before to access to a website, a social media platform, or a given mobile application individuals must agree to a privacy policy. Studies about how individuals responsibly interact with privacy disclosures reveal that web users do not have the time to read the document (Ploug & Holm, 2013), so they click directly on the "I agree" checkbox.

To explain the gap between privacy attitude and privacy protection behavior, that is, the so-called "privacy paradox," researchers have adopted several theoretical perspectives.

According to privacy calculus theory, individuals estimate the difference between the expected loss of privacy and the potential gain of disclosure (Dinev & Hart, 2006; Jiang et al., 2013; Xu et al., 2011). Benefits are in most cases intangible. For example, individuals give away personal information on social media to satisfy the need for diversion and entertainment, as well as the need for social relationships and identity construction (Debatin et al., 2009). Other benefits awarded by users are related to relationship development, social control, and self-representation (Lee et al., 2013).

As highlighted by the privacy calculus theory, individuals make decisions about their privacy in a rational way. However, research in the field of behavioral economics revealed that the decision-making process is influenced by heuristics and cognitive biases (Acquisti & Grossklags, 2007). According to Kokolakis (2017), heuristics and biases stand as one of the main drivers of the "privacy paradox."

Heuristics are mental shortcuts that help people to solve problems and make judgements in different decision-making contexts (Olivero & Lunt, 2004; Sundar et al., 2020). Cognitive heuristics are stored in one's memory in the format of schemata or general rules of thumbs (i.e., "if–then" statements). When possible, they are retrieved by individuals to support a decision-making process (Chen & Chaiken, 1999). Heuristics are helpful in many situations, but they can also lead to cognitive biases, such as optimism bias and affect bias (Kokolakis, 2017).

Optimism bias concerns the individual tendency to believe that he/she is less at risk of experiencing a negative situation compared to others. Cho et al. (2010) have observed this bias in privacy behavior. Specifically, their survey results suggested that people tend to show optimism bias about online privacy dangers and to judge themselves as less vulnerable than others to privacy issues. Similarly, Baek et al. (2014) confirmed that people perceive that the infringement of personal online privacy is a problem that considers other people.

According to Gilovich et al. (2002), affect heuristic is one of the most usual human decision-making and behavior biases. Affect heuristic involves making choices or judge a given situation based on the emotions that the individual is experiencing in that circumstance (Kokolakis, 2017). For example, research has shown that web users underestimate the risks of information disclosure when they are utilizing an interface that evokes positive affect (Kehr et al., 2015).

Other privacy heuristics are discussed by Sundar et al. (2020). For example, according to the authority heuristic, individuals tend to reveal their private information when they are interacting with a website created by an authoritative source such as a brand or a government office. In light of this shortcut, individuals believe that everything they reveal is secure, because authorities are credible and can guarantee quality (Sundar, 2008; Sundar et al., 2020).

Another theoretical lens employed to analyze privacy-related issues is the Elaboration Likelihood Model (ELM). The ELM theory, which was proposed by Petty and Cacioppo (1986), is useful to explain individuals' decision-making process (Bi et al., 2017), and provides a useful explanation about how individuals develop certain attitudes and behaviors (Bhattacherjee & Sanford, 2006). Specifically, it is widely employed by scholars in the information systems field to study specific contexts in which persuasion could occur, such as online marketing and user adoption (Cyr et al., 2018; Han et al., 2018; Zhou, 2012). According to the ELM theory, individuals can be persuaded or encouraged to take actions by means of two different routes: the central route and the peripheral route (Ho & Bodoff, 2014). The former concerns decision-making processes that involve high levels of cognitive effort. The latter deals with decision-making processes that often depend on cues, such as celebrity endorsements, charisma, or the attractiveness of the sender (Angst & Agarwal, 2009), and require less cognitive effort (Chen et al., 2018). As highlighted by Petty et al. (2002), decisions based on the central route are more stable and persistent than those from the peripheral route.

3. Methods

To investigate what Albanian and Italian college students think about the issues illustrated in the introductive section of this chapter (i.e., (i) awareness of the GDPR; (ii) actions to protect personal information online; and (iii) consideration

Table 4.1. Sample Characteristics.

Participant 1	23	Male	Albanian	Master's-degree student
Participant 2	23	Male	Albanian	Bachelors' degree
Participant 3	24	Female	Albanian	Master's-degree student
Participant 4	25	Female	Albanian-Italian	Master's-degree student
Participant 5	25	Male	Albanian-Greek	Master's-degree student
Participant 6	24	Female	Italian	Master's-degree student
Participant 7	24	Male	Italian	Master's-degree student
Participant 8	23	Female	Italian	Master's-degree student
Participant 9	22	Female	Italian	Bachelors'-degree student
Participant 10	24	Male	Italian	Master's-degree student

Source: The authors.

about the introduction of a property right to protect personal data), we opted for a qualitative method such as in-depth interviews. Focusing on the number of participants, we followed the guidelines suggested by Dworkin (2012). Specifically, the author highlights that from 5 to 50 participants is an appropriate number.

Ten in-depth interviews were conducted with both Albanian and Italian college students in the field of economics, business, and law. This specific sample was selected because of their educational background. Furthermore, individuals aged between 18 and 25 are generally described as technology savvy (Schrag et al., 2021) compared to older generational cohorts. Sample characteristics are illustrated in Table 4.1.

3.1. Data Analysis Process

The transcriptions of the 10 in-depth interviews were analyzed by using thematic analysis. This qualitative approach is mainly defined as "a method for identifying, analyzing and reporting patterns (themes) within data" (Braun & Clarke, 2006, p. 79). The first stage of data analysis consisted in transcribing the interviews. Then, transcripts were read several times to obtain the sense of the whole and to generate a list of ideas about the topics presented in the data. During this stage, the theoretical background and the list of questions (see Appendix 1) guided the coding process. After the coding phase, we started to sort the different codes into themes (see Appendix 2).

4. Results

4.1. Findings

The final output of the analysis consisted in the production of a thematic map (see Fig. 4.1). We identified four different themes, namely, (i) distrust towards the way personal data are used online, (ii) no change in behavior after the introduction of

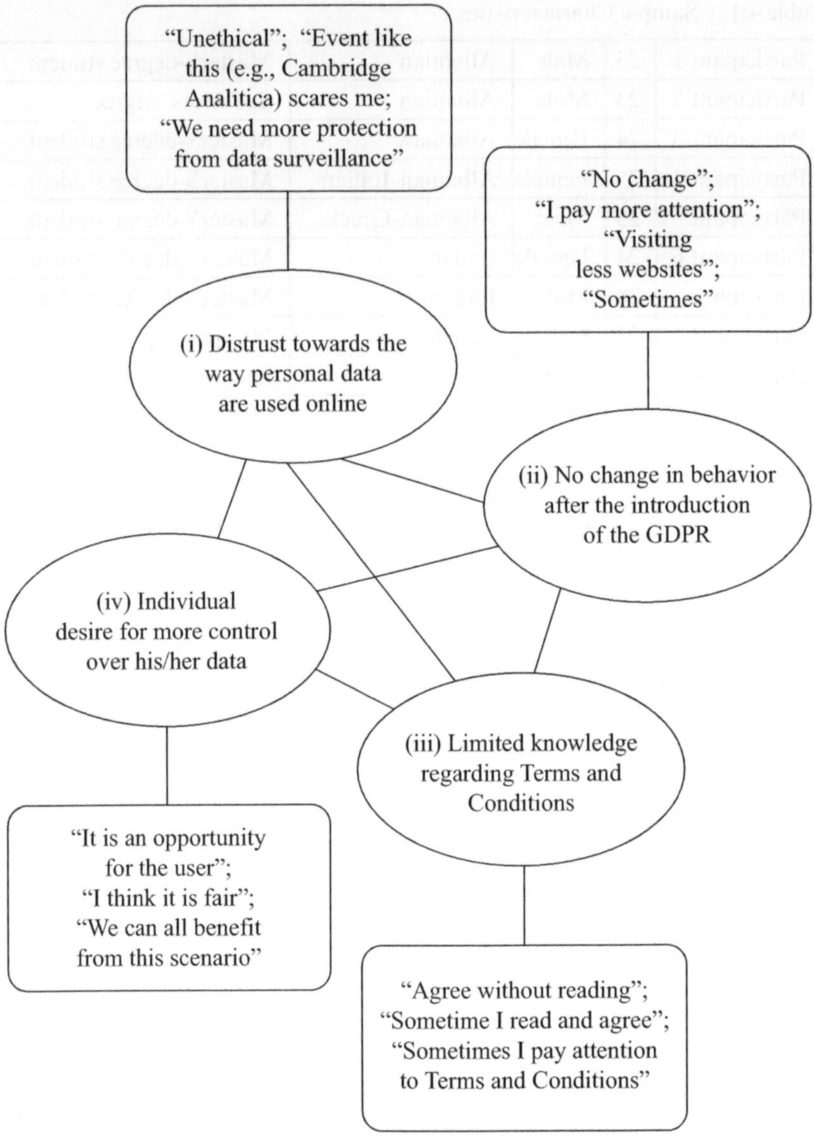

Fig. 4.1. Final Thematic Map, Showing Final Four Main Themes. *Source*: The authors.

the GDPR, (iii) limited knowledge regarding terms and conditions of websites, and (iv) individual desire for more control over his/her data.

One of the main topics that emerged from the analysis of the in-depth interviews is the suspicion or distrust of individuals regarding the way personal data are used online. Seven participants have mentioned the Cambridge Analytica scandal, five are Italian and two Albanian. Furthermore, among Albanian participants four of them have raised the E-Albania scandal. Participants expressed their sorrow about such events; data misuse represents a threat, as the following excerpts illustrate:

> After the implementation of the GDPR, I occasionally took a quick look at the terms of the online sites but in the end, I still gave my consent knowing that they would still manipulate people regardless of my acceptance or not.
>
> The way data were used, for example by Cambridge Analitica, is so unethical. Events like this scares me. We need more protection from data surveillance.

Another theme, which is in line with the extant literature about the "privacy paradox," considers the incapacity of the individual to take action to protect his/her personal information. Most participants answered to agree to the terms and condition page without reading its content. This situation is not changed even after the introduction of the GDPR regulations. To continue to use the website, respondents just click "I agree." This behavior is affected by lack of time, boredom, and the use of complex language, as illustrated below:

> I just agree without reading the "Terms and Conditions section" because I need to visit that site and I do not want to waste my time.
>
> The text of the "Terms and Conditions" page is too long, complex, and boring. So I just click the "I agree" button.

This behavior is also correlated to personal biases such as the authority heuristic. As illustrated in the excerpt below, individuals make decision by considering secure that given source because of the name of the company:

> Generally, I do not pay attention to the Term and Condition because I consider that website secure and trustworthy.

The incapacity to change behavior after the introduction of the GDPR is influenced by individuals' lack of knowledge. Almost all respondents have a vague knowledge of data protection laws, which leads to their insecurity to take a further step toward the protection of personal information. Against this backdrop, is paramount to increase the awareness of GDPR, for example, by adopting social media campaigns or traditional media that use central route. According to the ELM theory, adopt campaigns based on a central route rather than a peripheral route involve messages that can help the individual to think more critically and focus his/her attention on the possible consequences of privacy issues.

The last theme that emerged from data analysis considers the individual' desire for more control over his/her data. When asked to give their opinion about the possibility to introduce property rights to protect data, namely treating personal information as property to be licensed or sold, the majority of participants (nine) expressed a positive opinion, as illustrated below:

> I think it is an opportunity for the user to earn money and benefit of data control and management.
>
> This is definitely a good idea knowing that both parties benefit, that is, both the individuals and the party seeking the data of the individuals.
>
> It is a win–win relationship.

One Italian participant expressed some doubts, as the following excerpt illustrates:

> I have some doubts on the transactional model. Who decides the price? The service providers or the consumers throughout negotiation? Furthermore, I do not think data can be treated as a commodity. We cannot trade our personal information. This scenario seems to contradict the core principles of privacy protection.

This statement advances critical reflection about the pros and cons of applying property rights to protect data that individuals generate on the internet.

Focusing on the pros, a model based on property rights to protect data would give to individuals a total control over their personal information. In this scenario, individuals could license or sell their data to another party in exchange of a monetary benefit. At the same time, companies can benefit too, because they can collect information that are more accurate. However, this type of scenario presents several challenges. First, if personal information were to be embedded into property rights, each individual would have almost total control over his or her own data, but, on the other hand, he/she would be unable to make arrangements with any company that would utilize his/her data. Furthermore, stipulate a specific contract with all the companies that want to buy that given data would be a burden on the individuals.

Another challenge concerns the monetary evaluation of individuals' data. If pricing were set by internet users or through negotiation, the situation would be complex to handle. This complexity would also slow down the users' access to website. On the other hand, if pricing were set by service providers individuals would receive little payment.

4.2. Discussion

Findings suggest that the introduction of the GDPR represents an opportunity to avoid privacy scandals such as that involving Facebook and Cambridge Analytica. However, despite this regulation enhances individuals' data protection and rights, there is an intention–behavior gap, which is supported by themes (ii) and (iii).

This means that individuals can access a website by just clicking on "I agree" without paying attention to how their personal data will be used, such as the transfer of personal information to third parties. Lack of time, boredom, complex language, and personal biases are the main factors that influence such behavior. Especially for the personal bias, and in accordance with Kokolakis (2017), heuristics and biases stand as one of the main drivers of the "privacy paradox."

Focusing on the answers concerning the property regime, it emerges that individuals are favorable to treating privacy as property. However, making data into a specific form of property poses several challenges related to the transaction process, and this challenge is even bigger in e-commerce transactions (Dinev & Hart, 2006).

In the actual context, attention to both "terms and conditions" and the "consent form" published on the homepages of websites, social media platforms, and mobile applications, is a prerequisite for privacy protection. It follows that building a privacy culture in contemporary society is of paramount importance. Privacy breaches can be avoided when individuals are aware of the risks and possess knowledge, beliefs, and behaviors that can support them to make correct decisions, that is, pay attention to the disclaimer text before clicking "I agree." However, studies about how individuals responsibly interact with privacy disclosures reveal that web users do not have the time to read the document (Ploug & Holm, 2013), so they click directly on the "I agree" checkbox, creating again the case for "privacy paradox."

Regarding practical implications, educational institutions should launch awareness campaigns to educate the young generations about the issues of managing their personal data online. Best practices concerning the use and processing of personal information on the internet can also be promoted via social media by governments and other social actors. Furthermore, privacy legislations should empower internet users through transparency. In other terms, individuals should know their rights. For example, individuals do not know that the GDPR gives them the right to ask companies to delete their personal data, namely, the right to be forgotten. In addition, individuals should know their data can be shared with third parties, such as business partners, data brokers, and marketers, only if they give their consent.

5. Conclusions

This chapter attempted to understand what Albanian and Italian students think about privacy issues. Because of the COVID-19 emergency, we collected only a small number of interviews. Increasing the number of participants would have allowed the researchers to conduct a more accurate analysis. The study sample also consisted only of Albanian and Italian students in the field of economics, business, and law. Therefore, future research should consider larger sample size and incorporate different types of groups in order to analyze how the perception of issues related to privacy changes in response to socio-demographic variables, such as, age, education, and occupation. In one side, while aware of a limitation caused by the sample size which does not allow results generalizability, on the other side, we respect the threshold proposed by Dworkin (2012) with regard to the sample size policy for qualitative studies using in-depth interviews. Not only we match with Dworkin's criteria as derived from her meta-analysis, but we double the sample from 5 to 10 interviewees. In addition, we do not pretend to draw generalizations, but still we disclose some insights produced by the results which in any case might be subject to further studies.

References

Acquisti, A., & Grossklags, J. (2007). What can behavioral economics teach us about privacy. In A. Acquisti, S. Gritzalis C. Lambrinoudakis, & S. di Vimercati (Eds.), *Digital privacy: Theory, technology, and practices* (pp. 363–377). Auerbach Publications.

Angst, C. M., & Agarwal, R. (2009). Adoption of electronic health records in the presence of privacy concerns: The elaboration likelihood model and individual persuasion. *MIS Quarterly*, *33*(2), 339–370.

Baek, Y. M., Kim, E. M., & Bae, Y. (2014). My privacy is okay, but theirs is endangered: Why comparative optimism matters in online privacy concerns. *Computers in Human Behavior*, *31*, 48–56.

Bauer, P. C., Gerdon, F., Keusch, F., Kreuter, F., & Vannette, D. (2021). Did the GDPR increase trust in data collectors? Evidence from observational and experimental data. *Information, Communication & Society*, 1–21.

Becher, S. I., & Benoliel, U. (2021). Law in books and law in action: The readability of privacy policies and the GDPR. In K. Mathias & A. Tor (Eds.) *Consumer law and economics* (pp. 179–204). Springer.

Bhattacherjee, A., & Sanford, C. (2006). Influence processes for information technology acceptance: An elaboration likelihood model. *MIS Quarterly*, *30*(4), 805–825.

Bi, S., Liu, Z., & Usman, K. (2017). The influence of online information on investing decisions of reward-based crowdfunding. *Journal of Business Research*, *71*, 10–18.

Boussios E. (2021). Because of Snowden? The three leakers and privacy issues in the cyber matrix. In A. Visvizi, O. Troisi, & K. Saeedi (Eds.), *Research and innovation forum 2021. RIIFORUM 2021. Springer proceedings in complexity* (pp.513–528). Springer.

Boussios, E. (2019). ICT, politics, and cyber intelligence: Revisiting the case of Snowden. In A. Visvizi & M. D. Lytras (Eds.), *Politics and technology in the post-truth era* (Emerald Studies in Politics and Technology) (pp. 115–128). Emerald Publishing Limited.

Braun, V., & Clarke, V. (2006). Using thematic analysis in psychology. *Qualitative Research in Psychology*, *3*(2), 77–101.

Chen, S., & Chaiken, S. (1999). *The heuristic-systematic model in its broader context. Dual-process theories in social psychology*. Guilford Press.

Chen, Y., Yang, L., Zhang, M., & Yang, J. (2018). Central or peripheral? Cognition elaboration cues' effect on users' continuance intention of mobile health applications in the developing markets. *International Journal of Medical Informatics*, *116*, 33–45.

Cho, H., Lee, J. S., & Chung, S. (2010). Optimistic bias about online privacy risks: Testing the moderating effects of perceived controllability and prior experience. *Computers in Human Behavior*, *26*(5), 987–995.

Cyr, D., Head, M., Lim, E., & Stibe, A. (2018). Using the elaboration likelihood model to examine online persuasion through website design. *Information & Management*, *55*(7), 807–821.

Debatin, B., Lovejoy, J. P., Horn, A. K., & Hughes, B. N. (2009). Facebook and online privacy: Attitudes, behaviors, and unintended consequences. *Journal of Computer-mediated Communication*, *15*(1), 83–108.

Dimock, M. (2019). *Defining generations: Where Millennials end and Generation Z begins*. Pew Research Center, January 17, pp. 1–7.

Dinev, T., & Hart, P. (2006). An extended privacy calculus model for e-commerce transactions. *Information Systems Research*, *17*(1), 61–80.

Duguid, P. (2021). No more sucking up to Zuckerberg: Behavioural science plus profit-driven analytics equals disaster. *TLS. Times Literary Supplement* (6157), 26–27.

Dworkin, S. L. (2012). Sample size policy for qualitative studies using in-depth interviews. *Archives of Sexual Behavior*, *41*, 1319–1320.

Gerber, N., Gerber, P., & Volkamer, M. (2018). Explaining the privacy paradox: A systematic review of literature investigating privacy attitude and behavior. *Computers & Security*, *77*, 226–261.

Gilovich, T., Griffin, D., & Kahneman, D. (Eds.). (2002). *Heuristics and biases: The psychology of intuitive judgment*. Cambridge University Press.

Goddard, M. (2017). The EU General Data Protection Regulation (GDPR): European regulation that has a global impact. *International Journal of Market Research*, *59*(6), 703–705.

Han, J. T., Chen, Q., Liu, J. G., Luo, X. L., & Fan, W. (2018). The persuasion of borrowers' voluntary information in peer to peer lending: An empirical study based on elaboration likelihood model. *Computers in Human Behavior*, *78*, 200–214.

Ho, S. Y., & Bodoff, D. (2014). The effects of web personalization on user attitude and behavior: An integration of the elaboration likelihood model and consumer search theory. *MIS Quarterly*, *38*(2), 497–520.

Hummel, P., Braun, M., & Dabrock, P. (2020). Own data? Ethical reflections on data ownership. *Philosophy & Technology*, *34*, 545–572.

Jiang, Z., Heng, C. S., & Choi, B. C. (2013). Research note—Privacy concerns and privacy-protective behavior in synchronous online social interactions. *Information Systems Research*, *24*(3), 579–595.

Kayes, I., & Iamnitchi, A. (2017). Privacy and security in online social networks: A survey. *Online Social Networks and Media*, *3*, 1–21.

Kehr, F., Kowatsch, T., Wentzel, D., & Fleisch, E. (2015). Blissfully ignorant: The effects of general privacy concerns, general institutional trust, and affect in the privacy calculus. *Information Systems Journal*, *25*(6), 607–635.

Kokolakis, S. (2017). Privacy attitudes and privacy behavior: A review of current research on the privacy paradox phenomenon. *Computers and Security*, *64*, 122–134.

Kumar, S., & Kumar, P. (2021). Privacy preserving in online social networks using fuzzy rewiring. *IEEE Transactions on Engineering Management*.

Lee, H., Park, H., & Kim, J. (2013). Why do people share their context information on social network services? A qualitative study and an experimental study on users' behavior of balancing perceived benefit and risk. *International Journal of Human–Computer Studies*, *71*(9), 862–877.

Lytras, M., Visvizi, A., Zhang, X., & Aljohani, N. R. (2020). Cognitive computing, big data analytics and data driven industrial marketing. *Industrial Marketing Management*, *90*, 663–666.

Mayer-Schönberger, V., & Cukier, K. (2013). *Big data: A revolution that will transform how we live, work and think*. John Murray.

Olivero, N., & Lunt, P. (2004). Privacy versus willingness to disclose in e-commerce exchanges: The effect of risk awareness on the relative role of trust and control. *Journal of Economic Psychology*, *25*, 2.

Osservatorio Balcani e Caucaso Transeuropa. (2021). "Big Brother" privacy scandal exposes the fragility of Albanian democracy. https://www.balcanicaucaso.org/eng/Areas/Albania/Big-Brother-privacy-scandal-exposes-the-fragility-of-Albanian-democracy-210103

Petty, R. E., & Cacioppo, J. T. (1986). The elaboration likelihood model of persuasion. *Advances in Experimental Social Psychology*, *19*(4), 123–205.

Petty, R. E., Briñol, P., & Tormala, Z. L. (2002). Thought confidence as a determinant of persuasion: The self-validation hypothesis. *Journal of Personality and Social Psychology*, *82*, 722–741.

Ploug, T., & Holm, S. (2013). Informed consent and routinisation. *Journal of Medical Ethics*, *39*(4), 214–218.

Purtova, N. (2009). Property rights in personal data: Learning from the American discourse. *Computer Law & Security Review*, *25*(6), 507–521.

Rughiniş, R., Rughiniş, C., Vulpe, S. N., & Rosner, D. (2021). From social netizens to data citizens: Variations of GDPR awareness in 28 European countries. *Computer Law & Security Review*, *42*, 105585.

Saura, J. R., Ribeiro-Soriano, D., & Palacios-Marqués, D. (2021). From user-generated data to data-driven innovation: A research agenda to understand user privacy in digital markets. *International Journal of Information Management*, *60*, 102331.

Schrag, R. V., Hairston, D., Brown, M. L., & Wood, L. (2021). Advocate and survivor perspectives on the role of technology in help seeking and services with emerging adults in higher education. *Journal of Family Violence*, *37*, 123–136.

Stepanov, I (2020). Introducing a property right over data in the EU: The data producer's right – An evaluation. *International Review of Law, Computers & Technology*, *34*(1), 65–86.

Sundar, S. S. (2008). *The MAIN model: A heuristic approach to understanding technology effects on credibility. Digital media, youth, and credibility* (pp. 72–100). The MIT Press.

Sundar, S. S., Kim, J., Rosson, M. B., & Molina, M. D. (2020). Online privacy heuristics that predict information disclosure. In *Proceedings of the 2020 CHI conference on human factors in computing systems* (pp. 1–12).

Troisi, O., Grimaldi, M., & Loia, F. (2021). Redesigning business models for data-driven innovation: A three-layered framework. In A. Visvizi, M. D. Lytras, & N. R. Aljohani (Eds.), *Research and innovation forum 2020: Disruptive technologies in times of change* (pp. 421–435). Springer International Publishing.

Troisi, O., Maione, G., Grimaldi, M., & Loia, F. (2020). Growth hacking: Insights on data-driven decision-making from three firms. *Industrial Marketing Management*, *90*, 538–557.

Troisi, O., Visvizi, A., & Grimaldi, M. (2021). The different shades of innovation emergence in smart service systems: The case of Italian cluster for aerospace technology. *Journal of Business & Industrial Marketing*, ahead-of-print.

Urban, T., Tatang, D., Degeling, M., Holz, T., & Pohlmann, N. (2019). A study on subject data access in online advertising after the GDPR. In In C. Pérez-Solà, G. Navarro-Arribas, A. Biryukov, & J. Garcia-Alfaro (Eds.), *Data privacy management, cryptocurrencies and blockchain technology* (pp. 61–79). Springer.

Visvizi, A., & Lytras, M. D. (Eds.). (2019). *Politics and technology in the post-truth era* (pp. i–xix). Emerald Publishing.

Wagner, P. (2021). Data privacy – The ethical, sociological, and philosophical effects of Cambridge Analytica. https://ssrn.com/abstract=3782821 or http://dx.doi.org/10.2139/ssrn.3782821

Xu, H., Luo, X. R., Carroll, J. M., & Rosson, M. B. (2011). The personalization privacy paradox: An exploratory study of decision making process for location-aware marketing. *Decision Support Systems*, *51*(1), 42–52.

Zhou, T. (2012). Understanding users' initial trust in mobile banking: An elaboration likelihood perspective. *Computers in Human Behavior*, *28*(4), 1518–1525.

Zuboff, S. (2019). Surveillance capitalism and the challenge of collective action. *New labor forum 28*(1), 10–29.

Appendix 2: Interview Questions

Q1. How many web pages or apps do you visit throughout a day?
Q2. Are you targeted with different ads there?
Q3. Do you have knowledge on how online advertisement works?
Q4. Before GDPR, did you mostly agreed to terms and conditions of websites or apps to continue using them? How often have you read them? If yes, were they easy enough to understand?
Q5. Have you ever heard of any scandal regarding personal data misuse? If yes, which one?
Q6. What are your thoughts or feelings this kind of events?
Q7. To prevent related events in the future, GDPR aims to increase individual personal data control. Are you aware of any of these rights?
Q8. One of the rights is the right to consent in order for the companies to ask for permission for using your data and if one does not agree, he\she can't use that website. Do you agree by reading terms and conditions (TC) in that website? If you have read them, are they easier to understand?
Q9. After GDPR was introduced, have you changed your behavior regarding websites visits or TC?
Q10. Do you have any idea regarding property rights?
Q11. What do you think if personal data were about to be protected by those rights?
Q12. Would you license your personal data in exchange of a fee or monetary benefit?
Q13. Would this thing serve as a push or incentive for people to license or provide more data to other parties?

Appendix 2: Data Coding and Emerging Themes

	Participant 1	Participant 2	Participant 3	Participant 4	Participant 5	Participant 6	Participant 7	Participant 8	Participant 9	Participant 10
Q1	About 5	10	10	5–10	10–15	About 20	About 25	About 10	About 15	About 15
Q2	Yes	Yes, I am	Always	Yes	Targeted	Yes	Yes	Yes	Yes	Yes
Q3	General knowledge	Collecting personal data	Not at all	General knowledge	Build individual profile and then target adv.	General knowledge	General knowledge	No	General knowledge	General knowledge
Q4	Never	I just tap agree, long TC	Boring TC	Once when bored, didn't understand	Never ever, just accept	I just agree	I just agree, because I do not have the time to read term and conditions	I just agree	I just agree	I just agree to do not waste time
Q5	Cambridge Analytica, E-Albania	E-Albania	CA case, Yahoo case, E-Albania	E-Albania, Kate Clinic case from brother (Lawyer)	E-Albania	Cambridge Analytica	Cambridge Analytica and My space data breach	Cambridge Analytica	Cambridge Analytica	Cambridge Analytica and Yahoo
Q6	So unethical	Personal data so unprotected	Feel like we can do nothing to stop that	Unethical, they act like our data is their property	No one is blamed for this, no one will	I think it is an unethical activity	Potentially unethical behavior	Event like this scares me	We need more protection from data surveillance	So unethical
Q7	No	Vague knowledge	Vague knowledge	Right of consent	Very general info.	I'm aware of the GDPR	I know very little about it	Vague knowledge	I know its advantages	Vague knowledge

Q8	Agree without reading	Tap agree because I will use this site anyway	Just tap agree	Have a slight look on them, then agree, bullet points, easier	Don't have other opinions, therefore agree	Yes, sometimes I pay attention to TC	I just agree without reading	I just agree	Sometimes I read and agree	I just agree
Q9	Not at all	Sometimes	Do the same as before	Visiting less websites	No	Sometimes	No	No	I pay more attention	No
Q10	Hmm, no	General info		Little from my brother	Little things	Yes	I know very little about it	General info	You are the owner	No
Q11	Good idea	Why not	Good	It would be better I suppose	If it can, why not	It depends. Information can be treated as a commodity	It is the right thing to do	It is a good idea	It is an opportunity for the user	It is a good idea
Q12	Whatever they need, lol	Yes	Why not	Of course, as we all benefit from it	Definitely yes	Yes, it is an opportunity	Yes	Yes	I think it is fair	We can all benefit from this scenario
Q13	Probably	For sure	I think so	As a poor student of course	Yeah	Yes, it can help people to pay more attention	Yes	Yes	We need testing this scenario	Incentives may help motivate people

Themes:

Limited knowledge regarding terms and conditions of websites	Distrust toward the way personal data ar used online	No change in behavior after the introduction of GDPR	Individual desire for more control over his/her data

Chapter 5

NoSQL Security: Can My Data-driven Decision-making Be Influenced from Outside?

Anastasija Nikiforova, Artjoms Daskevics and Otmane Azeroual

Abstract

Nowadays, there are billions interconnected devices forming Cyber-Physical Systems (CPS), Internet of Things (IoT) and Industrial Internet of Things (IIoT) ecosystems. With an increasing number of devices and systems in use, amount and the value of data, the risks of security breaches increase. One of these risks is posed by open data sources, which are databases that are not properly protected. These poorly protected databases are accessible to external actors, which poses a serious risk to the data holder and the results of data-related activities such as analysis, forecasting, monitoring, decision-making, policy development, and the whole contemporary society. This chapter aims at examining the state of the security of open data databases representing both relational databases and NoSQL, with a particular focus on a later category.

Keywords: Database; NoSQL; vulnerability; security; OSINT; big data; secure by design; penetration testing; Internet of Things Search Engine; Search Engines for the Internet of Everything

Introduction

Today, with the technological advances affecting economic and socio-political landscapes, we deal with – create, generate, store, process, interpret and analyze – huge amounts of data on a daily basis in both private and public sectors (Visvizi &

Big Data and Decision-Making: Applications and Uses in the Public and Private Sector, 59–73

Published under exclusive licence by Emerald Publishing Limited
doi:10.1108/978-1-80382-551-920231005

Lytras, 2019). They can be structured, semi-structured and unstructured. Here, the concept of big data comes. These data, especially big data, form the basis for data-centric decision-making (Cui et al., 2014). This is all the more so in times of crisis, such as COVID-19 pandemics, since crisis management is typically a data-driven process of setting strategies, developing and coordinating actions and fiscal-, human-, time-resource allocation. This means that the data forms the basis for forecasting, predicting, mapping, tracking, monitoring and raising awareness about the events (Corsi et al., 2021), contributing to decision-making and policy development as well as the whole contemporary society. They have both direct and indirect values, which means that corrupted or modified data may affect the results of the actions carried out with them and lead to inaccurate or even completely incorrect results and decisions. If used as input, they can make even very advanced algorithms relatively useless.

Therefore, both database management and the security of data and data storage in particular are very important for both technicians and non-technicians. Unfortunately, NoSQL databases are often found to be weakly protected and secured, which leads to many breaches and data leakages (Daskevics & Nikiforova, 2021a; Derbeko et al., 2016; Goel & Ter Hofstede, 2021; Sahafizadeh & Nematbakhsh, 2015; Tran & Hu, 2019). However, nevertheless many companies like Google and Amazon have abandoned traditional database technology in favor of proprietary data stores called key-value stores (Chang et al., 2006; DeCandia et al., 2007).

As regards the latter, that is, data storages, one of the risks is posed by open data sources – databases, which are not properly protected, therefore they are available and accessible to external actors outside the organization. Although it may be surprising, the number of such databases is enormous. In many cases this is caused by misconfiguration, where the responsibility falls to database holders, in other cases there are vulnerabilities in the products, where apart of proper configuration additional security mechanisms are needed. Naturally, a series of questions arise: how to find out whether your database is visible and even accessible outside the organization? What information may be gathered from it? And whether stronger security mechanisms are needed or is the vulnerability rather related to internal configuration or the database in use? Although some questions may be partly answered by referring to Common Vulnerability and Exposure (CVE) Details and other sources summarizing vulnerabilities and patches on different services, this information may be too general. Therefore, penetration testing could be the answer.

The objective of this chapter is to provide an insight into the security of different databases, with a focus on NoSQL databases. First, the importance of this topic will be motivated by providing insight into data leaks by referring to some real-world examples (Section 1). Section 2 will provide a brief overview of the causes of these data leaks and some others database security concerns. Section 3 will provide an insight on techniques and methods used to assess and maintain the level of the data storage security in use. It will cover both very general and rather static, and dynamic solutions. It will give an insight into current knowledge about the security of some NoSQL databases. Then the Search Engines for the

Internet of Everything- (IoE-) also known as Internet of Things Search Engines- (IoTSE-) based tool called ShoBEVODSDT, which has been recently developed, will be presented in Section 4. Section 5 will present the results obtained by applying ShoBEVODSDT to eight types of data storage facilities. Then, the discussion on the current security state of these databases and potential bottlenecks that need to be considered when any of them is being used, or a choice should be made in favor of any of them, will be provided.

Data Leakages

The database is part of each system that is becoming even more popular as a result of digital transformations and Industry 4.0 reality (Kumar et al., 2019). With the increase of the usage of data and databases, particularly of NoSQL databases sometimes found to be most appropriate in the context of big data, IoT and IIoT, the topicality of database security increases as well. Unfortunately, NoSQL databases are mostly characterized by weak security, which leads to many cases of data leaks (Ferrari et al., 2020). Let us provide some evidences of this, that is, provide some examples of data leaks.

According to one of the most up-to-date lists on major security breaches compiled by Tunggal and UpGuard (Tunggal, 2021), a large number of data leaks occur due to unsecured databases. Let's look at some of these breaches that happened in the last five years:

(1) ZOOM data breach occurred in 2020 lead to the sale or free publication of 500,000 accounts' data in a dark web.
(2) Yahoo data breach in 2017 allowed hackers to compromise 3 billion user accounts. The investigation found that users' passwords in clear text, payment card data and bank information were not stolen. Yet, it remains one of the largest data breaches in history.
(3) Aadhaar data breach in 2018 resulted in the leakage of more than a billion Indian citizens' personal information stored in the world's largest biometric database, which could be purchased online, including data on names, their unique 12-digit identity numbers and bank details.
(4) LinkedIn data breach in 2021, when 700 million LinkedIn users' data were brought for sale in a dark web. That exposure affected 92% of the total users, that is, 756 million users.
(5) Starwood (Marriott) data breach in 2018, when approximately 500 million hotel customers' data were stolen, when the attackers had gained an access to the Starwood system in 2014 and remained in the system after Marriott acquired Starwood in 2016. What is more, this discovery was not made until 2018.
(6) Twitter data breach in 2018 and 330 million passwords exposed in an internal log, making all user passwords available to the internal network.
(7) Uber data breach in 2016 and personal information of 57 million Uber users and 600,000 drivers exposed.

The data leaks listed above give some insight on how frequently and how many users data were exposed, the level of detail of which may vary from IDs and name to addresses and bank details. However, this information does not provide an insight on fiscal losses resulting from these data leaks. This is because, firstly, it is difficult to assess such losses (although such assessments tend to be published). Secondly, financial losses are not the only ones affecting the organizations concerned, since, in addition to direct losses, they tend to suffer indirectly, that is, their reputation is affected negatively and can lead to losses of both clients/users and partners. In addition, although examples of users' data leakages have been covered here, it is clear that in many cases not only client/user data are the target of attackers and invaders, and other data make sense for attackers as well.

Perhaps the most provocative database in this respect is MongoDB, where 54,000 databases became accessible on the Internet in 2018, that lead to data leaks of 2.4 million of telemedicine vendor patients (Davis et al., 2021). According to Bizga (2020), it is a very common trend to target/compromise unprotected MongoDB servers for hackers, wiping out their data and leaving ransom notes outlining the threat of leaking stolen data and reporting to owners for general data protection regulation (GDPR) violations. Thus, in 2020 more than 22,000 ransom notes were left in the exposed MongoDB databases, that is, nearly 47% of all MongoDB databases that are accessible online.

A similar trend is also observed when the security of MongoDB databases is assessed using the IoTSE and searching for open databases accessible via the Internet (questions like "how it works?" and "what are the results?" will be answered a bit later). Recent findings showed that the most popular IoTSE – Shodan – lists more than 15,000 affected MongoDB, while another popular IoTSE – Binary Edge – around 23,000. However, although these results are mainly discussed referring to MongoDB, it is not the only vulnerable or easily accessible database. According to other studies, including lists of the largest data leaks, ElasticSearch is also found highly vulnerable, sometimes followed by Cassandra (Ferrari et al., 2020; Tunggal, 2021).

However, it should be acknowledged that some improvements have been made in this respect in recent years, although this remains a problem. In addition, although the low security level of NoSQL databases is widely discussed, it cannot be stated that SQL databases' holders do not risk their data leaking. Some evidence of this will be provided in the later sections. Moreover, given that MongoDB is not the only NoSQL database, more than the MongoDB will be referred to, covering some other NoSQL and SQL databases. This will be done using a tool based on the above mentioned IoTSEs that are described as relatively easy to use. This also explains their popularity and appropriateness for the purpose of this study.

Security Concerns

Let us now provide a brief overview of what might be the causes of these data leaks and some others database security concerns, primarily referring to NoSQL databases. It is not a secret that there exist some indexes and registries to be used to identify the weakest areas of the service, such as the database, and find out the latest "threats" by which is characterized the service in use. Perhaps the most popular of them is CVE Details (2022). It provides an index of registered vulnerabilities of various services dividing them in 13 categories, including Denial of Service, Code Execution, SQL injection, HTTP response splitting, Gain information, Gain Privileges, CSRF and File Inclusion, etc. However, although they are very valuable and useful, same as other registries such as VulDB and NVD – National Vulnerability Database, they are rather static and general and do not provide an information on the actual database in use, for example, whether the database is visible and can be accessed from outside of the organization. Thus, additional steps should be taken inspecting the particular database used within the organization. Before referring to this, another point to be elaborated on is related to database-specific security and privacy concerns, since the above listed categories used by the CVE are rather service agnostic.

For this purpose, let us refer to Goel and Ter Hofstede (2021), who have conducted a systematic analysis of privacy-related literature in the context of NoSQL databases, using a pattern-based approach to identify what the most widely occurring "privacy-breaching" issues are. The authors refer to them as "privacy-breaching patterns." Goel and Ter Hofstede have managed to identify six patterns:

- *Malicious query introduction* that occurs when a person with malicious intent interferes with the system and modifies a NoSQL query so that it can read or even modify a database or change data in a web application. Malicious queries allow users to manipulate the back-end of database by adding, modifying, or deleting data. They can be caused by either injection attacks or insider attacks. For injection attacks, perhaps the most commonly known are (a) tautologies injecting code in a conditional statement, (b) union queries used to bypass authentication and extract data, (c) JavaScript injections, which allows intruder to execute JavaScript to perform complex tasks, (d) piggy-backed queries that "exploits assumptions in the interpretation of escape sequences' special characters" to insert additional queries into the original one, and (e) origin violation that uses HTTP REST APIs to access database from another domain. Insider attacks, in turn, refers to "the use of queries to gain unauthorized access to information."
- *Accidental re-identification*, which refers to cases, where a person can be re-identified on the basis of the query output, despite the mechanisms in place to ensure data privacy. This, in turn, can happen by executing a complex query, resulting in a small output set, for example, advanced queries or data processing capabilities such as MapReduce and an aggregation are used, that allows to re-identify artifacts such as individuals that raise privacy concerns. In other words, this may disclose/reveal sensitive data stored in the database.
- *Weak authentication* that refers to cases when NoSQL databases provide poor password storage mechanisms or are limited to no authentication capabilities. As an example, MongoDB and Redis do not provide authentication by default, allowing an intruder to get an access to the system. It, in turn, can lead to "an

individual with malicious intent gaining access to the system," which can lead to attacks such as masquerade and hijacking.
- *Coarse-grained access control*, which is the process of "controlling access to data and resources in a system." It is usually done by associating different types of users with a certain set of rules based on their roles and responsibilities. NoSQL databases provide different levels of access control support, which typically can be divided in (a) role-based and (b) data-based.
- *Vulnerable data in motion* that poses a risk to the privacy of data, if the cluster uses poor security mechanisms that can compromise operations of the clusters.
- *Vulnerable data at rest* that refers to weak "data at rest" encryption or the use of data storage mechanisms susceptible to external attacks.

According to the authors' experiment, weak authentication and vulnerable data at rest were identified as the most widespread threats in eight NoSQL databases (MongoDB, CouchDB, Redis, Aerospike, Cassandra, Hbase, Neo4j and OrientDB), with weak authentication found to be the most significant among the assessed instances. Another study (Ferrari et al., 2020) investigated the use of the most popular NoSQL databases, focusing on misconfiguration analysis that can lead to security and privacy problems. The authors developed a tool that automatically scans IP subnets to identify exposed services, as well as performs security analyses. Their analysis showed that in 0.18% of IP addresses they have analyzed, database in use is misconfigured. The risks associated with the services exposed range from data leakages that can pose a significant threat to users' privacy, to manipulation of resource data stored in vulnerable databases, which can pose a significant threat to the reputation of web services.

To sum up, although the nature of attacks may vary significantly, one of the main security concern is related to the fact that many NoSQL databases are less likely to provide security measures, including sometimes very primitive and simple measures such as an authentication, authorization (Bada & Pete, 2020; Sahafizadeh & Nematbakhsh, 2015) and data encryption. They stand for the "open databases." As a result, according to recent observations, more than half of the known data leaks over the past years are leaks from open databases (Habr, 2022).

Methods and Techniques for Inspecting the Security of Data Storage Facility

There are many methods and techniques to check the overall security status of an artifact, such as a database. They mainly refer to vulnerability registries and indices/databases, as well as methods to assess the current state of the artifact in use, that is, the local database used in the organization. As for the approaches to testing the system in use, one of the most popular approaches is to perform an attack on a system such as an injection or CSRF (Cross-Site Request Forgery) as Ron et al. (2016) do. They demonstrate that while the emergence of new query formats makes old SQL injection techniques irrelevant, NoSQL databases are not immune to injections. To prevent breaches and data leaks, the authors recommend using Dynamic Application Security Testing (DAST) and static code analysis to find any injection vulnerabilities if coding guidelines were not followed. They stress that DAST should be seen as more credible and reliable, and allow a better understanding of the current state of the system and the need to improve security. Although they deal mainly with aspects not actually related to this study, the authors highlight the importance of a proper authentication mechanism and access control to avoid or at least reduce the risks of more advanced attacks they deal with. However, the source of these "more advanced" techniques, which often used to test the system used, is Open Web Application Security Project (OWASP), which collects examples of testing a specific product that meets the OWASP goal, that is, to improve the security of software (OWASP Foundation, 2013).

For registries, perhaps the most popular index used for a variety of services is the above mentioned CVE Details. CVE Details provide data not only on databases having a broader scope, however the number of databases covered by it is limited. More precisely, some popular databases, such as Memcahced and ElasticSearch, characterized by a high number of vulnerabilities and leaks in recent years, are not covered by it. This registry can therefore be used as a complimentary source, but in many cases it will not be applicable. Not least popular is NVD, the US government repository that includes databases of security checklist references, security-related software flaws, misconfigurations, product names and impact metrics. But as it was mentioned above, the nature of these sources is rather static and general. They provide information on the general database management system-related issues rather than on the database in use. Thus, the question on whether the database is visible and can be accessed from outside of the organization should be answered by database holders.

Here the blind and *double blind testing* (also called double blind penetration or pentesting) in particular comes. It is sometimes considered to be one of the most objective testing methods. This objectivity is ensured by the absence of preparatory works for testing, which may have affect the test results, while the pentester is an external actor without prior knowledge of the system and its specificities. Blind pentesting requires specific tools supporting testing, that is, tool to find basic information on a system under test (Daskevics & Nikiforova, 2021a). This stage is usually linked to the evaluation/assessment process that can be done for both the entire environment and each component forming it, where the assessment can be carried out by the internal or the external auditor (Ramadhan ct al., 2020). An internal audit may be carried out in a shorter time, providing information on existing threats and previous attacks, while external data audits and sources may help to facilitate knowledge of events in a broader cyberspace (Samtani et al., 2020). During the assessment process, the external auditors are expected to obtain as much information as possible in relation to the target. Perhaps the most valuable supporter of this task is vulnerability scanner (Burns et al., 2007). In order to be eligible to conduct more comprehensive analysis, it should conduct non-intrusive testing, mainly gathering information, which assist analysis and reporting of cyber security analysts.

Here, the concepts of Open Source Intelligence (OSINT) and IoTSE come, which are perfectly suited to collect and analyze publicly available data for investigation purposes (Maltego Team, 2020). The popularity of both concepts is increasing in a variety of areas, including but not limited to the detection of open databases (including leaked databases; Bada & Pete, 2020). For this reason, that is, being able to crawl and discover the network of the Internet-connected devices (such as web cameras, databases, industrial automation hardware, etc.), they are also known as Search Engines for the IoE. The inspection can be carried out at different levels, that is: (1) system level of only one organization or individual or (2) comprehensive, when overall insight on the state of the art can be gained.

Same as a pentesting by itself, they intend to facilitate identification of whether and at which extent the system tolerates real world-style attack patterns. This information, however, can be used to determine the level of sophistication an attacker needs to successfully compromise the system, countermeasures that could mitigate threats against the system and defenders' ability to detect attacks and respond appropriately if any are applied to the system, while in opposite case to identify the need for them and their further usability. The next section presents the tool, which follows this procedure to identify of open databases by means of IoTSE, demonstrating its potential, covering it from the less often covered viewpoint.

Search Engine for the IoE as a Tool for Detecting Vulnerable Open Data Sources

Search Engine for the IoE-based tool called Shodan- and Binary Edge-based vulnerable open data sources detection tool (ShoBEVODSDT) was originally presented in Daskevics and Nikiforova (2021a, 2021b). Therefore, it will not be described in detail, mainly covering its basics. ShoBEVODSDT is a tool for non-intrusive detection of vulnerable data sources, which is based on the use of OSINT tools, more precisely the Search Engine for the IoE (also known as IoTSE) – Shodan and Binary Edge. Both are considered to be passive information gathering applications and use Machine Learning (ML) and cybersecurity techniques to scan, acquire and classify public Internet data. In this solution, they complement each other, since their outputs tend to slightly differ. The tool conducts a passive assessment, which means that it does not intent to harm the databases – it rather checks for potentially existing bottlenecks or weaknesses which, if the attack would take place, could be exposed.

ShoBEVODSDT is designed to search for unprotected databases falling into the list of eight predefined data sources – MongoDB, Redis, Elasticsearch, CouchDB, Cassandra, Memcached, MySQL and PostgreSQL. These sources can be divided in two categories: NoSQL and SQL, while NoSQL can be divided in another three groups: key-value, document-oriented and column-oriented databases. ShoBEVODSDT source code is publicly available on https://github.com/zhmyh/Open-Databases, which allows to contribute to the development of this tool, including its enrichment with additional sources.

The tool overall action can divided into three steps: (1) IP address search (gathering), in scope of which the tool uses BinaryEdge and Shodan libraries to find service IP addresses according to predefined requirements, eliminates duplicates created by the use of these two services and saves the results in automatically created folders – one per service and country analyzed, (2) IP address check aimed at connecting to previously saved IP addresses and registering them depending on the status of the connection, (3) retrieving information from an IP address (parsing), which aims to retrieve the data (if possible) from those databases, to which it has managed to connect. These steps can be called either separately or one-by-one – sequentially.

The data gathered are then classified, by which is meant the examination of the data gathered on the level of their value. Here, previously introduced six categories referring to the "value" of the data gathered are used. According to this classification, the data can be matched to: (1) has managed to connect, but failed to gather data, (2) has managed to connect, but the database is empty, (3) has managed to connect by gathering system data or non-sensitive data, (4) has managed to connect and gather sensitive data and (5) compromised database.

Now, let us turn to the results of application of this tool and results demonstrated by the above mentioned databases. Whether MongoDB will be the less secure-by-design? And whether SQL databases will prove to be significantly less vulnerable compared to NoSQL databases?

Results: Whether My Database Is Secure?

In accordance with Daskevics and Nikiforova (2021b), the total number of unprotected or so-called "open" databases, which are available to external actors is less than 2% of the data sources scanned (slightly more than 15,000 IP addresses have been analyzed). This percentage is not very high representing 238 IP addresses. However, there are data sources that may pose risks to organizations, where information that can be used for further attacks can be easily obtained. What is more, 12% of identified open data sources have already been compromised. Thus, let us refer to more detailed results by the database and "value" of data, which is possible to retrieve from it (if any).

Table 5.1 provides an overall database-wise insight on the results, pointing on whether (1) ShoBEVODSDT has managed to connect to it, (2) has managed to connect, but the database was empty, (3) has managed to connect by gathering system data or non-sensitive information, (4) has managed to connect and gather sensitive data and (5) compromised database found. The first, that is, "managed to connect," and the latest three categories pointing on the data storage facilities, where the data and information useful for intruders and attackers data and information can be retrieved or have already been retrieved, are critical.

It is shown that CouchDB was the only database, which ShoBEVODSDT has not managed to access. Remaining seven databases were accessed and for every database at least one next "critical" level has been found.

However, this table provides very general results, pointing on the presence or absence of databases falling into one or another category rather than providing quantitative data. In addition, it does not allow to draw conclusion on the level of security neither by the service nor category, that is, SQL or NoSQL. Although it can be seen that SQL databases indeed cannot be considered as very secured as it could be assumed considering the frequency of debates on the low level of security and high vulnerability of NoSQL databases.

Table 5.1. General Results by Service.

	Mongo DB	Redis	Couch DB	Memcached	Elasticsearch	Cassandra	My SQL	Postegre SQL
Managed to connect	+	+	−	+	+	+	+	+
Failed to gather data	−	±	−	−	±	−	±	−
DB is empty	−	+	−	+	+	+	−	−
System data or non-sensitive	+	−	−	+	+	+	+	+
Sensitive data	+	+	−	+	+	−	−	−
Compromised DB	+	−	−	+	+	−	+	+

Source: Authors.

Table 5.2, however, provides more critical results, presenting a ratio of number of databases falling into particular category related to the total number of databases assessed. They are complemented with the ratio of databases falling into "failed to connect," that is, thereby proving to be capable not to allow the access to the data stored in it. Ratio instead of numbers should allow to reduce the potential bias of results provided on the basis of analysis of open databases accessible via the Internet, resulted in unequal number of databases found. However, it can still affect them. Therefore, the total number of found IP addresses and databases they refer to are also provided.

Memcached and ElasticSearch are the data sources to which ShoBEVODSDT has managed to connect most. To be more precise, ShoBEVODSDT was able to connect to all ElasticSearch instances and 80% of Memcached databases. As regards the sensitivity of the data, Redis is found to be less protected against intrusions and in 83% cases it is possible to obtain sensitive data. It is

Table 5.2. Quantitative Results by Service.

	Mongo DB	Redis	Memcached	Elasticsearch	Cassandra	My SQL
Total found	*177*	*122*	*116*	*86*	*7*	*1,347*
Connection successful	7.9%	9.8%	**80%**	**100%**	14%	0.14%
Compromised DB	**71%**	0	2.2%	**27%**	0	5.3%
Sensitive data	7.1%	**83%**	**24%**	8%	0	0
Failed to gather data	0	17%	0	3.5%	21%	21%

Source: Authors (partly adapted from Daskevics & Nikiforova, 2021a).

followed by Memcached, where, however the number of databases from which sensitive data could be gathered is significantly lower, that is, 24%. Cassandra and MySQL demonstrated the best results and was not possible to gather sensitive data from them.

However, as regards the *compromised databases*, here the results differ and the only facilities, where compromised instances have not been found are Redis and Cassandra, while in the case of MongoDB, 71% databases were already compromised, which is compliant with above mentioned findings made as a result of other studies. However, it is something unexpected that the same results have been demonstrated by PostgreSQL, which belongs to SQL databases. Even more, the next negative result in this respect is shown by MySQL (33%), which is also SQL database and Elasticsearch (27%). Some compromised databases were also found for Memcached, however their number is significantly lower compared to the above mentioned.

A good point is that the most popular categories are "has managed to connect by gathering system data or non-sensitive information" (45%) and "has managed to connect, but the database is empty" (21%). However, 18% of inspected data storage facilities had data that could be used by attackers. Even more, as mentioned above, 12% of them have been already compromised.

To sum up, MongoDB is characterized by a high number of cases where databases are compromised (83.3%), while some data sources are not protected from sensitive data gatherings, which can lead in the future to compromising these databases (4.2%), and some databases from which system and non-sensitive data can be gathered, which complies with Bada and Pete (2020) and Davis (2021). However, despite its popularity in different studies as the data source characterized by the lowest level of security, unfortunately, most databases inspected are not significantly better. Although PostgreSQL relates to SQL databases, it is still can be characterized by compromised databases, providing the next negative result after MongoDB that are worse than remaining NoSQL databases. In addition, PostgreSQL can be characterized by some databases, from which non-sensitive data or system data can be gathered.

The highest number of open data sources with higher "value" of gathered data were Memcached and ElasticSearch. The only exception is relatively poor result shown by MongoDB for compromised databases and Redis for accessibility to sensitive data. MySQL can be considered as more secure-by-design since in many cases, even if connection to databases was successful, data gathering failed. However, at the same time there were databases from which non-sensitive or system data can be gathered with a few cases of databases from which sensitive data can be gathered and even compromised databases.

According to the statistics provided, it can be assumed that the service with the smallest number of identified vulnerabilities, which may be considered "secure" compared to others, is Cassandra. But in our study CouchDB is the "most secure" because ShoBEVODSDT was unable to connect to any IP address. Although the most "vulnerable" database, according to CVE Details, is MySQL, information-gathering vulnerabilities represent only 2%, which is similar to the data obtained.

However, the highest number of the relevant vulnerabilities has been identified for Elasticsearch service (33.3%), which is also in line with our results, where it has managed to connect to all IP addresses and have managed to retrieve information from nearly all instances.

It should also be noted that some results should not be linked to the level of in-built security of the data sources concerned. In some cases, they should also be explained by the database holder's awareness of data security. This could be the reason for surprisingly positive results reported by MySQL, which contradicts the CVE Details. In other words, either MySQL is not characterized as an open database, which, in fact, does not exclude other security-related issues, or the holders of instances in question took care of their security. Otherwise, databases with weaker or any in-built mechanisms are more likely to be vulnerable. What is more, some data sources even do not have authentication mechanism as is the case for Redis, Memcached, while MongoDB and ElasticSearch do not have them enabled by default. MySQL, CouchDB and Cassandra, in turn, require authentication and in most cases show better results when ShoBEVODSDT is used. This makes it possible to argue that even such a primitive and obvious approach as authentication mechanisms leads to a significant reduction of the risk of intrusion, data leakage or even corruption. This does not mean that NoSQL databases should be avoided, but rather points to what Sollins (2019) emphasized in his work that a compromise between IoT big data security and privacy, and innovation should be made and additional security mechanisms should be considered.

Discussion and Conclusions

Companies and individuals, as well as the increasing number of actors representing CPS, IoT and IIoT applications (Oppl & Stary, 2022), today create, generate, store, interpret and analyze huge amounts of data. These data and big data, in particular, serve as an input for data-driven processes of decision-making, personalization of services, marketing purposes, crisis management, strategy setting and policy-making and overall performance in both private and public sectors, as well as the whole contemporary society.

The question of the most appropriate data management system is vital. However, when selecting the data storage and management facility, the performance and efficiency of data processing so that they can cope with data that are unmanageable with the traditional/conventional database management systems (Dash et al., 2019; Visvizi & Lytras, 2019) may become the decisive factors.

However, when deciding to use the database, security criteria should also be taken into account in addition to performance, interoperability and cost aspects. Not least important are the four key policies – access control, encryption, data masking and inspection and reporting. In accordance with the principle of security by design and privacy by design, these functions should be provided at all levels: data level (core), connectivity level (middle) and user level (edge) on end devices. The integration of security measures into the database management system is important for the implementation of a consistent cybersecurity concept. It also reduces the necessary efforts to be put at the level of database development, its use/operation and ensuring compliance with legal and internal requirements. This may be perceived by users as a self-evident prerequisite, which would explain why additional security mechanisms are not provided in databases in use, as demonstrate the results of the previous section. It is not least important that the security should be an ongoing priority, constantly checking of both the current security, safety and privacy status of the artifact, and the emerging trends and their appropriateness for further deployment. Today, many emerging technologies are being used in various domains, including security. As a result, more and more promising advanced techniques and solutions based on big data (Azeroual & Fabre, 2021), ML (Azeroual & Nikiforova, 2022) or distributed ledger technologies and blockchains (Abdullah et al., 2022), in particular, appear. They should be constantly examined and included in security policy development, implementation and maintenance, if found appropriate, thereby ensuring sustainable security and safety of the system and its components.

Moreover, it is obvious that the database is not the only asset, whose security should be taken into account. A recent study by Verizon (2021) revealed that in 2021 web application and mail servers were the most popular assets affected by incidents, followed by a desktop or laptop, mobile phone (user), a database (server). In terms of patterns, the most popular threats were social engineering, basic web application attacks, system intrusion, miscellaneous errors, privilege misuse, lost and stolen assets, denial of service. This means that the security of IS is very multi-dimensional question, where the questions such as more secure-by-design database management system is probably one of the first questions to be asked. It is even more the case given that, if database security is low, the invention of other even very advanced security mechanisms and users education can fail.

This is the case for data storage and processing facilities, particularly in the context of the widespread databases accessible from outside the organization, which pose the risk to the data holder. These databases can be accessed by external actors, while their data can be both retrieved and even manipulated, including compromising the database. The access to the open databases is simpler than ever before beforehand IoTSEs, such as Shodan, Binary Edge, Censys etc. However, they can also be used for pentesting purposes. In this Chapter one of such tools has been presented. It allows to inspect eight predefined data sources representing both NoSQL and SQL databases.

Although some data storage facilities can be described as sufficiently protected, some of them face serious challenges in this respect. From the "most secure" service viewport, CouchDB has demonstrated very good results in the context of security as the NoSQL database and MySQL as a relational database. However, if the developer needs to use Redis or Memcached, additional security mechanisms and/or activities should be introduced to protect them. It must be understood, however, that these results cannot be broadly disseminated with regard to the security of the open data storage facility, mostly by demonstrating how many data storage holders were concerned about the security of their data storage facilities, since many data storage facilities have the potential to apply a series of built-in mechanisms.

For the "most unsecure" service, Elasticsearch is characterized by weaker and less frequently used security protection mechanisms. This means that the database holder should be wary of using it. Similar conclusion can be drawn on Memcached (although it contradicts to CVE Details), where the total number of vulnerabilities found was the highest. However, the risk of these vulnerabilities was lower compared to ElasticSearch, so it can be assumed that CVE Details either does not respect such "low-level" weaknesses or have not yet identified them. Here in the future, an in-depth analysis of what CVE Details counts as vulnerability, and further exploration of the correlation with our results, could be carried out.

References

Abdullah, S., Arshad, J., Mubashir Khan, M., Alazab, M. & Salah, K. (2022). PRISED tangle: a privacy-aware framework for smart healthcare data sharing using IOTA tangle. *Complex and Intelligent Systems*. https://doi.org/10.1007/s40747-021-00610-8

Azeroual, O., & Fabre, R. (2021). Processing big data with Apache Hadoop in the current challenging era of COVID-19. *Big Data and Cognitive Computing*, *5*(1), 12. https://doi.org/10.3390/bdcc5010012

Azeroual, O., & Nikiforova, A. (2022). Apache Spark and MLlib-based intrusion detection system or how the big data technologies can secure the data. *Information*, *13*(2), 58. https://doi.org/10.3390/info13020058

Bada, M., & Pete, I. (2020, December). An exploration of the cybercrime ecosystem around Shodan. In L. Boubchir, E. Benkhelifa, Y. Jararweh & I. Saleh (Eds.), 2020 *7th international conference on internet of things: Systems, management and security (IOTSMS)* (pp. 1–8). IEEE.

Bizga, A. (2020). *Bad actors target MongoDB databases, threatening to contact GDPR legislators unless ransom is paid*. Retrieved December 2, 2021, from https://www.bitdefender.com/blog/hotforsecurity/bad-actors-target-mongodb-databases-threatening-to-contact-gdpr-legislators-unless-ransom-is-paid

Burns, B., Killion, D., Beauchesne, N., Moret, E., Sobrier, J., Lynn, M., Markham, E., Iezzoni, C., Biondi, P., Stisa Granick, J., Manzuik, S., & Guersch, P. (2007). *Security power tools*. O'Reilly Media, Inc.

Chang, F., Dean, J., Ghemawat, S., Hsieh, W. C., Wallach, D. A., Burrows, M., Chandra, T., Fikes, A., & Gruber, R. E. (2006). Bigtable: A distributed storage system for structured data. *In* B. Bershad & J. Mogul (Eds.), *Proceedings of the 7th USENIX symposium on operating systems design and implementation, OSDI'06* (Vol. 7, p. 15). USENIX Association.

Corsi, A., de Souza, F. F., Pagani, R. N., & Kovaleski, J. L. (2021). Big data analytics as a tool for fighting pandemics: A systematic review of literature. *Journal of Ambient Intelligence and Humanized Computing*, *12*(10), 9163–9180.

Cui, B., Mei, H., & Chin Ooi, B. (2014). Big data: The driver for innovation in databases. *National Science Review*, *1*(1), 27–30.

CVE Details. (2022). Retrieved January 12, 2022, from https://www.cvedetails.com/

Daskevics, A., & Nikiforova, A. (2021a, November). ShoBeVODSDT: Shodan and binary edge based vulnerable open data sources detection tool or what Internet of Things search engines know about you. In *2021 second international conference on intelligent data science technologies and applications (IDSTA)* (pp. 38–45). IEEE.

Daskevics, A., & Nikiforova, A. (2021b). IoTSE-based open database vulnerability inspection in three Baltic countries: ShoBEVODSDT sees you. In *8th international conference on internet of things: Systems, management and security (IOTSMS)*, in print.

Dash, S., Shakyawar, S. K., Sharma, M., et al. (2019). Big data in healthcare: Management, analysis and future prospects. *Journal of Big Data*, *6*, 54.

Davis, J. (2021). *Telemedicine vendor breaches the data of 2.4 million patients in Mexico*. Retrieved December 2, 2021, from https://www.healthcareitnews.com/news/telemedicine-vendor-breaches-data-24-million-patients-mexico

DeCandia, G., Hastorun, D., Jampani, M., Kakulapati, G., Lakshman, A., Pilchin, A., Sivasubramanian, S., Vosshall, P., & Vogels, W. (2007). Dynamo: Amazon's highly available key-value store. *In* T. C. Bressoud & M. F. Kaashoek (Eds.), *Proceedings of twenty-first ACM SIGOPS symposium on operating systems principles, SOSP'07* (pp. 205–220). ACM.

Derbeko, P., Dolev, S., Gudes, E., & Sharma, S. (2016). Security and privacy aspects in MapReduce on clouds: A survey. *Computer Science Review*, *20*, 1–28.

Ferrari, D., Carminati, M., Polino, M., & Zanero, S. (2020, December). NoSQL breakdown: A large-scale analysis of misconfigured NoSQL services. In R. Perdisci, M. Lindorfer & G. Stringhini (Eds.), *Annual computer security applications conference* (pp. 567–581).

Goel, K., & Ter Hofstede, A. H. (2021). Privacy-breaching patterns in NoSQL databases. *IEEE Access*, *9*, 35229–35239.

Habr. (2022). *How to discover MongoDB and Elasticsearch open databases*. Retrieved January 12, 2022, from https://habr.com/en/post/443132/

Kumar, S., Tiwari, P., & Zymbler, M. (2019). Internet of Things is a revolutionary approach for future technology enhancement: A review. *Journal of Big Data*, *6*, 111

Maltego Team. (2020). *What is open source intelligence (OSINT) & how to conduct OSINT investigations in Maltego*. Retrieved December 2, 2021, from https://www.maltego.com/blog/what-is-open-source-intelligence-and-how-to-conduct-osint-investigations/

Oppl, S., & Stary, C. (2022). Motivating users to manage privacy concerns in cyber-physical settings—A design science approach considering self-determination theory. *Sustainability*, *14*(2), 900. https://doi.org/10.3390/su14020900

OWASP Foundation. (2013). *OWASP risk rating methodology*. Retrieved January 12, 2022, from https://www.owasp.org/index.php/OWASP_Risk_Rating_Methodology

Ramadhan, R. A., Aresta, R. M., & Hariyadi, D. (2020, March). Sudomy: information gathering tools for subdomain enumeration and analysis. *In IOP Conference Series: Materials Science and Engineering* (Vol. 771, No. 1, p. 012019). IOP Publishing.

Ron, A., Shulman-Peleg, A., & Puzanov, A. (2016). Analysis and mitigation of NoSQL injections. *IEEE Security & Privacy*, *14*(2), 30–39.

Sahafizadeh, E., & Nematbakhsh, M. A. (2015). A survey on security issues in big data and NoSQL. *Advances in Computer Science: An International Journal*, *4*(4), 68–72.

Samtani, S., Kantarcioglu, M., & Chen, H. (2020). Trailblazing the artificial intelligence for cybersecurity discipline: a multi-disciplinary research roadmap. *ACM Transactions on Management Information Systems (TMIS)*, *11*(4), 1–19.

Sollins, K. R. (2019). IoT big data security and privacy versus innovation. *IEEE Internet of Things Journal*, *6*(2), 1628–1635.

Tran, H. Y., & Hu, J. (2019). Privacy-preserving big data analytics a comprehensive survey. *Journal of Parallel and Distributed Computing*, *134*, 207–218.

Tunggal, A. (2021). *The 61 biggest data breaches* (Updated for December 2021). Retrieved December 2, 2021, from https://www.upguard.com/blog/biggest-data-breaches

Visvizi, A., & Lytras, M. D. (2019). Politics and ICT: Issues, challenges, developments. In *Politics and technology in the post-truth era*. Emerald Publishing Limited.

Verizon. (2021). *Data breach investigations report*. Retrieved January 17, 2022, from https://www.verizon.com/business/resources/reports/dbir/

Part 2

Big Big Data and Its Application Across Policy Fields

Chapter 6

Big Data, Knowledge Sharing, and the Innovation Process: A Systematic Literature Review

Gianluca Maria Guazzo and Vilma Çekani

Abstract

The purpose of this chapter is to investigate how big data influences the diffusion of knowledge in firms and how it influences the firms' innovation process. The chapter identifies gaps that exist in the current literature on the topic. This study is conducted by using a qualitative methodology. PRISMA methodology is used to carry out a systematic literature review. The results shown in this study indicate the positive influence that technology has on knowledge sharing and innovation and on the other hand how good management of knowledge can benefit small and medium enterprises (SMEs). The limitation of this study is related to the methodology, whereas it is considered that a quantitative methodology can be incorporated into the other research resources. The chapter's aim is to fill a gap in the current literature and to be a new starting point for scholars and managers. Through this work, managers can better understand how to improve the innovation process through knowledge sharing in their organizations. The originality of the present study represents a first step in understanding the mechanisms of knowledge sharing within firms, how it supports the innovation process, and what role big data plays in this context.

Keywords: Knowledge management; knowledge sharing; big data; innovation, PRISMA, SMEs

1. Introduction

The recent development of information communication technologies (ICT), as well as digital transformations, has a significant impact on new knowledge.

Big Data and Decision-Making: Applications and Uses in the Public and Private Sector, 77–92

Published under exclusive licence by Emerald Publishing Limited
doi:10.1108/978-1-80382-551-920231006

ICT acts as a tool to collect data (Adam & Alhassan, 2021; Çekani, 2021; Mansoor, 2021) and turn it into knowledge, which is spread within the organization with the aim to positively influence the decision-making process. In the last decades, businesses are relying more on digitalization which gives them a competitive advantage even in the global markets. This reliance on digitalization has made the firms focus and realize more the importance and relationship of big data and knowledge (Dennis et al., 2001). On the other hand, it should be emphasized that a company's culture, its abilities, skills, and competencies play an important role in the adaptation of a digital organization (Brynjolfsson & McAfee, 2012; Sivarajah et al., 2017). In addition, taking into consideration that data value is not found only in the data itself but also to what extent it can support the company, it is concluded that it is the next step to innovation. Gobble (2013) stated that big data stimulates business value creation. Furthermore, for market-oriented companies, there is a possibility to collaborate closely with their customers, generating new shared value, and consequently new knowledge, through the co-creation of value (Akram et al., 2011). In this regard, knowledge management plays a significant role in the organization (Ekambaram et al., 2018). Therefore, enterprise-wide knowledge flow management enables improved performance by having a significant impact on three key areas, customer experience, operational systems, and business models (Polese & Guazzo, 2021). Overall, there is a need to support managerial practices related to business decision-making with big data. Big data is an important asset for companies as it enables the firms to integrate procedures, policies, processes, skills, and experiences that constitute knowledge. In this regard, Prahalad and Hamel (1990) conclude that the increase and comprehension of knowledge as a core competency is a survival factor for enterprises. Furthermore, taking into consideration the perspective that different scholars give regarding big data, knowledge sharing, and innovation, this chapter's aim is to review and investigate the existing literature by giving a panorama in how big data supports the flow of business knowledge and to understand the dynamics which facilitate the sharing of business knowledge. It is needed to underline that there is a gap in current literature, defining these three elements as a chain in a firm. Therefore, taking into consideration this gap, the research goal of this chapter is to identify the drivers that foster knowledge sharing and to indicate the importance of data in supporting knowledge sharing and innovation.

Following the objectives of this chapter, this chapter's research questions are:

- What are the main business characteristics (physical and non-physical) that act as drivers able to foster knowledge sharing?
- To what extent does the use of data support knowledge sharing and innovation, namely in the service offered by firms?

This is a qualitative research. The systematic literature is conducted by using PRISMA methodology, which will show different relationships caused by different drivers that foster knowledge sharing and the importance of data in the firms. The originality of this research consists in revealing the importance of this new digitalization area. Firstly, by identifying the genesis of knowledge management/knowledge sharing. Secondly, by analyzing what triggers the innovation process and knowledge sharing. In this regard, taking into consideration that there exists a gap in the literature studied in this research, this systematic literature review can help scholars and managers to have a better understanding of the big data – knowledge sharing – innovation chain. This chapter is divided into six sections: 1. Introduction, 2. Literature Review, 3. Methodology, 4. Findings, 5. Discussions, and 6. Conclusions and Implications.

2. Literature Review

This section gives a brief overview of knowledge sharing as a concept. To gain a better understanding of the impact that big data has on it and innovation, this second section of the chapter is dedicated to knowledge sharing and innovation by giving different insights.

2.1. Theoretical Background

The study made by Cummings (2003) revealed that the term "knowledge sharing" has its roots within the technology transfer and innovation studies in the middle of the 1970s. In this period, the research area in which knowledge sharing is contextualized is related to the different nations' success or failures to increase economic growth through the development of technologies. In this regard, Nelson (1993) stated that knowledge sharing has a positive impact on firms mastering and getting into practice product designs, manufacturing processes, and organizational designs. In addition, knowledge sharing takes place through a dynamic learning process, whereas firms consistently interact with customers and suppliers to innovate or creatively imitate (Kim & Nelson, 2000). Moreover, scholars have seen knowledge sharing in two different theoretical perspectives. Rogers et al. (2014) studied knowledge sharing in the adaption of technology and innovations, whereas Szulanski (1996) studied the best practice transfers within the organizations, also known as communication theory. Furthermore, linking knowledge sharing and innovation scholars, Birkinshaw and Morrison (1995) found out in their study that firms that use organizational structures that support combining activities and sharing resources have the tendency to be more innovative than the firms that lack this collaboration or link within themselves.

On the other hand, other scholars (Gupta & Govindarajan, 1991) emphasized how different administrative controls, such as delegation of decision-making authority are assigned to a subsidiary manager and affect both knowledge flows as well as other activities that can be taken to support knowledge sharing. Hendriks (1999) defined knowledge sharing as an act of externalization by individuals that have knowledge (knowledge owners). Referring to externalization, different forms can be noticed, for example, codifying knowledge in a written document or explaining the meaning of an idea (Savolainen, 2017), therefore knowledge sharing presumes an act of internalization by those acquiring knowledge, which is knowledge reconstruction. In addition, it is important to mention that knowledge sharing comes as part of knowledge management which is defined

> as an organizational process aimed at innovation, which enables the acquisition, assimilation, distribution, integration, sharing, retrieval and reuse of internal and external knowledge in the form of the product, through people and within organization processes. (Akram et al., 2011)

In this regard, several scholars contributed to defining a framework that helps to understand how the knowledge process is structured. Shujahat et al. (2019) stated that it is designed with three phases, namely knowledge creation, knowledge sharing, and knowledge utilization. Furthermore, knowledge creation refers to the ability of an organization to generate new knowledge, which can be represented in the form of practical knowledge, "know-how," theoretical knowledge, "know-what," or a combination of them (Singh & Gupta, 2014). This creation of new knowledge starts from the intuition of one or more actors, considered as the result of both imagination and experience and observation/exploration of the context to which one belongs (Crossan et al., 1999; Gupta et al., 2006). This allegedly refers to the four processes of socialization, externalization, combination, and internalization, identified by different scholars (Nonaka et al., 1995), also defined together as the *SECI model.* Moreover, following up this framework innovation takes place, which is defined as the number of significant changes that have an impact on different areas and departments of the company, such as product development (R&D), manufacturing, human resources, sales, and marketing (Troisi et al., 2021). In addition, the literature on the topic of knowledge applied to the innovation process (Machlup, 1962, Cohen & Levinthal, 1990) includes knowledge as a fundamental prerequisite for innovation, but not an initiator. Dougherty (1992) argues that knowledge disseminated within the organization is a key attribute for promoting innovation. At the same time, scholars (Quintane et al., 2011) claim that knowledge, that is generated during the innovation process, contributes to understanding how innovation occurs, and how it can be replicated in the future. In this regard, Cavusgil et al. (2003) explain that knowledge management is a mechanism through which the complexity of innovation can be addressed. Therefore, it supports not only the management of new knowledge, created through the innovation process but also the management of existing knowledge, which acts as an input in the innovation process (Du Plessis, 2007).

In the section below, the PRISMA methodology is used to conduct this systematic literature research, which indicates the gap that exists in the literature related to the data – knowledge share – innovation chain. This systematic literature review gives a panorama of the impact that data have on the knowledge sharing and innovation process within the organization in the digitalization area.

3. Methodology

The purpose of this study is to investigate how big data influences the diffusion of knowledge firms, and how they can be a catalyst in the innovation process triggered by knowledge sharing. A systematic literature review is conducted according to the guidelines established by the PRISMA statement; the purpose of this methodology is to identify the lack of information on the topic by critically evaluating studies already available (Burry, 2000).

The process of selection of final studies is conducted by different steps, which precisely define the relevance of the topic, including the development of a protocol to revise papers, acknowledgment of both inclusion and exclusion criteria, analysis, and discussion of results.

It is important to highlight that this chapter has been divided into two timelines: the first one is related to the theoretical background whereas it will be 1962 and 1999, and the second timeline is the studies published between 2000 and 2021, relevant to the topic, in order to observe how the phenomenon has been changing over time.

The research is conducted through online libraries, including Science Direct, Scopus, Web of Science, and Emerald Insight; in addition, keywords were also searched on the Google Scholar engine for more specific analyses.

Articles published in both national and international journals were considered, as well as company reports, to have a more detailed view of the knowledge management (KM) framework, thanks to the contribution of both scholars and managers; while conference papers, reviews, and notes were not selected English were excluded.

The research began in August 2021 and was completed in January 2022. In the first phase, 478 publications were identified and selected by using keywords, namely, "knowledge management," "knowledge sharing," "big data," "innovation," and "ICT" within titles, abstracts, and paper keywords.

In the second phase, all authors reviewed the titles of the first phase to determine their relevance to the research objectives. In this phase, studies that were not consistent with research objectives and/or not written in English were excluded and discipline areas (business management, information management, computer science, and communication) were included. Thus, the number of articles selected was 184. In the third phase, all remaining articles were reviewed and evaluated by reading the abstracts; their consistency with the proposed research objectives was assessed. In fact, some articles lacked information related to the topic, while others proved to be not relevant to the stated research questions. At this stage, the abstract of each article was reviewed independently by each author. Of the 184 abstracts evaluated, 151 were excluded for irrelevance, leaving 33 articles for further analysis. Fig. 6.1 illustrates the pipeline of the employed research methodology.

This study shows several limitations. Firstly, it would have been better if the systematic literature review conducted would be integrated with quantitative research, for example, a survey to SMEs. Secondly, it does not take into consideration the gray literature which could have given a contribution to this chapter as well. Thirdly, it would have been better if this study would have considered papers

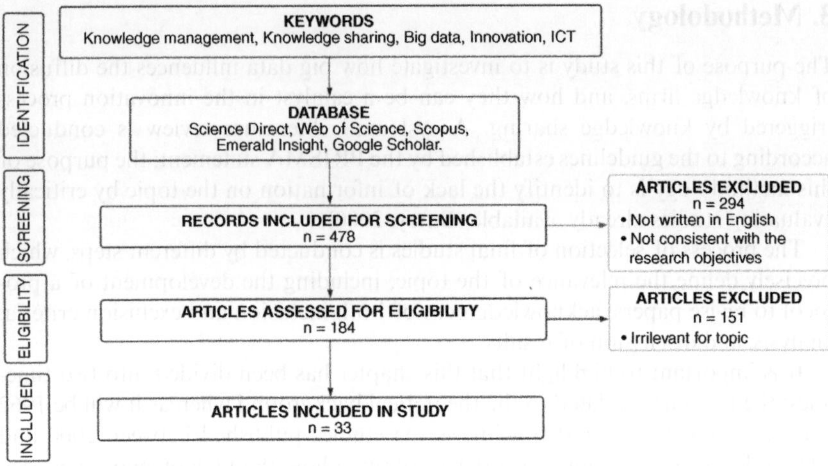

Fig. 6.1. Flowchart Illustrating the Articles Selection Process for Review.
Source: The authors.

that are available even in other databases to increase the validity of this research. Furthermore, it can be proposed as future research that it is necessary to study not only the internal knowledge that exists within the organizations (e.g., between employees) but also the external knowledge which comes from the customers.

4. Findings

This section illustrates some of the main findings of this chapter. The purpose of this section is to show how different relationships between technology, knowledge, and innovation can affect firms. The reason why these studies are specifically collected is that they are part of the scope of this chapter and give a brief panorama of the firm's structure as well.

Table 6.1 shows the relationships that are caused by technology and knowledge sharing which implies the benefits. Its aim is to present in general how this relationship evolves. In this table, it can be noticed that there is a close relationship between IT and knowledge sharing which increases the competitive advantage and it positively influences innovation. Another phenomenon to be pointed out is the fact that ICT and knowledge management collect, create, and distribute knowledge in an efficient way, which helps to add value to the new/product or service.

Table 6.2 shows the relationship between SMEs with knowledge sharing and its impact on the organization. In this table, a close relationship that exists within the knowledge sharing and innovation can be noticed, taking into consideration also the SMEs' behavior or human capital. On the other hand, SMEs have the tendency to rely on internal knowledge sharing and the external information which comes from customers, different from other typologies of companies. Furthermore, one of the factors why SMEs do not give importance to big data/technology is related to the volume of the data which is relatively smaller than others enterprises (Singh et al., 2021).

Table 6.1. Technology and Knowledge Sharing (Authors' Elaboration).

Authors	Titles	Contributions	Main Concepts
Eidizadeh et al. (2017)	Analyzing the role of business intelligence, knowledge sharing, and organizational innovation on gaining competitive advantage	1. Business intelligence (BI) positive impact on knowledge sharing 2. Knowledge sharing impact competitive advantage	Knowledge sharing, competitive advantage, organizational innovation, and business intelligence
Kumar et al. (2022)	Organizational IT support and knowledge sharing behavior affecting service innovation performance: empirical evidence from the hospitality industry	1. Organization IT supports influence on knowledge sharing and service innovation performance. 2. Managerial-level knowledge sharing motivation increases organization performance and knowledge sharing culture 3. Knowledge management role in acquisitions, creating, sharing, and storing knowledge	Competitive advantage, knowledge sharing behavior, organizational excellence, hospitality services, organization IT support, and service innovation performance
Lin (2007a)	Knowledge sharing and firm innovation capability: an empirical study	-Relationship: ICT and knowledge collecting 1. Firm innovation and knowledge sharing culture 2. Top management support and employees sharing knowledge	Knowledge sharing, organizational innovation, and ICT, competitive advantage
Saleem et al. (2021)	Big data use and its outcomes in supply chain context: the roles of information sharing and technological innovation	1. Big data use (BDU) impact on innovation in SMEs 2. Knowledge sharing impact on BDU and technological innovation 3. Knowledge management and firm performance impact the innovation process	Big data use, technological innovation, supply chain performance, SMEs performance, and information/knowledge sharing

Source: The authors.

Table 6.2. SMEs and Knowledge Sharing.

Authors	Title	Contributions	Main Concepts
Harel et al. (2020)	Sharing knowledge processes for promoting innovation in small businesses	1. Knowledge sharing to promote innovation in SME 2. Knowledge Management important in SMEs innovation process	Small businesses, innovation, sharing knowledge, and managerial process
Hanifah et al. (2021)	Effect of intellectual capital and entrepreneurial orientation on innovation performance of manufacturing SMEs: mediating role of knowledge sharing	1. Human capital and external relational capital impact on knowledge sharing and innovation performance in SMEs 2. Knowledge sharing impact on firm innovation performance in SMEs	Innovation performance, structural capital, human capital, rational capital, entrepreneurial orientation, and knowledge sharing
Sulistiyani and Harwiki (2016)	How SMEs build innovation capabilities based on knowledge sharing behavior? Phenomenological approach	1. SMEs behavior on knowledge share and product innovation capabilities 2. Knowledge sharing impact: 2.1 innovative product 2.2 improved production techniques 2.3 improved quality	Innovation capabilities, knowledge sharing behavior, phenomenology, and SMEs
Singh et al. (2021)	Top management knowledge value, knowledge sharing practices, open innovation and organizational performance	1. Knowledge sharing practices play a vital role in open innovation SMEs 2. Critical role of top management and knowledge sharing practices to support open innovation 3. SMEs' reliance on internal knowledge sharing practices and external information	Top management knowledge value, knowledge sharing practices, open innovation, organizational performance, and SMEs

Source: The authors.

5. Discussions

In general, there is a need for companies to adopt a data-oriented strategic orientation which requires the active role of leadership in fostering a culture oriented toward innovation and data management at every stage of the decision-making process. As knowledge sharing is considered as transferring knowledge within/out organization, employees, or groups, scholars (Lee et al., 2012; Tong et al., 2015) emphasize the fact that this is the starting point whereas big data plays a vital role in the company. Knowledge is the accumulation of the big data which comes from different sources, shared in the firms it can have an important role in the innovation process. In this way, the performance of the firm increases, and consequently, value creation is enabled (Polese et al., 2019; Visvizi et al., 2021). Furthermore, the role of business management must be proactive and focused on changing and trying to encourage decision-making based on data analysis. In this regard, the strategic choices are not the result of mere intuitions but a careful interpretation of the surrounding phenomena and variables, therefore fostering an innovation-oriented culture and data management at every stage of the decision-making process (Lytras & Visvizi, 2019; Troisi et al., 2020). As firms try to implement these strategies, different scholars (Ardichvili et al., 2003; Gupta & George, 2016; Lin, 2007b; Van den Hooff et al., 2012) studied knowledge sharing and considered it "as an important process of social interaction in an organization, and it occurs at the individual, group, or organizational levels." In this regard, Foss et al. (2010) state that knowledge sharing is designed to transform an individual into organizational knowledge. Therefore, firms by understanding the importance of knowledge sharing, time after time try to discover new drivers that influence the efficiency of sharing the knowledge within the company.

Scholars (Barile et al., 2017) argue that if there is better management of technology it can lead to stimulating knowledge exchange, the latter brings the creation of new knowledge, and it leads managers to increase service innovation which is improved by a better technology management strategy. Hence, taking into consideration what the scholars professed it can be noticed that the knowledge exchange and knowledge sharing are synonyms which consequently brings new knowledge within the organization itself. Therefore, a good technology management infrastructure is considered as a physical characteristic to foster knowledge sharing. This implies that there is better management of data whereas thanks to a better technology infrastructure it helps the process of knowledge sharing. On the other hand, a non-physical example of knowledge sharing is enterprise social media, which is described by Anchara et al. (2018) and Leonardi et al. (2013). They describe it as web-based platforms that allow workers to communicate messages with specific coworkers/broadcast messages to everyone in the organization, post, edit, and sort text and files linked to themselves and others, view messages, connections, text, and files communicated, posted, edited, and sorted by anyone in the organization at any time of their choosing, and also to explicitly indicate or implicitly reveal particular coworkers as communication partners. These platforms facilitate knowledge sharing by fastening the sharing of knowledge.

Moreover, this is an exchange data platform where good management of it within the coworkers helps in sharing the knowledge. Furthermore, firms can have more efficiency in producing/improving a new product or service which adapts to the needs/wants of the customers. Moreover (Razmerita et al. (2016) based on Lin (2007b) categorized the factors that impact knowledge sharing in three dimensions: individual which includes employee's self-determination theory (extrinsic and intrinsic motivation) (Deci & Ryan, 2000), organizational factors, and technological. In this regard, Lepore et al. (2021) argued that organizational culture can be an important driver for knowledge sharing as it can influence by creating; firstly, an environment where strong social norms are for knowledge sharing and secondly, a trustable environment that can encourage everyone in the enterprise to share knowledge with others. Knowledge comes from different sources and the way it is shared shows its efficiency and increases the collaborative spirit with the employees. A good IT system that acts as a generator of different data that can come from online communication within the organization can facilitate the processes of innovation.

Different scholars (Alavi & Leidner, 2001; Alavi et al., 2005; Baskerville & Dulipovici, 2006) agree when it comes to the theory of knowledge management whereas knowledge itself is seen as an intangible asset of firms. In addition, scholars (Chión et al., 2019) in their study noticed that there is a significant relationship between knowledge sharing and process improvement, organizational culture and knowledge sharing, and organizational structure and knowledge sharing. In this sphere, as is knowledge sharing can help in improving processes which can be important when it comes to managing knowledge or sharing it faster. Ciasullo and Troisi (2013) analyze in their research a case study of Sabox company whereas it is concluded that knowledge sharing is part of the encouragement of the corporate, for example, teamwork innovation or customized projects. In this sphere, it is understandable that sharing knowledge between members has a significant impact as it stimulates innovation. Furthermore, Ye et al. (2021) affirmed that the innovation behavior of the firm is positively impacted by the creative leadership ability, emotional reaction, innovation climate, and knowledge sharing. Therefore, knowledge sharing itself is found to be functioning as a balance between innovation climate and innovation behavior which helps a product or service to develop or perform better in the future.

Harel et al. (2020) acknowledge that in the context of research on SMEs, there is a lack of studies regarding types of innovation as they are considered as one cohesive group. Furthermore, the sharing knowledge process is found to be important for them to promote innovation. They should implement processes for sharing knowledge. Another important factor in knowledge sharing besides the ones discussed above is big data support. In this regard, scholars (Bechina & Bommen, 2006) noted that IT infrastructure gives significant support to knowledge sharing by using different technology tools, where managing the data can help companies to process it faster and will have an impact on their product or service which will fulfill the needs and wants of their customers by improving them. In support of this affirmation, Tippins and Sohi (2003) add that this technological support helps the communication between individuals which

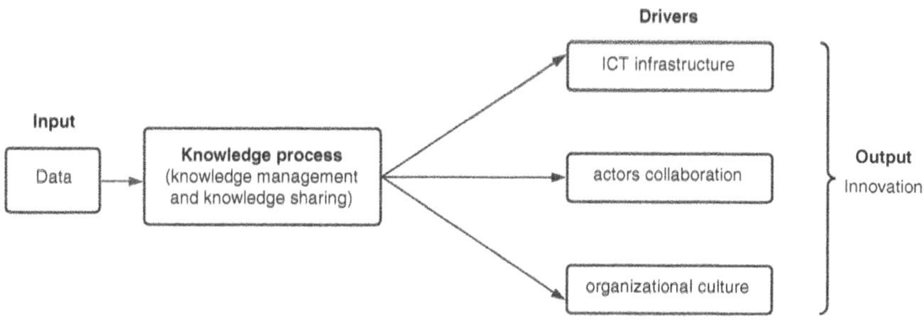

Fig. 6.2. SMEs and the Knowledge Sharing and Diffusion Process. *Source*: The authors.

subsequently will promote and facilitate the knowledge exchange process, which was highlighted above also by Barile et al. (2017) who summarized that IT usage and support, knowledge sharing, and innovation performance are correlated with each other. If this relationship can be described as statistic, it would be a covariant relationship, taking into consideration that if a change happens in one of the variables aforementioned (IT support/usage, knowledge sharing, and innovation) it can influence the others.

Most of the studies are concentrated on studying innovation whereas an IT support/usage that helps the company in organizing the data or managing it better can be a trigger to invent a new product/service which can open a new segment in the market. In addition, Castaneda and Cuellar (2020) highlight the fact that innovation and knowledge sharing is the "exchange of expertise oriented to create or improve products and service value." According to them, the relationship between knowledge sharing and innovation is collaboration whereas they see a strong relationship between knowledge sharing with internet of things (IoT) and artificial intelligence (AI) as stimulators of innovation. It is important to emphasize that most scholars find knowledge sharing efficiency within the management structure of the company which will have an aftereffect on the innovation, rather than taking big data more into consideration. Furthermore, if there is not a system that can manage the data or filter it, the impact that it will have on knowledge sharing will not be as efficient as it is supposed to be (Fig. 6.2).

6. Conclusions and Implications

The aim of this chapter is to give a panorama of how big data impacts the knowledge sharing and innovation process. The means chosen to show the impact is by using a systematic literature review which showed the relationships between data, knowledge sharing, and innovation. This chapter took into consideration 33 papers to prove that there exists a gap in the literature regarding the data influence in knowledge processes within SMEs. Some of the studies affirmed that technological changes could help in the creation of new knowledge and use this knowledge as a catalyst to facilitate the innovation process of firms. Accordingly, the improvement of these processes increases the efficiency and efficacy of the production of a product or a service by improving it or by bringing a new one.

Different organizations use various channels and platforms as means of communication to improve knowledge sharing. Furthermore, this study takes into consideration also different factors that have a significant impact on increasing knowledge sharing such as organization culture, openness between employees, and motivation of the employees. As big data generates valuable information, firms use knowledge sharing as a means to transfer knowledge within the organization whose aim is to positively influence the innovation process.

This chapter's goal is to fill a gap in the literature, whereas the scholars can use this chapter as a guiding line to understand how big data impacts the innovative process of enterprises by taking advantage of knowledge sharing. On the other hand, for the managers, this study can have a significant value because it shows the importance of big data as an asset capable to improve innovation capabilities. Therefore, knowledge sharing can not only help in the dissemination/transferring the information within the organization but it goes beyond, also between different organizations, which precipitates the innovation process. Furthermore, sharing knowledge between different groups/departments in the organization can help to facilitate different processes that lead to innovation in SMEs. Managers through this study can understand that big data is seen as a first step that leads to innovation. On the other hand, there are also other factors that can influence knowledge sharing such as the culture of the firms and a data support structure which are capable to facilitate the exchange of information, competencies, and experiences within firms. Finally, SMEs create value not only outside but also within the organization.

References

Acharya, A., Singh, S. K., Pereira, V., & Singh, P. (2018). Big data, knowledge co-creation and decision making in fashion industry. *International Journal of Information Management*, *42*, 90–101.

Adam, I. O., & Alhassan, M. D. (2021). Bridging the global digital divide through digital inclusion: The role of ICT access and ICT use. *Transforming Government: People, Process and Policy*, *15*(4), 580–596.

Akram, K., Siddiqui, S. H., Nawaz, M. A., Ghauri, T. A., & Cheema, A. K. H. (2011). Role of knowledge management to bring innovation: An integrated approach. *Cell*, *92*(333), 6183035.

Alavi, M., Kayworth, T. R., & Leidner, D. E. (2005). An empirical examination of the influence of organisational culture on knowledge management practices. *Journal of Management Information Systems*, *22*(3), 191–224. https://doi.org/10.2753/MIS0742-1222220307

Alavi, M., & Leidner, D. E. (2001). Review: Knowledge management and knowledge management systems: Conceptual foundations and research issues. *MIS Quarterly*, *25*(1), 107–136. https://doi.org/10.2307/3250961

Ardichvili, A., Page, V., & Wentling, T. (2003). Motivation and barriers to participation in virtual knowledge-sharing communities of practice. *Journal of Knowledge Management*, *7*(1), 64–77. https://doi.org/10.1108/13673270310463626

Barile, S., Ciasullo, M. V., Troisi, O., & Sarno, D. (2017). The role of technology and institutions in tourism service ecosystems: Findings from a case study. *The TQM Journal*, *29*(6), 811–833. https://doi.org/10.1108/TQM-06-2017-0068

Baskerville, R., & Dulipovici, A. (2006). The theoretical foundations of knowledge management. *Knowledge Management Research & Practice*, *4*(2), 83–105. https://doi.org/10.1057/palgrave.kmrp.8500090

Bechina, A. A., & Bommen, T. (2006). Knowledge sharing practices: Analysis of a global Scandinavian consulting company. *The Electronic Journal of Knowledge Management*, *4*(2), 109–116.

Birkinshaw, J. M., & Morrison, A. J. (1995). Configurations of strategy and structure in subsidiaries of multinational corporations. *Journal of International Business Studies*, *26*(1), 729–753. https://doi.org/10.1057/palgrave.jibs.8490818

Brynjolfsson, E., & McAfee, A. (2012). *Race against the machine: How the digital revolution is accelerating innovation, driving productivity, and irreversibly transforming employment and the economy* (pp. 1–8). MIT Sloan Management.

Burry, C. (2000). What is concurrent planning, and how do i do it? In H. Dubowitz, & D. DePanfilis (Eds.), *Handbook for child protection practice* (pp. 387–389). SAGE Publications, Inc., https://dx.doi.org/10.4135/9781452205489.n80

Castaneda, D. I., & Cuellar, S. (2020). Knowledge sharing and innovation: A systematic review. *Knowledge and Process Management*, *27*(3), 159–173.

Cavusgil, S. T., Calantone, R. J., & Zhao, Y. (2003). Tacit knowledge transfer and firm innovation capability. *Journal of Business & Industrial Marketing*, *18*(1), 6–21.

Çekani, V. (2021, April). The Role of Blockchain Technology During Covid-19 in the Healthcare Sector. In A. Visvizi, O. Troisi, & K. Saeedi (Eds.), *Research and innovation forum 2021, RIIFORUM 2021* (pp. 35–43). Springer, Cham.

Chión, S. J., Charles, V., & Morales, J. (2019). The impact of organisational culture, organisational structure, and technological infrastructure on process improvement through knowledge sharing. *Business Process Management Journal*, *26*(6), 1443–1472. https://doi.org/10.1108/BPMJ-10-2018-0279

Ciasullo, M. V., & Troisi, O. (2013). Sustainable value creation in SMEs: A case study. *The TQM Journal*, *25*(1), 44–61. https://doi.org/10.1108/17542731311286423

Cohen, W. M., & Levinthal, D. A. (1990). Absorptive capacity: A new perspective on learning and innovation. *Administrative Science Quarterly*, *35*(1), 128–152.

Crossan, M. M., Lane, H. W., & White, R. E. (1999). An organizational learning framework: From intuition to institution. *Academy of Management Review*, *24*(3), 522–537.

Cummings, J. (2003). Knowledge sharing: A review of the literature. In *OED working paper series* (pp. 3–6). World Bank.

Deci, E. L., & Ryan, R. M. (2000). The 'what' and 'why' of goal pursuits: Human needs and the self-determination of behavior. *Psychological Inquiry*, *11*(4), 227–268. https://doi.org/10.1207/S15327965PLI1104_01

Dennis, C., Marsland, D., & Cockett, T. (2001). Data mining for shopping centres – Customer knowledge-management framework. *Journal of Knowledge Management*, *5*(4), 368–374. https://doi.org/10.1108/13673270110411797

Dougherty, D. (1992). Interpretive barriers to successful product innovation in large firms. *Organization Science*, *3*(2), 179–202.

Du Plessis, M. (2007). The role of knowledge management in innovation. *Journal of Knowledge Management*, *11*(4), 20–29.

Eidizadeh, R., Salehzadeh, R., & Esfahani, A. C. (2017). Analysing the role of business intelligence, knowledge sharing and organisational innovation on gaining competitive advantage. *Journal of Workplace Learning*, *29*(4), 250–267. https://doi.org/10.1108/JWL-07-2016-0070

Ekambaram, A., Sørensen, A. Ø., Bull-Berg, H., & Olsson, N. O. (2018). The role of big data and knowledge management in improving projects and project-based organizations. *Procedia Computer Science*, *138*, 851–858.

Foss, N. J., Husted, K., & Michailova, S. (2010). Governing knowledge sharing in organizations: Levels of analysis, governance mechanisms, and research directions. *Journal of Management Studies*, *47*(3), 455–482. https://doi.org/10.1111/j.1467-6486.2009.00870.x

Gobble, M. A. (2013). Big data: The next big thing in innovation. *Research and Technology Management*, *56*(1), 64–66.

Gupta, M., & George, J. F. (2016). Toward the development of a big data analytics capability. *Information & Management*, *53*(8), 1049–1064.

Gupta, A. K., & Govindarajan, V. (1991). Knowledge flows and the structure of control within multinational corporations. *Academy of Management Review*, *16*(4), 768–792. https://doi.org/10.5465/amr.1991.4279628

Gupta, A. K., Smith, K. G., & Shalley, C. E. (2006). The interplay between exploration and exploitation. *Academy of Management Journal*, *49*(4), 693–706.

Hanifah, H., Abd Halim, N., Vafaei-Zadeh, A., & Nawaser, K. (2021). Effect of intellectual capital and entrepreneurial orientation on innovation performance of manufacturing SMEs: Mediating role of knowledge sharing. *Journal of Intellectual Capital*, ahead-of-print. https://doi.org/10.1108/JIC-06-2020-0186

Harel, R., Schwartz, D., & Kaufmann, D. (2020). Sharing knowledge processes for promoting innovation in small businesses. *European Journal of Innovation Management*, *24*(5), 1860–1882.

Hendriks, P. (1999). Why share knowledge? The influence of ICT on the motivation for knowledge sharing. *Knowledge and Process Management*, *6*(2), 91–100.

Kim, L., & Nelson, R. R. (2000). *Technology, learning, and innovation: Experiences of newly industrializing economies*. Cambridge University Press.

Kumar, M., Mamgain, P., Pasumarti, S. S., & Singh, P. K. (2022). Organizational IT support and knowledge sharing behaviour affecting service innovation performance: Empirical evidence from the hospitality industry. *VINE Journal of Information and Knowledge Management Systems*, ahead-of-print. https://doi.org/10.1108/VJIKMS-07-2021-0124

Lee, A., Hobson, J., Bienkowski, M., Midgley, S., Currier, S., Campbell, L. M., & Novoselova, T. (2012). Towards networked knowledge: The learning registry, an infrastructure for sharing online learning resources. *Educational Technology*, *52*(6), 14–19.

Leonardi, P. M., Huysman, M., & Steinfield, C. (2013). Enterprise social media: Definition, history, and prospects for the study of social technologies in organizations. *Journal of Computer-mediated Communication*, *19*(1), 1–19. https://doi.org/10.1111/jcc4.12029

Lepore, D., Dubbini, S., Micozzi, A., & Spigarelli, F. (2021). Knowledge sharing opportunities for Industry 4.0 firms. *Journal of the Knowledge Economy*, *13*(3), 1–20. https://doi.org/10.1007/s13132-021-00750-9

Lin, H. F. (2007a). Knowledge sharing and firm innovation capability: an empirical study. *International Journal of Manpower*. *28*(3–4), 315–332.

Lin, H.-F. (2007b). Effects of extrinsic and intrinsic motivation on employee knowledge sharing intentions. *Journal of Information Science*, *33*(2), 135–149. https://doi.org/10.1177/0165551506068174

Lytras, M. D., & Visvizi, A. (2019). Big data and their social impact: Preliminary study. *Sustainability*, *11*(18), 5067.

Machlup, F. (1962). *The production and distribution of knowledge in the United States* (Vol. 278). Princeton University Press.

Mansoor, M. (2021). An interaction effect of perceived government response on COVID-19 and government agency's use of ICT in building trust among citizens of Pakistan. *Transforming Government: People, Process and Policy*, *15*(4), 693–707.

Nelson, M. W. (1993). The effects of error frequency and accounting knowledge on error diagnosis in analytical review. *Accounting Review*, 804–824.

Nonaka, I., Ikujiro, N., & Takeuchi, H. (1995). *The knowledge-creating company: How Japanese companies create the dynamics of innovation* (Vol. 105). OUP USA.

Polese, F., & Guazzo, G. M. (2021, April). Business Governance in Emergent Contexts: Firms and Artificial Intelligence During the Covid-19 Pandemic. A Systematic Literature Review. In A. Visvizi, O. Troisi, & K. Saeedi (Eds.), *Research and innovation forum 2021, RIIFORUM 2021* (pp. 343–351). Cham: Springer.

Polese, F., Troisi, O., Grimaldi, M., & Romeo, E. (2019). A big data-oriented approach to decision-making: A systematic literature review. In *22nd international conference proceedings* (pp. 472–496).

Prahalad, C. K., & Hamel, G. (1990). The core competence of the corporation. *Harvard Business Review*, May–June, pp. 79–91.

Quintane, E., Casselman, R. M., Reiche, B. S., & Nylund, P. A. (2011). Innovation as a knowledge-based outcome. *Journal of Knowledge Management*, *15*(6), 928–947.

Razmerita, L., Kirchner, K., & Nielsen, P. (2016). What factors influence knowledge sharing in organizations? A social dilemma perspective of social media communication. *Journal of Knowledge Management*, *20*(6), 1225–1246. https://doi.org/10.1108/JKM-03-2016-0112

Rogers, E. M., Singhal, A., & Quinlan, M. M. (2014). *Diffusion of innovations* (pp. 432–448). Routledge.

Saleem, H., Li, Y., Ali, Z., Ayyoub, M., Wang, Y., & Mehreen, A. (2021). Big data use and its outcomes in supply chain context: The roles of information sharing and technological innovation. *Journal of Enterprise Information Management*, *34*(4), 1121–1143. https://doi.org/10.1108/JEIM-03-2020-0119

Savolainen, R. (2017). Information sharing and knowledge sharing as communicative activities. *Information Research: An International Electronic Journal*, *22*(3), paper 767.

Shujahat, M., Sousa, M. J., Hussain, S., Nawaz, F., Wang, M., & Umer, M. (2019). Translating the impact of knowledge management processes into knowledge-based innovation: The neglected and mediating role of knowledge-worker productivity. *Journal of Business Research*, *94*, 442–450.

Singh, R. M., & Gupta, M. (2014). Knowledge management in teams: Empirical integration and development of a scale. *Journal of Knowledge Management*, *18*(4), 777–794.

Singh, S. K., Gupta, S., Busso, D., & Kamboj, S. (2021). Top management knowledge value, knowledge sharing practices, open innovation and organizational performance. *Journal of Business Research*, *128*, 788–798. https://doi.org/10.1016/j.jbusres.2019.04.040

Sivarajah, U., Kamal, M. M., Irani, Z., & Weerakkody, V. (2017). Critical analysis of big data challenges and analytical methods. *Journal of Business Research*, *70*, 263–286.

Sulistiyani, R., & Harwiki, W. (2016). How SMEs build innovation capability based on knowledge sharing behavior? Phenomenological approach. *Procedia-Social and Behavioral Sciences*, *219*, 741–747.

Szulanski, G. (1996). Exploring internal stickiness: Impediments to the transfer of best practice within the firm. *Strategic Management Journal*, *17*, 27–43 https://doi.org/10.1002/smj.4250171105

Tippins, M. J., & Sohi, R. S. (2003). IT competency and firm performance: Is organizational learning a missing link?. *Strategic Management Journal*, *24*(8), 745–761. https://doi.org/10.1002/smj.337

Tong, C., Tak, W. I. W., & Wong, A. (2015). The impact of knowledge sharing on the relationship between organizational culture and job satisfaction: The perception of information communication and technology (ICT) practitioners in Hong Kong. *International Journal of Human Resource Studies*, *5*(1), 19.

Troisi, O., Maione, G., Grimaldi, M., & Loia, F. (2020). Growth hacking: Insights on data-driven decision-making from three firms. *Industrial Marketing Management*, *90*, 538–557.

Troisi, O., Visvizi, A., & Grimaldi, M. (2021). The different shades of innovation emergence in smart service systems: The case of Italian cluster for aerospace technology. *Journal of Business & Industrial Marketing*, 1–25.

Van den Hooff, B., Schouten, A. P., & Simonovski, S. (2012). What one feels and what one knows: The influence of emotions on attitudes and intentions towards knowledge sharing. *Journal of Knowledge Management*, *16*(1), 148–158. https://doi.org/10.1108/13673271211198990

Visvizi, A., Troisi, O., Grimaldi, M., & Loia, F. (2021). Think human, act digital: Activating data-driven orientation in innovative start-ups. *European Journal of Innovation Management*, *25*(6), 452–447.

Ye, P., Liu, L., & Tan, J. (2021). Creative leadership, innovation climate and innovation behaviour: The moderating role of knowledge sharing in management. *European Journal of Innovation Management*, *25*(4), 1092–1114.

Chapter 7

Transparency in AI Systems for Value Co-creation in Healthcare

Antonietta Megaro

Abstract

This conceptual chapter aims to understand the role of artificial intelligence (AI) in value co-creation phenomena in a healthcare service ecosystem, through a literature review and the definition of a conceptual framework. AI, as an operant resource, can stimulate a completely patient-centered, adaptive and resilient healthcare system, and governance models in healthcare based on data-driven decision-making (DDDM), ensuring faster choices, more timely diagnosis and more personalized treatment paths. However, the full implementation of AI in healthcare is inhibited by some frictions, mainly related to the risk that the AI black box may generate an inadequate automatic decision, also due to the quality of data used, often partial and unstructured given the reluctance to share them by patients concerned by privacy threats. The co-design (multi-part and multi-level) of a predictive decision model based on the functional transparency of the AI algorithm would allow for augmented decision as result of an effective human–machine interaction. Healthcare actors could thus make decisions using the information detected by the software (based on clear cause-and-effect correlations and modifiable variables in case of mistakes), integrated with their professional knowledge. This would also help to strengthen the patient's perception of the decision's reliability and accuracy and the safety of the tool (factors that can affect his/her trust). AI may be considered as a driver for value co-creation in healthcare, thanks to transparency. It would allow the promotion of collaborative behaviors involving actors by generating new institutions and new resource integration practices among them.

Keywords: AI; healthcare service ecosystem; value co-creation; transparency; data-driven decision-making; big data; service innovation

Big Data and Decision-Making: Applications and Uses in the Public and Private Sector, 93–105

Published under exclusive licence by Emerald Publishing Limited
doi:10.1108/978-1-80382-551-920231007

1. Introduction

The use of new tools based on AI in healthcare spreads. There are several benefits related to the use of AI in healthcare: it allows the management of a large amount of electronic data for each patient and identifies calculation and analysis models at a scale and speed higher than the capacity of human analysis, supporting healthcare professionals in diagnosis, interpreting a greater amount of data and with significantly reduced timing to obtain more precise diagnoses and new treatment paths.

The biggest challenge for AI in healthcare is its full applicability in daily clinical practice. A challenge that must necessarily be integrated with the need to always ensure the centrality of the patient's experience and the patient's active participation in therapy. A need that should already be considered by programmers who develop an AI system intended to be inserted into the infrastructure of a health system. By centralizing the patient's role in the course of his or her therapeutic path, they can lead to a collection of inclusive data, which takes into account the experience lived by the same, as well as their symptoms, and allow to reduce the time needed to carry out bureaucratic activities and routine and investing more time in the relationship with the patient.

However, one of the main obstacles is certainly the fragmentation of data in the information and communication technology (ICT) systems of healthcare facilities, further complicated by the reluctance to share data on the part of patients, concerned about the problem of privacy. Having little data available, of poor quality and unstructured, complicates the implementation of projects and models and delivers inaccurate results. In fact, it is believed that cases of medical malpractice in healthcare activities are increasingly linked to incorrect data collection due to often incomplete, incorrect or distorted health data.

The application of AI encounters various obstacles among medical operators and to overcome this resistance it is necessary that the algorithms used as "transparent" as possible, that is, they allow to fully understand the cause–effect relationship on which they are based, such as they work and how they make the final decisions that will then be used in healthcare. When the algorithms are understandable, operators have a greater chance of easily interpreting and correcting any errors and the certainty that the decisions made are ethical and scientific.

For this reason, this conceptual work aims to respond to the following *RQ*:

> *RQ*. Is it possible to consider transparency in AI systems as a driver to enable healthcare actors to co-create value?

To pursue this aim, the contribution is structured by initially presenting the theoretical framework used, then the healthcare system is deepened through the analysis of the phenomena stimulated by the introduction of AI systems (Section 3) in terms of opportunities and threats. Finally, links were drawn between the literature on transparency in AI and the literature on value co-creation to understand if the first one could be a lever for the other (Section 4). The work ends with non-conclusive considerations (Section 5).

2. The Conceptual Background

2.1. Service Ecosystem and Value Co-creation: Insights for the Healthcare Sector

Service ecosystems are relatively autonomous systems. They are composed of different heterogeneous actors, stratified on different levels (micro, meso and macro), which autonomously integrate resources with the aim of co-creating value (Vargo & Lusch, 2016). Any change in one level that has an impact on other levels (Ciasullo et al., 2020).

The service ecosystem is a self-regulating system as the players make it up to adapt to changes at each level by obtaining resources from the environment and thus shape the ecosystem as a whole (Polese et al., 2021).

The service ecosystem functioning is based on shared institutions, that is, rules, tacit norms, beliefs, and emerging social practices (Koskela-Huotari & Vargo, 2016) which modify the behavior of actors, allow their interactions and affect the integration of resources among them (Vargo & Akaka, 2012). The set of institutions constitutes the institutional arrangements, or provisions, which favor coordination between the different levels of the eco-service system (Vargo et al., 2015).

The system approach can improve understanding of value co-creation phenomena and help managers think about how multiple perspectives and actors contribute to the creation of value (Polese, Mele, et al., 2017). Value is phenomenological, multi-dimensional and emergent, so firms cannot create it on their own.

It is the continuous recombination of operant resources, between actors linked in systems through value propositions (Frow et al., 2014), and interaction between the ecosystem layers that leads the co-creation of value (Chandler & Vargo, 2011). All social or economic actors, according to the A2A perspective, act with the aim of creating value for themselves and for others through the mutual integration of resources and the provision of service. This implies the dynamic and systemic nature of social and economic exchange (Wieland et al., 2012). In a service ecosystem where actors are adaptive and seek reciprocal relationships in order to co-create value, as they believe they have a much greater opportunity to meet their needs by acting for the system instead of acting alone (Polese, Pels, et al., 2017).

Value co-creation includes actors involved in the integration of resources and the exchange of service, enabled and bound by endogenously generated institutions and institutional agreements (Barile et al., 2017), and is tickled by factors such as greater access, sharing and recombination, monitoring and institutions (Beirão et al., 2017).

The healthcare system is patient-centered; it may be considered as a service ecosystem (Polese & Carrubbo, 2017) as it embeds a set of heterogeneous actors, nested at different layers (Beirão et al., 2017), interconnected by value propositions (Frow et al., 2016) and interacting based on shared tacit norms, the institutions (Polese et al., 2018).

2.2. DDDM – Insights for Healthcare

DDDM involves the use of metrics and data to guide corporate decision-making in line with objectives, purposes and initiatives (Brynjolfsson & McElheran, 2016), to favor more effective and timely decisions (Provost & Fawcett, 2013).

Data-driven is a mind-set, a new culture that is wrecking companies' business models, according to which data are conceived as strategic resources useful for decisions, rather than as output of intuitions and experiences (Polese et al., 2019). However, it is necessary to create a data-driven corporate culture, which pervades the entire organization, to optimize the information flows and the interactions between the actors that must be based on data (Troisi et al., 2021) and to allow the spread of DDDM governance it is necessary to train specialized skills in data analysis for in-depth knowledge of the context and its growth potential (Lytras et al., 2020).

A DDDM process can improve the competitiveness of companies and enable them to pursue their marketing aims, such as customer relationship management, improvement of the quality of the product or service proposed (Troisi et al., 2020).

DDDM can also support healthcare actors to improve their performance. The healthcare system is today increasingly patient-centered and, for example, patient data, if correctly interpreted, could improve knowledge, allowing a doctor/patient co-learning process (McColl-Kennedy et al., 2012). This process would support doctors-decision makers to intervene in an ever timelier and precise manner (Sakr & Elgammal, 2016), with an improvement in overall performance and in response times (Dautov et al., 2019)

The goal to aim for is the implementation of predictive governance models in favor of precision medicine, which can be achieved through AI systems.

3. AI as Operant Resource for Value Co-creation in Healthcare

AI, understood as a set of software techniques and combined ICT infrastructures, allows tasks with performances comparable to the experience of human intelligence (cf. Visvizi, 2021). In this section of the work, it will be in-depth whether it is possible to consider that AI, understood as an engine of digital transformation and implementation of DDDM processes (Sarirete et al., 2021), can be considered as an operant resource for value co-creation by enabling actors to effectively integrate resources (Bassano et al., 2020).

AI is gradually changing medical practice, offering healthcare professionals the possibility to modify and update the healthcare offer thanks to a requalification of the healthcare service delivery process which would be based on data-driven decisions; AI, which aims to mimic human cognitive functions, is bringing about a paradigm shift in healthcare, fueled by the increasing availability of health data (structured and unstructured) and the rapid advancement of analytical techniques (Jiang et al., 2017).

With recent advances in digitized data acquisition, machine learning (ML) and IT infrastructure, AI applications are expanding into areas previously thought to be within the purview of only human experts (Yu et al., 2018), among those where there is greater influence: patient administration, clinical decision support, patient monitoring and health interventions (Reddy et al., 2019). One of the most interesting and impactful AI applications distorts the doctor–patient relationship through a review of virtual assistance from doctors to patients. The partial automation of this relationship would allow, for the former, to avoid boring and repetitive tasks and concentrate on operations with higher added value, for the latter, to receive adequate answers from suitably trained chatbots through a large multitude of data that could even allow to understand some symptoms starting from the questions received and activating, if necessary, an alert system for particular pathologies, as well as streamlining administrative processes.

Thus, AI implicitly promises to improve accessibility to healthcare by creating an efficient healthcare environment. Some applications allow patients to understand their symptoms (without self-diagnosis) and to communicate with their doctors, without visiting a health facility, helping to decongest the facilities, but still receiving the treatment they need. AI also helps detect early disease risks as the system uses past and present information about health problems, executes it through the system, and can identify whether the patient is at risk of contracting a disease or not (Becker, 2019).

It could also allow patients to take greater control of their healthcare and better understand the evolution of their health needs. It is the basis for the first clinical decision support systems (CDSS) that were developed in the 1980s.

Their main contribution lies in the possibility of improving the decision-making process of doctors. There are two different types of CDSS: knowledge-based CDSS and non-knowledge-based CDSS. The former is made up of rules (IF–THEN statements which can also be very complex), which the system evaluates according to the patient's data to produce an action or an output. Rules can be defined using evidence-based on literature, practice or patient. CDSS that are not knowledge-based still require a data source, but the decision relies on AI, ML or statistical pattern recognition, rather than being programmed to follow the medical knowledge of experts (Alugubelli, 2016).

Careful design, implementation and evaluation of these AI-enabled systems will be important in understanding how AI can improve healthcare (Li et al., 2020).

The implementation of AI system, which enables risk prediction with greater accuracy based on available multi-dimensional clinical and biological data sets, also favors the design of health models based on precision medicine practices. The purpose of precision medicine is to design and improve diagnosis, therapy and prognosis with large complex data sets that incorporate individual genes, functions and environmental variations; AI-based precision medicine offers clinicians the opportunity to tailor early interventions to each individual (Subramanian et al., 2020).

AI in healthcare can be understood as an operant resource as it influences how value can be determined and co-created between the actors (Akaka & Vargo, 2014). The technology illustrated involves a review of practices, processes and symbols, which contribute to the creation of value as well as the factors of co-creation of value (Beirão et al., 2017). The value co-creation, as well as innovation, understood in the service ecosystem perspective (Koskela-Huotari et al., 2016), is driven by iterative processes of collaboration and learning between suppliers and beneficiaries of the service (Polese, Pels, et al., 2017) which, according to what has been illustrated so far, can be favored by AI. Kaartemo and Helkkula (2018) identify the first series of literature on AI in the co-creation of value, finding in it co-creation factors in the generic advancement in the field, support to service providers, enabling the integration of resources between suppliers of services and beneficiaries and support for the welfare of beneficiaries.

However, some critical issues could slow down or even fail the adoption of these applications: data quality, data protection and privacy issues, cybersecurity, a huge amount of data and interoperability between various data collector systems. Furthermore, a problem often arises in terms of transparency on the operating mechanisms of these algorithms, which can lead to serious biases that can negatively affect the final quality of the results.

3.1. Problems in Terms of Transparency

While new technologies using AI hold great promise for improving diagnosis, treatment, health research and drug development, and to support governments performing public health functions, the World Health Organization (WHO, 2021) published guidelines to clarify how ethics and rights should be placed at the center of the design, distribution and use of AI systems.

The most difficult problem to address concerning the full adoption of AI technologies in healthcare is transparency as many AI algorithms are practically impossible to interpret or explain. AI systems could make mistakes in diagnosing and treating patients and it could be difficult to establish accountability (Davenport & Kalakota, 2019).

Ensuring transparency, explainability and intelligibility is one of the six principles identified by the WHO to ensure that AI works for the public interest in all countries. Transparency requires that sufficient information be published or documented prior to the design or implementation of AI technology. Such information must be easily accessible and facilitate meaningful public consultation and debate on how the technology is designed and how it should or should not be used (World Health Organization, 2021).

Problems in terms of transparency and poor explainability of black box AI algorithms affect all the key dimensions of trust in inter-company relationships (reliability, fairness and goodwill) and they can affect the opportunity for value co-creation (Das, 2020).

It's believed that to prevent negative outcomes and achieve accountable systems it's necessary to open the "black box" of AI decision-making and make it more transparent, to ensure high-quality, fair and reliable decisions (de Fine Licht & de Fine Licht, 2020). However, it may be useful to supply justifications, both about the design of AI assistants and the decisions taken may have the potential to ensure greater perceived legitimacy by the public concerning transparency in the decision-making process.

Felzmann et al. (2020) proposed the transparency by design model to support organizations in designing transparent AI systems.

The model focuses on three fundamental pillars, understood as general planning/design requirements of AI systems, on the provision of user-oriented information on the system and on the management of transparency for systems in the organizational sense, from which nine indicators have been formulated.

The first phase concerns the design of AI systems, it implies the need to consider transparency in the design process, bearing in mind the ethical issues raised with respect to such systems, primarily in terms of epistemic concerns about the quality of evidence on which a system is based, regulations such as unfair results and the traceability of a system decision.

- *Proactivity* (need to be proactive, non-reactive): it would be advisable from the very beginning of the development of the AI system to decide on how to make information on decision-making standards accessible and understandable to those interested parties involved in the decisions of the system, including the different categories of users and, for example, regulators.
- *Integration*: transparency should be understood as an integrative process. Transparency measures should be defined with respect to standards governing decision making in the system. Companies should therefore be able to explain the standards of what they consider acceptable inferences.
- *Focus on the public*: developers of AI systems must consider the relational nature of transparency communications and, taking into account that the goal is to improve the perception of reliability, it is necessary not only to disclose information on transparency but also to do so considering the characteristics of the audience that will receive and interpret them.

The second phase concerns the disclosure of information about data processing and analysis to interested parties about what data is being processed, how it is being processed and what risks are associated with this processing. The goal is to achieve the explainability of the system, that is, to ensure that algorithmic decisions, as well as all the data guiding those decisions, can be explained in non-technical terms. Its indictors:

- *Data processing*: it requires providing an understandable description of what data are used by the system and the ways in which it is used.
- *Decision standards*: explain the decision criteria and their justifiability. These criteria are normative. Their explanation and justification can be understood as the first step toward accountability and also includes an assessment of the link between data sources and inferences must be critically evaluated. In the context of the justification, it could also be useful to ask about the degree of invasiveness of the privacy of the processing, the specific intentions underlying the processing, the use of potentially discriminatory characteristics, the potential impact of the derivation of sensitive data from data harmless, the regulatory acceptability of deriving information from source data created for different purposes and the reliability of inferences.

- *Risk disclosure*: explain the risks and risk mitigation measures. This principle focuses on the transparency of the risks associated with the operation of the AI system. Automated decision making poses risks in terms of discrimination, invasion of privacy, the obscurity of data processing and insufficient ability of users to understand the risks associated with automated decision-making from the system. Knowledge of risks is essential to foster increased autonomy and control for users of AI systems.

The third phase of managing organizational and stakeholder-oriented transparency presupposes the traceability and verifiability of AI systems. Traceability means that systems are designed in a way that allows them to retrace their decision-making process, with a record that allows for the reliable reconstruction of the processes and relevant decision-making factors and therefore the determination of responsibility for certain decisions. Audibility means that systems must be designed in such a way as to allow qualified external parties to access information on relevant processes and decision-making factors and to make judgments on their adequacy. Its indictors:

- *Inspectability*: AI systems should allow inspection of the system's decision-making process through audits. The principle also includes collaboration with third parties responsible for verification.
- *Reactivity*: this principle requires responsiveness to individual and social stakeholders beyond the question of the inspectionability of individual decisions. Responsiveness means being open to being approached and scrutinized by interested parties such as journalists, civil society organizations, public administrators and the general public.
- *Reporting*: AI system designers should make their activities transparent through detailed reports published to provide descriptive and aggregated information about the AI system.

However, there is a diatribe on the concept of transparency as it is believed that while the external forms of transparency, relating to the relationship between an AI system, its developers, users and media, can be reached directly, functional transparency, about the internal functioning of a system is, in many cases, much more difficult to achieve, which is why the right of contestability is relevant, according to which, when users cannot understand how a system has produced a particular output, they can at least challenge it (Walmsley, 2021).

4. Toward an "Augmented Decision"-based Model for Value Co-creation in Healthcare: The Role of Transparency

It can be assumed that actors operating within the healthcare context can be assisted by AI in their decision-making process, but this determines the need to understand how AI can influence the ability of these healthcare professionals to stimulate the emergence of phenomena of value co-creation, in order to lead to the pursuit of healthcare service ecosystem well-being (Beirão et al., 2017; Frow et al., 2019).

Mele et al. (2021) conceptualize smart nudge, understood as the use of cognitive technologies to influence people's behavior predictably. According to their approach, cognitive technologies make it possible to expand the accessibility of resources by providing cognitive resources and data that would otherwise not be available and content of choice based both on data collected in real-time and on forecasts. They also make it possible to extend the engagement of actors and their proactive predisposition to establish cognitive bonds. They help improve the action and agency of actors.

The architectures of choice built into AI push humans to make informed and relevant decisions: it is not cognitive technologies that alone generate intelligent results, but they allow the design of an intelligent behavioral context that promotes intelligent actions by the actors involved.

However, as noted above, the full implementation of AI in healthcare is inhibited by some frictions, mainly related to problems in terms of transparency. It may generate an inadequate automatic decision, also due to the quality of data used, often partial and unstructured given the reluctance to share them by patients concerned by privacy threats. In this case, fears in terms of transparency can inhibit the ability of the actors to stimulate the emergence of value co-creation phenomena and undermine the potential of smart nudging.

Questioning how to make AI an effective winning tool in healthcare means asking how it can improve and enhance the bond of trust between doctor and patient, the central cornerstone of the therapeutic relationship, overcoming the concept of the dominance of one over the other (Langeard et al., 1981) and information asymmetry (Tellis & Wernerfelt, 1987), in favor of increasingly collaborative relationships that can be enhanced by digitization.

To respond to this need and to face conditions of complexity determined by the increasingly pervasive dissemination of information online and by the pressures on the responsibility of healthcare professionals toward patients and the general public, motivated transparency could be understood as a potential tool that can guide and stimulate collaboration between the parties.

Reasoned transparency invites physicians to communicate to patients and communities of reference about the use of digital tools and devices, reassure patients about data confidentiality, increase patient awareness of treatment (Mabillard et al., 2021) and may ensure a favorable environment to encourage value co-creation practices.

To overcome the critical issues posed by transparency and ensure that conceptualized smart nudging with respect to the influence of AI in the predisposition of actors to co-create value is effective, it may be useful to observe how the transparency by design model (Felzmann et al., 2020) can, through its indicators, generate levers to maximize the result of smart nudges (Mele et al., 2021) and ensure that they are effectively able to allow the design of an intelligent behavioral context in health that promotes intelligent actions.

AI systems allow for the retrieval and analysis of enormous quantities of data, but doubts arise in terms of the quality of the data analyzed (Earley, 2016; Tao et al., 2019). A design of AI systems, carried out in compliance with the indicators of proactivity, integration and focus on the public, can help improve accessibility to good quality resources that can enable actors to make increasingly timely and effective decisions.

Doubts about the adequacy of the information released by AI systems increasingly discourage healthcare professionals from using them in the provision of their services (Shinners et al., 2020), while fears in terms of privacy protection, decision reliability and accuracy and the safety of the tool (Lytras & Visvizi, 2021), increasingly discourage patients from releasing their data to systems of this type (Reddy et al., 2020). The solutions proposed as part of the transparency by design model, in phase two, can help mitigate these perplexities and reduce the perception of risk by the actors involved, this could, on the other hand, stimulate greater involvement and engagement on their part.

Finally, the indicators provided for in the third phase relating to the traceability and verifiability of AI systems can help improve the agency of the actors who feel more and more protagonists and managers in carrying out their actions; healthcare professionals can control the automated process and adapt their decision-making process. This condition increases their empowerment and makes them able to continuously monitor, update and refine their decisions. It lays the foundations for decision-making models in healthcare that are increasingly data-driven and based on an "augmented decision" (Burton et al., 2020); it implies that not the software decides but the human expert who, fully aware of the functioning of the AI system used, makes a decision based on the evidence proposed by the technology, integrated with the baggage of his own previous knowledge.

A relevant training of AI systems can support healthcare actors in overcoming the functioning of black box medicine which provides accurate but difficult to interpret methods. The possibility of making these systems transparent and explaining their functioning as well as the logic that led to the decision improves the predisposition of these actors to integrate resources in a positive and proactive way with the aim of co-creating value and contributing to the well-being of the healthcare ecosystem, intended as a whole. It can therefore be assumed that the transparency in AI systems in healthcare can be understood as a driver for value co-creation (*RQ*).

5. Concluding Remarks

The use of the transparency by design model to understand how smart nudges can be spread, based on AI systems, in healthcare, has made it possible to understand that transparency can enable the factors of value co-creation in healthcare, understood as a service ecosystem. It can mitigate the resistance factors recorded up to now due to the perplexities of the involved actors about the functioning of the black box and safety, privacy and accuracy issues.

In this sense, it was found that transparency in AI systems in healthcare can be understood as a driver for the co-creation of value.

The main limitation of this work lies in its conceptual nature, an empirical study, carried out through a case study or a participatory observation, could be useful to validate the effectiveness of this insight.

The main implication lies in the always multi-disciplinary approach that requires the study of value co-creation through AI: to pursue transparency aims means to contaminate skills that pertain to the system design phase, as well as management that concern the tool implementation phase, in an all-encompassing, multi-actor, multi-part and multi-level dialogue.

References

Akaka, M. A., & Vargo, S. L. (2014). Technology as an operant resource in service (eco) systems. *Information Systems and E-business Management*, *12*(3), 367–384.

Alugubelli, R. (2016). Exploratory study of AI in healthcare. *International Journal of Innovations in Engineering Research and Technology*, *3*(1), 1–10.

Barile, S., Ciasullo, M. V., Troisi, O., & Sarno, D. (2017). The role of technology and institutions in tourism service ecosystems: Findings from a case study. *The TQM Journal*, *29*(6), 811–833.

Bassano, C., Barile, S., Saviano, M., Pietronudo, M. C., & Cosimato, S. (2020). AI technologies & value co-creation in luxury context. In Proceedings of the 53rd Hawaii International Conference on System Sciences, 1618–1627.

Becker, A. (2019). AI in medicine: What is it doing for us today?. *Health Policy and Technology*, *8*(2), 198–205.

Beirão, G., Patrício, L., & Fisk, R. P. (2017). Value cocreation in service ecosystems: Investigating health care at the micro, meso, and macro levels. *Journal of Service Management*, *28*(2), 227–249.

Brynjolfsson, E., & McElheran, K. (2016). The rapid adoption of data-driven decision-making. *American Economic Review*, *106*(5), 133–139.

Burton, J. W., Stein, M. K., & Jensen, T. B. (2020). A systematic review of algorithm aversion in augmented decision making. *Journal of Behavioral Decision Making*, *33*(2), 220–239.

Chandler, J. D., & Vargo, S. L. (2011). Contextualization and value-in-context: How context frames exchange. *Marketing Theory*, *11*(1), 35–49.

Ciasullo, M. V., Troisi, O., Grimaldi, M., & Leone, D. (2020). Multi-level governance for sustainable innovation in smart communities: An ecosystems approach. *International Entrepreneurship and Management Journal*, *16*(4), 1167–1195.

Das, A. (2020). Trust in "trust-free" digital networks: How inter-firm algorithmic relationships embed the cardinal principles of value co-creation. *AIS Transactions on Human–Computer Interaction*, *12*(4), 228–252.

Davenport, T., & Kalakota, R. (2019). The potential for AI in healthcare. *Future Healthcare Journal*, *6*(2), 94.

Dautov, R., Distefano, S., & Buyya, R. (2019). Hierarchical data fusion for smart healthcare. *Journal of Big Data*, *6*(1), 1–23.

de Fine Licht, K., & de Fine Licht, J. (2020). AI, transparency, and public decision-making. *AI & Society*, *35*(4), 917–926.

Earley, S. (2016). There is no AI without IA. *IT Professional*, *18*(3), 58–64.

Felzmann, H., Fosch-Villaronga, E., Lutz, C., & Tamò-Larrieux, A. (2020). Towards transparency by design for AI. *Science and Engineering Ethics*, *26*(6), 3333–3361.

Frow, P., McColl-Kennedy, J. R., Hilton, T., Davidson, A., Payne, A., & Brozovic, D. (2014). Value propositions: A service ecosystems perspective. *Marketing Theory*, *14*(3), 327–351.

Frow, P., McColl-Kennedy, J. R., & Payne, A. (2016). Co-creation practices: Their role in shaping a health care ecosystem. *Industrial Marketing Management*, *56*, 24–39.

Frow, P., McColl-Kennedy, J. R., Payne, A., & Govind, R. (2019). Service ecosystem well-being: Conceptualization and implications for theory and practice. *European Journal of Marketing*, *53*(12), 2657–2691.

Jiang, F., Jiang, Y., Zhi, H., Dong, Y., Li, H., Ma, S., … & Wang, Y. (2017). AI in healthcare: Past, present and future. *Stroke and Vascular Neurology*, *2*(4), 230–243.

Kaartemo, V., & Helkkula, A. (2018). A systematic review of AI and robots in value co-creation: Current status and future research avenues. *Journal of Creating Value*, *4*(2), 211–228.

Koskela-Huotari, K., Edvardsson, B., Jonas, J. M., Sörhammar, D., & Witell, L. (2016). Innovation in service ecosystems—Breaking, making, and maintaining institutionalized rules of resource integration. *Journal of Business Research*, *69*(8), 2964–2971.

Koskela-Huotari, K., & Vargo, S. L. (2016). Institutions as resource context. *Journal of Service Theory and Practice*, *26*(2), 163–178.

Langeard, E., Bateson, J., Lovelock, C. H., & Eiglier, P. (1981). *Marketing of services: New insights from consumers and managers* (pp. 81–104). Marketing Science Institute.

Li, R. C., Asch, S. M., & Shah, N. H. (2020). Developing a delivery science for AI in healthcare. *NPJ Digital Medicine*, *3*(1), 1–3.

Lytras, M. D., & Visvizi, A. (2021). *AI and cognitive computing: Methods, technologies, systems, applications and policy making*. MDPI.

Lytras, M., Visvizi, A., Zhang, X., & Aljohani, N. R. (2020). Cognitive computing, big data analytics and data driven industrial marketing. *Industrial Marketing Management*, *90*, 663–666.

Mabillard, V., Demartines, N., & Joliat, G. R. (2021). How can reasoned transparency enhance co-creation in health care and remedy the pitfalls of digitization in doctor–patient relationships?. *International Journal of Health Policy and Management*, 1–5.

McColl-Kennedy, J. R., Vargo, S. L., Dagger, T. S., Sweeney, J. C., & Kasteren, Y. V. (2012). Health care customer value cocreation practice styles. *Journal of Service Research*, *15*(4), 370–389.

Mele, C., Spena, T. R., Kaartemo, V., & Marzullo, M. L. (2021). Smart nudging: How cognitive technologies enable choice architectures for value co-creation. *Journal of Business Research*, *129*, 949–960.

Polese, F., & Carrubbo, L. (2017). Eco-sistemi di servizio in sanità (Vol. 65). G Giappichelli Editore.

Polese, F., Carrubbo, L., Caputo, F., & Sarno, D. (2018). Managing healthcare service ecosystems: Abstracting a sustainability-based view from hospitalization at home (HaH) practices. *Sustainability*, *10*(11), 3951.

Polese, F., Mele, C., & Gummesson, E. (2017). Value co-creation as a complex adaptive process. *Journal of Service Theory and Practice*, *27*(5), 926–929.

Polese, F., Payne, A., Frow, P., Sarno, D., & Nenonen, S. (2021). Emergence and phase transitions in service ecosystems. *Journal of Business Research*, *127*, 25–34.

Polese, F., Pels, J., Tronvoll, B., Bruni, R., & Carrubbo, L. (2017). A4A relationships. *Journal of Service Theory and Practice*, *27*(5), 1040–1056.

Polese, F., Troisi, O., Grimaldi, M., & Romeo, E. (2019). A big data-oriented approach to decision-making: A systematic literature review. In *22nd international conference proceedings* (pp. 472–496), Toulon-Verona Conference.

Provost, F., & Fawcett, T. (2013). Data science and its relationship to big data and data-driven decision making. *Big Data*, *1*(1), 51–59.

Reddy, S., Allan, S., Coghlan, S., & Cooper, P. (2020). A governance model for the application of AI in health care. *Journal of the American Medical Informatics Association*, *27*(3), 491–497.

Reddy, S., Fox, J., & Purohit, M. P. (2019). AI-enabled healthcare delivery. *Journal of the Royal Society of Medicine*, *112*(1), 22–28.

Sakr, S., & Elgammal, A. (2016). Towards a comprehensive data analytics framework for smart healthcare services. *Big Data Research*, *4*, 44–58.

Sarirete, A., Balfagih, Z., Brahimi, T., Lytras, M. D., & Visvizi, A. (2021). Artificial intelligence and machine learning research: Towards digital transformation at a global scale. *Journal of Ambient Intelligence and Humanized Computing*, *13*, 3319–3321.

Shinners, L., Aggar, C., Grace, S., & Smith, S. (2020). Exploring healthcare professionals' understanding and experiences of AI technology use in the delivery of healthcare: An integrative review. *Health Informatics Journal*, *26*(2), 1225–1236.

Subramanian, M., Wojtusciszyn, A., Favre, L., Boughorbel, S., Shan, J., Letaief, K. B., Pitteloud, N., & Chouchane, L. (2020). Precision medicine in the era of AI: Implications in chronic disease management. *Journal of Translational Medicine*, *18*(1), 1–12.

Tao, C., Gao, J., & Wang, T. (2019). Testing and quality validation for AI software – perspectives, issues, and practices. *IEEE Access*, *7*, 120164–120175.

Tellis, G. J., & Wernerfelt, B. (1987). Competitive price and quality under asymmetric information. *Marketing Science*, *6*(3), 240–253.

Troisi, O., Maione, G., Grimaldi, M., & Loia, F. (2020). Growth hacking: Insights on data-driven decision-making from three firms. *Industrial Marketing Management*, *90*, 538–557.

Troisi, O., Visvizi, A., & Grimaldi, M. (2021). The different shades of innovation emergence in smart service systems: The case of Italian cluster for aerospace technology. *Journal of Business & Industrial Marketing*, 1–25.

Vargo, S. L., & Akaka, M. A. (2012). Value cocreation and service systems (re) formation: A service ecosystems view. *Service Science*, *4*(3), 207–217.

Vargo, S. L., Wieland, H., & Akaka, M. A. (2015). Innovation through institutionalization: A service ecosystems perspective. *Industrial Marketing Management*, *44*, 63–72.

Vargo, S. L., & Lusch, R. F. (2016). Institutions and axioms: an extension and update of service-dominant logic. *Journal of the Academy of marketing Science*, *44*(1), 5–23.

Visvizi, A. (2021). Artificial intelligence (AI): Explaining, querying, demystifying. In A. Visvizi & M. Bodziany (Eds.), *Artificial intelligence and its contexts. Advanced sciences and technologies for security applications* (pp. 13–26). Springer. https://doi.org/10.1007/978-3-030-88972-2_2

Walmsley, J. (2021). AI and the value of transparency. *AI & SOCIETY*, *36*(2), 585–595.

Wieland, H., Polese, F., Vargo, S. L., & Lusch, R. F. (2012). Toward a service (eco) systems perspective on value creation. *International Journal of Service Science, Management, Engineering, and Technology (IJSSMET)*, *3*(3), 12–25.

World Health Organization. (2021). *Ethics and governance of AI for health: WHO guidance*. Health Ethics and Governance Unit Research for Health Department Digital Health and Innovation Department Division of the Chief Scientist.

Yu, K. H., Beam, A. L., & Kohane, I. S. (2018). AI in healthcare. *Nature Biomedical Engineering*, *2*(10), 719–731.

Chapter 8

Big Data and Its Impact on Tourism and Entrepreneurship

Antonio Botti and Antonella Monda

Abstract

The progressive increase in the size of datasets has given life to the so-called big data that provides researchers with the opportunity to extract a greater amount of useful information in many sectors, especially in the tourism industry.

The chapter aims to demonstrate that sustainable tourism (ST) could be particularly favored by using big data and a data-driven approach. Furthermore, as ST appears in line with a new type of responsible entrepreneurship, called Humane Entrepreneurship (HumEnt), this chapter investigates the link between ST and HumEnt and the impact of big data and data-oriented approaches on ST and HumEnt.

The research adopts a qualitative approach, applying the case study technique. The authors conducted ten semi-structured interviews with key informants from a specific form of hospitality: Albergo Diffuso. Findings show the advantages of the data-driven approach to tourism and entrepreneurship highlighting how using data creates new opportunities for decision making in ST and HumEnt.

Keywords: Humane entrepreneurship; sustainable tourism; data-driven approach; Albergo Diffuso; entrepreneurial orientation; sustainability orientation

Big Data and Decision-Making: Applications and Uses in the Public and Private Sector, 107–119

Published under exclusive licence by Emerald Publishing Limited
doi:10.1108/978-1-80382-551-920231008

1. Introduction

Over the last few years, the progressive increase in the size of datasets has given life to the so-called big data. Big data is a collection of large data, even unstructured and fast-moving, which cannot be managed with traditional approaches. The processing and storage of big data provide researchers with the opportunity to extract a greater amount of information than could be obtained by analyzing small sets of data. For this reason, big data and data-driven approaches represent the basis for improving knowledge and understanding the needs and desires of consumers and creating increasingly personalized products able to build customer loyalty. The revolution brought by big data in each sector is particularly significant in the tourism industry (Ciccarelli & Scarsella, 2017). Some companies, such as Swiss Air, Air France-KLM and Lufthansa, use big data to improve revenue management strategies and several hotel chains have also begun to implement interventions based on the use of big data. Some hotels use platforms that – through big data analysis algorithms that continuously analyze the climate, the building and the use of electricity – favor efficient energy management, reducing costs by at least 10–15%.

In this sense, the use of big data appears to be an opportunity also for ST. New technologies make it possible to implement new business models (Bouwman & Van Den Ham, 2004) that can be considered facilitators of ST (Ali & Frew, 2010).

ST is tourism capable of taking into account present and future economic, social and environmental impacts to satisfy the needs of visitors, businesses, the environment and host communities (United Nations Environment Program, World Tourism Organization (UNEP-UNWTO), 2005, p. 12). A particularly representative form of ST is the Albergo Diffuso (AD) (Droli, 2019). AD is a model of ST that aims at the exploitation of local resources both tangible and intangible (Vallone et al., 2013). It is a model that takes into account at the same time: the orientation toward sustainability, as defined starting from the Bruntland report (1987), and the attention for the stakeholders involved in the tourism supply chain (Waligo et al., 2013).

At the same time, AD can be considered an example of "Humane Entrepreneurship" (or HumEnt, Feola et al., 2021).

HumEnt (Kim et al., 2018; Parente et al., 2018, 2020) is an emerging theory which propose a new model of entrepreneurship, based on the integration of three elements: entrepreneurial orientation (EO), sustainability orientation (SO) and human resource orientation (HRO). From the perspective of HumEnt, the concept of sustainability is not understood only in environmental terms, but in broader terms as attention to the local community and society (Parente et al., 2018, 2020). Starting from these premises, this research has the objective of investigating the link between AD and HumEnt and the impact of the data-oriented approach on ST and HumEnt. Therefore, this chapter aims to answer the following research questions:

RQ1: AD, understood as a form of ST, can be considered an example of HumEnt?

RQ2: Can the data-driven approach favor the development of ST?

RQ3: Can the data-driven approach favor the development of HumEnt?

To address these questions, the argument in this chapter shall be structured as follows. First, the concepts of HumEnt, ST and the data-driven approach and their connections are analyzed from a theoretical point of view. Then, in the empirical part, the work analyzes the AD as an innovative business model in the field of hospitality, identifiable as a form of ST (Vallone et al., 2013) and in line with the principles of HumEnt. In particular, using a qualitative approach and applying the case study technique (Feagin et al., 1991; Yin, 2003), the role that technology play in defining a business model that combines a purely economic dimension with a more strictly ethics, able to look at the needs of stakeholders, is investigated.

2. Methodology

The research adopts a qualitative approach, based on the methodology of the case study (Yin, 2003). This methodology is suitable for examining the dynamics underlying a complex context (Eisenhardt, 1989; Feagin et al., 1991; Tellis, 1997) and for this reason it was considered the most appropriate for investigating the characteristics of AD, chosen as a case of study due to the growing tourist demand which has led to its progressive diffusion.

From a methodological point of view, the semi-structured interview technique was adopted, which is based on the administration of some predefined topics to key informants. In this research, the key informants are AD managers in the Italian territory. In line with the methodology chosen, we selected the respondents in a "strategic" way, according to their direct experience and knowledge of the phenomenon studied (Rubin & Rubin, 2011). Each respondent is considered a peculiar individual, influenced by the context in which he lives, for this reason, the previous experiences, knowledge and attitudes of the interviewees should be preserved by the researchers in the transcription of the interviews (Addeo & Montesperelli, 2007). The transcription and interpretation of data are mainly guided by the personal skills and knowledge of the researchers since the topics investigated with semi-structured interviews are mainly theoretical, intangible or concern sensitive issues.

In line with the main objectives of the research, the interview outline was divided into two main sections. The first part of the interview aims to perceive whether AD managers adopt a HumEnt. Specifically, it aims at analyzing AD, as a form of ST, to bring out the presence or absence of the three dimensions of HumEnt. Therefore, this part of the interview is divided into three macro-areas that correspond to the three orientations of HumEnt (EO, SO and HRO).

Questions relating to EO aim to investigate the entrepreneur's innovativeness, proactivity and risk orientation. In particular, questions try to obtain information on the role of innovation within the AD; the level of proactivity of the company in the relationship with competitors; the degree of risk orientation of the company in the decision-making process.

Questions relating to SO focus on the element of sustainability. In particular, we asked interviewees: (1) if they understand sustainability purely from an environmental point of view; and (2) what actions do they take to respond to the challenges of sustainability, or what are the practices implemented for environmental protection and the reduction of pollution.

Questions relating to HRO focus on the four elements of this orientation, namely empathy, equity, enablement and empowerment. About empathy, we try to obtain information about the company climate and the interactions that develop between employees and the company. The questions relating to equity want to bring out information about the company's policy regarding the recruitment of personnel and any distinctions by gender, age and experience. Questions regarding the enablement aim to investigate the possible presence of programs for the development of staff skills through training courses. Questions focused on empowerment examine the management style adopted in the company. The aim is to understand whether delegation or centralization of responsibilities is favored in the organization.

The second part of the interview focused on the opinions that managers have of the data-driven approach. We asked respondents to talk about the role that ICT in the creation and dissemination of AD and how the data-driven approach affects their EO, SO and HRO.

We submitted the interview outline to 10 managers of ADs that use data-driven tools, to understand their inclination to adopt data-driven approaches and models of sustainable entrepreneurship.

The interviews were conducted in September and October 2020, lasted on average 30 minutes, were recorded, transcribed and analyzed based on the main hypotheses deriving from the theoretical background and research questions.

3. The Conceptual Background

3.1. Humane Entrepreneurship

HumEnt (Kim et al., 2018; Parente et al., 2018) is a new entrepreneurship model based on the idea that entrepreneurs should extend their priorities beyond their profit, toward their employees, environment and society in which the company lives.

It is a strategic approach in which performance is faced as a complex problem, whose evaluation must take into account not only an EO, as defined in the classic definition of Covin and Slevin (1989) (i.e., as a sum of innovativeness, assumption of risks and proactivity), but also an orientation toward sustainability and human resources.

Humane Entrepreneurship Theory proposes an entrepreneurship model based on the integration of three elements Parente et al. (2018): EO, SO and HRO.

In the conceptualization of Parente et al. (2018), each dimension considers different sub-dimensions. The sub-dimensions of EO are (Covin & Slevin, 1989):

innovativeness, risk-taking and proactivity. The sub-dimensions of SO concern the definition of sustainability and the sustainability activities carried out by the company. In the HumEnt perspective, the concept of sustainability is not only understood in environmental terms but also in broader terms as attention to the local community (Parente et al., 2018, 2020). The local community is a central player in entrepreneurial processes: its involvement in the implementation of these processes plays a key role in the creation of a society commitment capable of activating a virtuous circle between the development of the company and the generation of returns for the company itself. Finally, the sub-dimensions of HRO are (Kim et al., 2018): empathy, equity, enablement and empowerment.

3.2. Sustainable Tourism

The UNEP and the WTO define the ST as a "tourism that takes full account of its current and future economic, social and environmental impacts, addressing the needs of visitors, the industry, the environment and host communities" (UNEP-UNWTO, 2005, p. 12). This definition highlights the three pillars of sustainability: economic, social and environmental (UNEP-UNWTO, 2005, p. 9). Economic sustainability concerns the generation of prosperity at different levels of society and essentially concerns the ability of a business to survive in the long term. Social sustainability is about respect for human rights and equal opportunities for everyone in society, it emphasizes local communities, maintaining and strengthening their reference systems, and recognizing and respecting cultural diversity. Environmental sustainability concerns the management and preservation of resources, in particular, non-renewable ones, including biological diversity and natural heritage.

There is no commonly accepted definition of ST in the literature (Dimoska & Petrevska, 2012). Various definitions express the concept of sustainability in very different terms. According to Diamantis and Ladkin (1999), ST is a form of tourism

> leading to management of all resources in such a way that we can fulfil economic, social and aesthetic needs while maintaining cultural integrity, essential ecological processes, biological diversity and life support systems. (Diamantis & Ladkin, 1999, p. 35)

In this perspective, the main objective of the ST is to improve the quality of life of residents and the experience of tourists, as well as safeguard the environmental resources on which tourism is based.

Other definitions emphasize the ecological, social and economic elements to achieve a "balanced or wise use of natural resources" (Rämet et al., 1985, p. 2). In this definition, ST is linked to the concept of resources and their "wise use".

Furthermore, the development of the ST requires meeting the needs of tourists, tourism businesses, the host community and the needs of environmental protection at the same time. As Bramwell and Lane (2000) argue, it requires effective planning and implementation of collaborations between all stakeholders in the tourism development process. Only by integrating and reconciling these different needs, it is possible to obtain benefits for all those involved in the sector: a better quality of life for the local communities, more satisfying experiences for tourists, greater profits for the tourism industry and benefits for the environment and its conservation.

Based on the conceptualization of the ST in literature, we decided to deepen a particular form of ST: the AD. It represents a network model, which brings together different service proposals and takes the form of a hospitality hotel proposal integrated into the territory and its community, which become basic components of the hospitality services offered (Dall'Ara, 2002, 2010). The AD is an example of the enhancement of territory in terms of sustainability. It aims at the exploitation of local resources both tangible (cultural heritage, agriculture and crafts, and small businesses) and intangible (traditions, knowledge and social ties) (Vallone et al., 2013).

Moreover, the small businesses that constitute AD support the territory both in terms of employment and prosperity of the local community. Therefore, all subjects operating in the local tourism system take advantage of AD (Paniccia, 2012).

The crucial role of innovation, the environment and stakeholders in the realization of ST (Waligo et al., 2013) and AD appear in line with the emerging HumEnt Theory (Kim et al., 2018; Parente et al., 2018) and led us to formulate our first research question (*RQ1*).

3.3. Data-driven Approach and HumEnt in Tourism

The advent of ICT and the spread of big data redefine business processes, strategies and decision-making. At the same time, the growing complexity of the markets leads companies to evaluate the need to adopt big data analysis and big data analytics as strategic levers, resources and key operational drivers for the effectiveness and efficiency of decisions (Polese et al., 2022; Visvizi et al., 2021).

In general, good data can lead to good decisions. However, in addition to the quality of the data, companies have to make the best possible use of the explorative tool analysis (Capellá et al., 2012). Therefore, to manage data in a way that improves decisions, companies need to take a strategic approach to data (Botti & Monda, 2021; Troisi et al., 2017). The data-driven approach is an integrated, proactive data-oriented approach to improve decisions and stimulate knowledge (Gupta & George, 2016; McAfee et al., 2012). It requires companies to adopt a culture based on data, which are seen as strategic resources for decisions.

This approach requires the active role of leadership in promoting an innovation-oriented culture and a strong focus on data management at every stage of the decision-making process (Brynjolfsson et al., 2011). Adopting an innovative and proactive mindset can favor the effectiveness of the decision-making process based on data analysis. Therefore, the data-driven approach is stimulated by the adoption of EO, as understood by Covin and Slevin (1989).

To effectively exploit and implement the data-driven approach, large data-driven organizations must, on the one hand, acquire new skills and talents and, on the other hand, enrich and develop the existing knowledge of employees (Adrian et al., 2018). In this sense, a data-driven approach pushes managers to pay attention to human resources and, specifically, to enablement. Consequently, we notice a strict connection between the data-driven approach and the HRO.

In addition to the link with EO and HRO, the data-driven approach also allows the achievement of sustainable objectives. Over time, the progressive proposition of new technologies seems to pursue broader and more complex marketing objectives. While in past times, the use of data tended to achieve mere economic objectives (e-commerce, marketing and profiling activities), more and more companies pursue relational objectives (data collection and user-generated content from social networks, forums and blogs) and social objectives (e-government and e-health or security) (Troisi et al., 2020, 2021). Large amounts of data are collected to achieve different sustainable goals, such as smart education, e-health and ending poverty (see Agenda 2030, UN; Botti & Monda, 2020). Adopting the data-driven approach also fosters sustainable objectives representing the solution to environmental issues generated by the impact of tourism (Polese et al., 2022).

In fact, data-driven segmentation studies are typically conducted in the field of tourism research (Barile et al., 2017; Polese et al., 2018; Troisi et al., 2019).

In this field, a data-driven approach promotes the collection and analysis of online data to offer a complete and detailed picture of any destination or business: from the preferences and behaviors of visitors to the comparison with competitors. Data access and analysis allow the identification of KPIs (Key Performance Indicators) and market trends that let companies and destinations to improve and attract new visitors, invest safely and reduce risks.

The main advantages of the data-driven approach in tourism are (Ali & Frew, 2010; Dolnicar, 2002): forecasting tourist demand and flows; measuring the performance of the hospitality and catering; identifying the specific target and the right channels for marketing strategies; identify the strengths that attract visitors; compare the destination with competitors.

Although there are studies that analyze the relationship between data generated by ICT and tourism (Ali & Frew, 2010; Dolnicar, 2002), nevertheless the line of studies relating to the role of digital technologies in support of ST development is only limitedly analyzed (Ali & Frew, 2010). Consequently, in line with what emerged from the review of the literature and to fill a knowledge gap caused by the scarce literature in force on managing big data through data-driven decision-making and ST, this work aims to deepen the relationship between these two concepts, answering our second research question (*RQ2*).

Furthermore, given the links between the data-driven approach and the EO, SO and HRO, the chapter aims to answer our third research question (*RQ3*).

4. Results

The analysis of the results shows that AD has several elements in common with HumEnt. The results show that, in most cases, the managers of ADs strategically use data and adopt a HumEnt model. They are attentive to the issues of socio-environmental sustainability, respect for employees and the safeguarding of the territory in which the company operates.

Below are the results for the first and second parts of the interview.

The Role of ICT and Data-Driven Approach:

We asked the interviewees to talk about the role of ICT in the creation and dissemination of AD. The interviewees affirm that technology has had and still has a fundamental role in the spread of AD. Since AD is a hospitality model born and developed away from traffic, the use of intelligent transport systems is essential to reach the chosen destination. The AD10 states:

> If there was no advanced technology, it would be impossible to think of sustainable development of the business. It is, in fact, impossible to reach these places without GPS because in most cases they are remote villages.

ICTs also can foster community participation. During their stay, guests become part of the community and, subsequently, the interaction between the local community and guests is fueled by the exchange of intangible resources or those linked to the intangible cultural heritage of the place, such as typical recipes or updates on the offer of typical seasonal products. Social networks allow you to create a digital environment similar to "a virtual square".

Subsequently, the interviewees were asked what role had the data obtained through ICT; if such data would improve the business; how data are managed. The main utility of the data obtained through ICT is manifested mainly in the ability to obtain valuable information, regarding global hospitality trends. AD4 states:

> Destination intelligence tools that provide information on tourist intentions, visitor opinions and the online performance of destinations, are useful for photographing reality. They help both destinations and individual operators to better organize the work at a strategic level.

AD7 says:

> To manage the huge amount of data we use a tool that supports our administration. It is an app that allows us to know the online reputation trends in real-time and virtually instantaneously. It offers a 360-degree view of our property and the market, making it the perfect tool for multiple objectives. From review management to market positioning, we're able to critically understand our

> business from every angle. [...] the use of the app allowed us to increase the number of reviews, 80% of which are positive!

Entrepreneurial Orientation:

All managers interviewed stated that innovation plays a fundamental role in managing AD. In particular, the innovation concerns the offer of services generally not present in other ADs. The use of intelligence tools helps hoteliers to integrate innovative services into the offer, based on market trends and consumer tastes. The AD2, for example, in addition to the services available in a classic AD, offers yoga courses and Italian courses for foreigners. AD4 activated a social inclusion project aimed at children with disabilities. The project makes AD4 a multifunctional social center, which offers courses to children with problems, and at the same time an AD who offers disabled children the opportunity to work on their own indoor. AD8 is developing routes for e-bike to renew its offer.

With regard to the relationship with competitors, five out of 10 ADs do not feel the direct pressure of competing companies, as they see all the hotels "disconnected", even geographically. The manager of AD9 states "we perceive a comparison rather than actual competition". In the other five cases, however, the answers show that a proactive attitude is preferred. Managers of ADs try to anticipate the possible actions of competitors. An example is provided by the manager of AD10, who was the first entrepreneur to create AD in Cilento. He states:

> Thanks to the collection and use of a large amount of data, we are able to understand the behavior of competitors. This allows us to stay up to date and anticipate our competitors and not make the mistakes they have made.

Regarding the degree of risk orientation of the individual company in the decision-making process, the interviewees are asked to provide examples of investments made that highlight the policy adopted by the company regarding this element and how an approach to data can be useful. The answers show that six out of 10 scattered hotels are risk-oriented. The use of a strategic approach to data helps to orient investments toward market trends. However, in several cases, the problems linked to the Covid-19 pandemic have meant that the investments of individual companies have not produced the desired effects. In particular, AD3 claims to have concluded a large investment for the renovation of buildings just before the Covid-19, and that the months of non-activity caused economic losses because of cancelation of bookings.

Sustainability Orientation:

About sustainability and the sustainability practices adopted by each AD, we distinguish three types of sustainability: structural, environmental and social. ADs are born in old pre-existing structures which are given new life (structural sustainability). All the ADs interviewed practice separate waste collection, plus the AD3 and AD10 are plastic-free; only glass bottles and containers are used in the rooms (environmental sustainability). AD10 also invested in a rainwater collection system for irrigation. AD1, AD2 and AD6 are equipped with solar panels for the use of solar energy. AD8 has installed doors with a card that allows the automatic shutdown of heaters and lights when the customer leaves the room.

Two of the 10 managers interviewed believe they have a social impact (social sustainability). AD4 offers courses aimed at the social inclusion of children with disabilities and AD10 mainly buys zero-kilometer products to support small local companies.

The data-driven approach is useful for hoteliers to consider solutions that meet the needs related to projects that improve the analysis of territorial information and promote sustainable mobility.

Humane Resource Orientation:

Regarding the corporate climate, nine out of 10 ADs establish a family relationship between employees and the company. Only in the case of AD5, the manager prefers a professional climate in his company.

About the "equity" sub-dimension, all respondents state that there is no discrimination based on sex, age and experience among employees and that there is an equal distribution between men and women.

About the under-dimension of "enablement", we asked respondents about the presence of programs aimed at developing staff skills. Five out of 10 respondents say there are both internal and external training programs. Furthermore, the adoption of a data-driven approach seems to stimulate enablement. Hotel managers are encouraged to enrich and develop employees' existing knowledge of marketing and management of big data through data-driven decision-making. In the months immediately preceding the interview, AD7 and AD8 offered e-Marketing and Big Data management courses to employees; AD10 organized an external English language course for the receptionist and specific courses for the staff in charge of cleaning the rooms; AD2 organized a course for security related to Covid-19. AD7 states:

> The app we use was immediately integrated into the daily activities. Not only did all the staff find the tool intuitive and easy to use, but it immediately had a positive effect on the facilities, especially on saving time and reducing noise, allowing us to focus only on important information.

About "empowerment", eight ADs favor delegation, leaving employees ample autonomy in carrying out the work assigned to them. However, two managers, those of AD5 and AD9, prefer a management style more oriented toward the centralization of responsibilities.

In line with the three research questions, the analysis of the results obtained from the case study reveals: (1) the presence of a link between AD, an innovative model of ST and the theory of HumEnt; (2) the ability of the data-driven approach to favor both the development of ST and (3) HumEnt (see Fig. 8.1). In particular, the results obtained allow us to highlight how the data-driven approach affects ST and HumEnt.

		Advantages of Data-driven Approach
ST		Manage the complexity of customer feedback, design marketing strategies, thoughtful communication
HumEnt	EO	Profits, productivity and comparison with competitors
	SO	Energy saving, promoting sustainable mobility, community development and transparency
	HRO	Employee enablement

Fig. 8.1. The Advantages of Data-driven Approach on ST and HumEnt. *Source*: Authors' elaboration.

As for the ST, the results show that the data obtained through ICT and the tools that allow their collection and analysis are crucial elements to optimize the management of the AD. They also facilitate the creation and maintenance of relationships between service providers and guests. Knowing potential tourists' intentions, opinions and tastes helps hoteliers to adapt the offer to the demand and to direct the offer toward the specific target. Furthermore, knowing the visitors' opinions helps to monitor and improve the hotel online reputation.

As for HumEnt, the results show how the use of a strategic approach to data can be useful to stimulate HumEnt. A data-driven approach is an element of innovation, useful for understanding the behavior of competitors and being able to anticipate them (EO). The use of semantic analysis, artificial intelligence and data science tools helps ADs to explore solutions that promote structural, environmental and social sustainability (SO) and stimulate employee enablement (HRO).

5. Conclusions

Starting from a critical discussion of the main characteristics of ST and the link between ST and the data-driven approach, the work analyzes the role of data generated by ICT in the development of a particular form of ST: AD. Using a qualitative approach, the case of AD, an innovative business model of hospitality, is examined. To detect a possible link between the ST and HumEnt, the research also focuses on the presence of the components of the HumEnt model (EO, SO and HRO) and their strategic use in the AD business strategies. The results allow us to recognize in AD many elements of the HumEnt theory, as well as the benefits of a data-driven approach to ST and HumEnt.

According to this study, AD could be understood as a ST model that has the potential to encourage and express HumEnt.

The link between this type of accommodation (AD) and HumEnt could originate from the nature of the AD which generally stands in small historic centers and ancient villages, allowing guests to stay in contact with nature and discover the history and traditions of the territory, enriching itself culturally. These small businesses benefit the territory both in terms of employment and in terms of the prosperity of the local community. Therefore, all the subjects operating in the local tourism system take advantage of AD (Paniccia, 2012).

We can assume that adopting a strategic orientation toward HumEnt fosters new value for companies and improvements for the community, creating new social value for companies and territories.

Furthermore, the results reveal that the use of a strategic approach to data favors the development of a business model capable of combining a purely economic dimension with a more strictly ethical one. In particular, the use of data allows hoteliers to (1) improve their online reputation; (2) better manage feedback and monitor the progress of online reviews; (3) reduce noise by focusing only on important information; (4) evaluate competitors; (5) evaluate commercial policies.

The results provide managers and scholars insights and discussions on the challenges and opportunities associated with the new data-driven models in the ST and the impacts that data have on the adoption of HumEnt.

The identification of the main advantages brought by technology in the field of ST can theoretically contribute to the development of the literature on data-driven decision-making and allows the identification of possible practices that can direct future entrepreneurs to adopt a coherent approach with the AD model and with the HumEnt framework (Kim et al., 2018; Parente et al., 2018).

Showing different ways in which the data obtained by ICT are used in AD, the work tries to fill a gap in the literature regarding the description of the function of these elements in ST – a topic little dealt within the literature (Ali & Frew, 2010).

From a management point of view, the analysis of the functions of data-driven tools can help managers understand how to use technology more efficiently, engage guests to be part of the community and manage information flows.

However, the work shows some limitations relating to the adoption of the case study methodology, which does not allow any generalization to be drawn from the results obtained and implies some problems in extending the results to the population.

References

Adrian, C., Abdullah, R., Atan, R., & Jusoh, Y. Y. (2018). Conceptual model development of big data analytics implementation assessment effect on decision-making. *International Journal of Interactive Multimedia and Artificial Intelligence*, *5*(1), 101–106.

Addeo, F., & Montesperelli, P. (2007). *Esperienze di analisi di interviste non direttive*. Rome: Aracne.

Ali, A., & Frew, A. J. (2010). ICT and its role in sustainable tourism development. In *Information and communication technologies in tourism 2010* (pp. 479–491). Vienna: Springer.

Barile, S., Ciasullo, M. V., Troisi, O., & Sarno, D. (2017). The role of technology and institutions in tourism service ecosystems: Findings from a case study. *The TQM Journal*, *29*(6), 811–833. https://doi.org/10.1108/TQM-06-2017-0068.

Botti, A., & Monda, A. (2020). Sustainable value co-creation and digital health: The case of trentino eHealth ecosystem. *Sustainability*, *12*(13), 5263.

Botti, A., & Monda, A. (2021). ICT platforms and the restaurant business in times of Covid-19: The case of Italy. In A. Visvizi, O. Troisi, & K. Saeedi (Eds.), *Research and Innovation Forum 2021 Managing continuity, innovation, and change in the post-Covid world: Technology, politics and society*. Springer International Publishing. ISBN 978-3-030-84311-3. https://doi.org/10.1007/978-3-030-84311-3

Bouwman, H., & Van Den Ham, E. (2004). Business models and e-metrics, a state of the art. In B. Priessl, H. Bouwman, & C. Steinfield (Eds.), *Life after the Dot Com bust* (pp. 83–100). Springer Verlag.

Bramwell, B., & Lane, B. (2000). *Tourism collaboration and partnerships. Politics, Practice and Sustainability*. Clevedon, OH: Channel View.

Brynjolfsson, E., Hitt, L. M., & Kim, H. H. (2011). Strength in numbers: How does data-driven decisionmaking affect firm performance? https://ssrn.com/abstract=1819486https://doi.org/10.2139/ssrn.1819486

Capellá, J., Horne, A., & Shah, S. (2012). *Good data won't guarantee good decisions'*. Harvard Business Review.

Ciccarelli, A., & Scarsella, E. (2017). Le potenzialità dei Big Data nel Turismo. In G. De Paulis (Ed.), *In viaggio con un click. Nuovi strumenti di marketing digitale per il settore turistico* (pp. 103–116). Duende.

Covin, J. G., & Slevin, D. P. (1989). Strategic management of small firms in hostile and benign environments. *Strategic Management Journal*, *10*(1), 75–87.

Dall'Ara, G. (2002). Albergo diffuso: un'idea che piace, *La Rivista del Turismo*, N. 1.

Dall'Ara, G. (2010). *Manuale dell'Albergo Diffuso. L'idea, la gestione, il marketing dell'ospitalità diffusa*. Milano: Franco Angeli.

Diamantis, D., & Ladkin, A. (1999). The links between sustainable tourism and ecotourism: A definitional and operational perspective. *Journal of Tourism Studies*, *10*(2), 35–46.

Dimoska, T., & Petrevska, B. (2012). Indicators for sustainable tourism development in Macedonia. *Conference proceedings, first international conference on business, economics and finance "from liberalization to globalization: Challenges in the changing World," September 13–15*, Macedonia (pp. 389–400).

Dolnicar, S. (2002). A review of data-driven market segmentation in tourism. *Journal of Travel & Tourism Marketing*, *12*(1), 1–22.

Droli, M. (2019). The Albergo Diffuso Model. In *The Albergo Diffuso Model*. De Gruyter Oldenbourg.

Eisenhardt, K. M. (1989). Making fast strategic decisions in high-velocity environments. *Academy of Management Journal*, *32*(3), 543–576.

Feagin, J., Orum, A., & Sjoberg, G. (1991). *A case for case study*. University of North Carolina Press.

Feola, R., Monda, A., Crudele, C., Celenta, R., Botti, A., & Parente, R. (2021). Turismo Sostenibile e Humane Entrepreneurship: Il Caso dell'Albergo Diffuso. In *Electronic conference proceedings of Sinergie – Sima Management Conference "Leveraging intersections in management theory and practice*", June 10–11, Palermo (pp. 569–575). ISBN 97888943937-9-8.

Gupta, M., & George, J. F. (2016). Toward the development of a big data analytics capability. *Information & Management*, *53*(8), 1049–1064.

Kim, K. C., Eltarabishy, A., & Bae, Z. T. (2018). Humane entrepreneurship: How focusing on people can drive a new era of wealth and quality job creation in a sustainable world. *Journal of Small Business Management*, *56*(S1), 10–29.

McAfee, A., Brynjolfsson, E., Davenport, T. H., Patil, D. J., & Barton, D. (2012). Big data: the management revolution. *Harvard Business Review*, *90*(10), 60–68.

Paniccia, P. (2012). Nuovi fermenti di sviluppo sostenibile nel turismo: l'esempio dell' "albergo diffuso". Tra borghi storici, residenze d'epoca e antichi casali rurali. *Impresa Progetto-Electronic Journal of Management*, *1*, 1–26.

Parente, R., El Tarabishy, A., Botti, A., Vesci, M., & Feola, R. (2020). Humane entrepreneurship: Some steps in the development of a measurement scale. *Journal of Small Business Management*, 1–25.

Parente, R., El Tarabishy, A., Vesci, M., & Botti, A. (2018). The epistemology of humane entrepreneurship: Theory and proposal for future research agenda. *Journal of Small Business Management*, *56*(S1), 30–52.

Polese, F., Botti, A., Grimaldi, M., Monda, A., & Vesci, M. (2018). Social innovation in smart tourism ecosystems: How technology and institutions shape sustainable value co-creation. *Sustainability*, *10*(1), 140.

Polese, F., Botti, A., & Monda, A. (2022). Value co-creation and data-driven orientation: Reflections on restaurant management practices during COVID-19 in Italy. *Transforming Government: People, Process and Policy*, *16*(2), 172–184. https://doi.org/10.1108/TG-07-2021-0119

Rämet, J., Tolvanen, A., Kinnunen, I., & Laapio, A. (2005). Sustainable Tourism. In A. Jalkanen, P. Nygren (Eds.), *Sustainable use of renewable natural resources: from principles to practices*, (3.3, pp. 1–10). Helsínquia: University of Helsinki, Department of Forest Ecology.

Rubin, H. J., & Rubin, I. S. (2011). *Qualitative interviewing: The art of hearing data*. Beverly Hills, CA: Sage.

Tellis, W. (1997). Application of a case study methodology. *The Qualitative Report*, *3*(3), 1–19.

Troisi, O., Grimaldi, M., & Monda, A. (2019). Managing smart service ecosystems through technology: How ICTs enable value cocreation. *Tourism Analysis*, *24*(3), 377–393.

Troisi, O., Maione, G., Grimaldi, M., & Loia, F. (2020). Growth hacking: Insights on data-driven decision-making from three firms. *Industrial Marketing Management*, *90*, 538–557.

Troisi, O., Sirianni, C. A., Monda, A., & Grimaldi, M. (2017). ICTs and engagement platforms in resource integration: Threat or opportunity for value co-creation? *Esperienze d'impresa*, *25*(1), 99–123. ISSN: 1971-5293.

Troisi, O., Visvizi, A., & Grimaldi, M. (2021). The different shades of innovation emergence in smart service systems: The case of Italian cluster for aerospace technology. *Journal of Business & Industrial Marketing* (ahead-of-print).

United Nations Environment Program, World Tourism Organization (UNEP-UNWTO). (2005). *Making tourism more sustainable – A guide for policy makers*. Madrid: UNWTO.

Vallone, C., Orlandini, P., & Cecchetti, R. (2013). Sustainability and innovation in tourism services: The Albergo Diffuso case study. *Eurasian Journal of Social Sciences*, *1*(2), 21–34.

Visvizi, A., Troisi, O., Grimaldi, M., & Loia, F. (2021). Think human, act digital: Activating data-driven orientation in innovative start-ups. *European Journal of Innovation Management*, *25*(6), 452–478. https://doi.org/10.1108/EJIM-04-2021-0206

Waligo, V. M., Clarke, J., & Hawkins, R. (2013). Implementing sustainable tourism: A multi-stakeholder involvement management framework. *Tourism Management*, *36*, 342–353.

Yin, R. K. (2003). *Case study research: Design and methods* (3rd ed.). Thousand Oaks, CA: Sage Publications.

Chapter 9

Big Data and Digital Technologies for Circular Economy in the Agri-food Sector

Benedetta Esposito, Ornella Malandrino, Maria Rosaria Sessa and Daniela Sica

Abstract

The improvement of the agri-food supply chain sustainability plays pivotal role in the planet's survival and in overcoming of climate disasters. Digital technologies that support the collection of Big Data produced along the agri-food supply chain (SC) emerge as powerful tools to accelerate the ecological transition of the sector. Digital technologies can support the implementation of circular business models by sharing data across the SC, monitoring in real time the materials flow, automatizing some agricultural practices and improving the decision-making through the development of decision support systems. Despite the relevance of these arguments, there is a lack of shared frameworks and guidelines for the effective development of a "data-driven circular economy" in the agri-food SC. In this scenario, this chapter examines how scholars investigate data-oriented strategies to accelerate the ecological transition and the adoption of circular economy (CE) models in the agri-food sector (AFS). To this end, a systematic literature review (SLR) was performed. Twenty-nine papers were selected following a rigorous sampling process. Both bibliometric and descriptive results are provided in the first part of this chapter. According to the analytical framework developed, the selected papers were examined in light of the "reduce, reuse and recycle" (3R) paradigm. Moreover, an additional R was retrieved from the systematic review (i.e., redesign), broadening the analytical perspective. The results indicate that scholars have predominantly provided theoretical contributions concerning the role of digital technologies and big data for the agri-food circular transition from a macro-perspective. The findings are useful for policy-makers and managers, who can promote and implement the big data-oriented approach to facilitate the circular transition. Limitations and future research directions are also provided.

Big Data and Decision-Making: Applications and Uses in the Public and Private Sector, 121–141

Published under exclusive licence by Emerald Publishing Limited
doi:10.1108/978-1-80382-551-920231009

Keywords: Circular economy; sustainability; agri-food; big data; digital technologies; information and communication technology

1. Introduction

During the last decade, the AFS has experienced numerous challenges, such as the overproduction of food waste, excessive food losses at all stages of the SC and a resource shortage (Sica et al., 2019). Scholars have demonstrated that improper agri-food SC management is one of the main causes of these problems (Food and Agriculture Organization of the United Nations, 2019, 2019). Accordingly, there is a need to redesign the traditional linear economic model based on the "take–make–dispose" paradigm to address these critical issues. From this perspective, it has been argued that the CE model is crucial for fighting against climate change and supporting the sector's long-term survival. Based on the main principles of "reuse," "recycle" and "reduce," the CE model should support the AFS in optimizing resource management. Furthermore, a circular approach toward the agri-food processes should maximize the energetic performance and reduce greenhouse gas emissions and the food loss and waste generated along with the whole SC (Merli et al., 2017).

However, the implementation of CE strategies presents several barriers that make the transition toward the closed-loop economy model very slow and critical (Su et al., 2013). The correct adoption of the CE model requires strong collaboration among all the actors of the agri-food SC from a co-creation value perspective (Cosimato & Troisi, 2015; Troisi et al., 2021; del Hoyo et al., 2021). The lack of information about the stakeholders involved in the processes represents one of the main barriers to achieving this purpose (Chui et al., 2018). Effective and rapid communication among the actors – such as customers, producers and investors – of the SC and the simultaneous analytics of all issues related to agri-food operations should support the sector in activating control mechanisms at every stage of the SC (Barile et al., 2017; Troisi et al., 2018). Indeed, insightful information can inform the establishment of sustainable business systems that consider environmental and social issues in the decision-making processes and, in turn, also achieve significant economic benefits (Lytras & Visvizi, 2019, 2020; Troisi et al., 2020). In addition, a large amount of data, generally known as big data, is generated from agri-food SC operations, which must be systematically collected and analyzed to provide strategic information for managers and policymakers (Troisi et al., 2022; Visvizi et al., 2018). The awareness of the potential of digital technologies in improving sustainability has led to the growing utilization of these technologies in productive processes (Malik et al., 2021; Troisi et al., 2020; Segura et al., 2021). Rethinking strategies is increasingly easy thanks to consequential data collection and analysis. Data provide useful insights for drawing new processes, considering how foods, arrived at the end of their life cycle, can be transformed into secondary raw materials and be inserted into new production processes in a circular perspective. However, unlike other production sectors, the AFS is characterized by some peculiarities that make the various agri-food chains completely different. This – in turn – requires the need to develop ad hoc circular production models for the needs of individual SCs. Therefore, the possibility of having data in real time and having a trace of the single operations, of the quantities of material flow thanks to the use of advanced sensors systems, can help the management in rethinking business processes. Starting from this background, the role of big data analytics becomes pivotal for the transition from a linear economy to a circular one (Esposito et al., 2021).

Considering its relevance, scholars have started to investigate this topic (e.g., Belaud et al., 2019; Kamble et al., 2020; Vernier et al., 2021). However, there is a lack of systematization in the scientific literature. Accordingly, the following research question has been developed: How do scholars investigate big data and digital technologies for CE transition in the AFS?

Aiming to address this research question, a SLR has been performed to investigate the state of the art related to adopting big data and digital technologies in the AFS as enablers for the transition toward a circular agri-food SC. This chapter is divided into five sections. Section 1 discusses the introduction. Section 2 describes the research methodology adopted. Section 3 provides a descriptive overview of the articles analyzed. Section 4 presents and discuss the results of the SLR. Section 5 includes the conclusions, limitations and future research directions.

2. Methodology

2.1. Data Collection and Sampling Process

Following previous studies on the SLR methodology (Moher et al., 2009; Polese et al., 2019), this chapter has been developed according to the PRISMA (Preferred Reporting Items for Systematic Reviews and Meta-Analysis) method. This systematic approach allows researchers to avoid the shortcomings of a narrative literature review and provide a structured contribution (Esposito et al., 2021). Accordingly, the sampling process – based on four steps – was characterized by clarity, transparency and replicability in reporting (Esposito et al., 2020; Tranfield & Denyer, 2003). Fig. 9.1 details the sampling process adopted.

In the first step, the search process, performed on the Scopus database, was developed using the following search string: ("BIG DATA" OR "DIGITAL TECHNOLOGIES") AND ("AGRIFOOD" OR "FOOD" OR "AGRIFOOD") AND ("CIRCULAR ECONOMY" OR "ECOLOGICAL TRANSITION"). This database was chosen for its broader range of scientific journals to reduce the criticalities and potential omissions related to a smaller set of journals (Pizzi et al., 2020). Moreover, an additional cross-validation analysis was performed using the Google Scholar and Emerald databases. The keywords were selected according to the research questions developed at the beginning of the analysis to address the purpose of the study. No temporal filters were adopted to identify the year in which scholars began to explore this topic. Books, chapters, conference papers and theses were excluded from the analysis to ensure high-quality research. At the end of this step, 150 papers were retrieved from the databases. In the second step, defined as the "screening step," 54 duplicates were

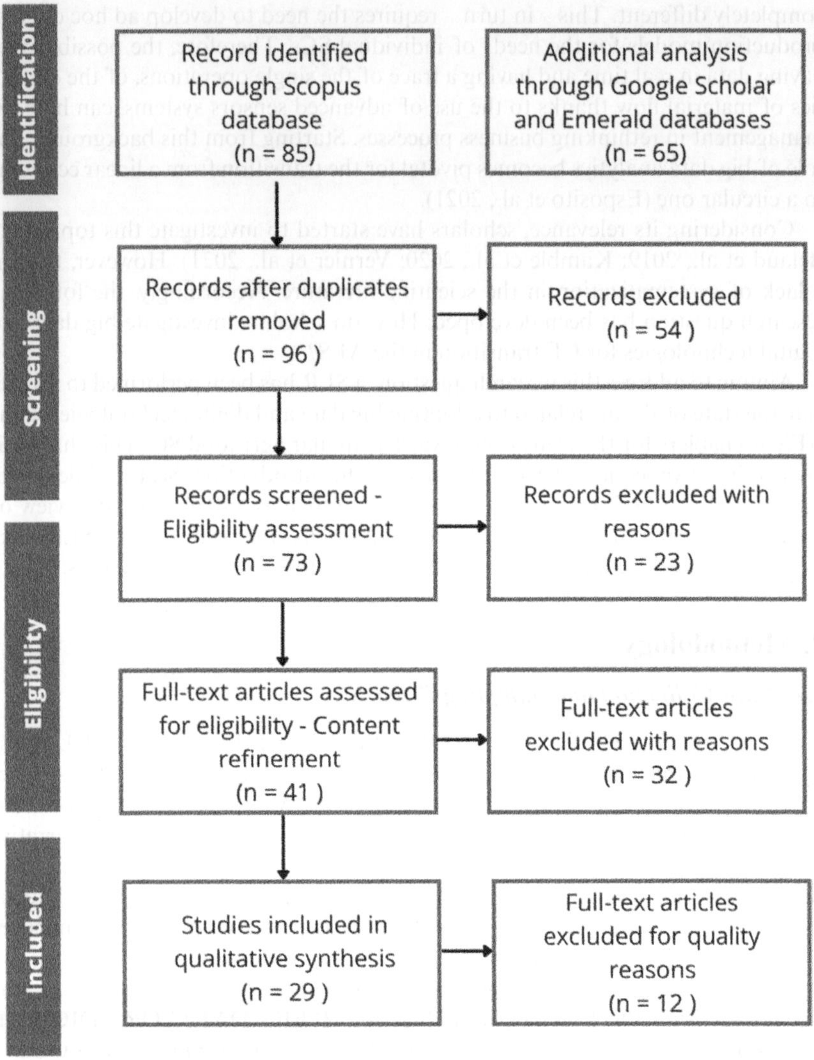

Fig. 9.1. Sampling Process Following the PRISMA Methodology. *Source*: Authors.

removed from the analysis. Subsequently, the title and abstract of each contribution were inspected to eliminate papers that were unsuitable for this study. The "eligibility" step involved two sub-stages. First, inclusion criteria were formulated in order to select relevant contributions with methodological rigor (Petticrew & Roberts, 2008). Studies were selected based on the following criteria: (a) empirical studies focused on enabler technologies for Industry 4.0 in the AFS for sustainable production processes; (b) review papers and comment letters on big data or enabler technologies in the agri-food SC; and (c) multidisciplinary articles available in full text. Moreover, articles focused on chemicals and agronomy issues were excluded.

Following these guidelines, a full text screening was performed to select only papers matching the criteria defined as *ex ante* and suitable to address the research question. Finally, the total number of selected papers was 29 articles. Following these guidelines, the second stage of the eligibility assessment was performed based on the full-text screening. This stage aims to address the research question and extrapolate the final sample article.

The articles retrieved from the database were analyzed separately by two independent coders to ensure the study's reliability. Specifically, the coders independently analyzed the titles, abstracts and keywords (Krippendorff, 201). This enabled the researchers to avoid subjectivity biases and perform a reliable analysis (Polese et al., 2017). Moreover, several briefings were held to overcome the uncertainties and doubts of the coders.

2.2. Data Analysis

The developed analytical framework was structured in two parts. In the first part, the following bibliometric information was collected to assess the volume and the research impact of the work: (a) year of publication; (b) journal's impact factor; (c) journal's *h*-index; (d) Scimago journal ranking index; and (e) number of citations. To this end, a performance analysis was carried out based on keyword frequency analysis and citation analysis. The citation analysis was performed using the InOrdinatio index (Pagani et al., 2015), which includes the journal's impact factor, the number of citations received by the article and the year of publication, implementing the following equation:

$$\text{InOrdinatio} = (\text{IF}/1{,}000) + \alpha * [10 - (\text{ResearchYear} - \text{PublishYear})] + (\Sigma\ \text{Cit})$$

where "IF" is the impact factor, divided by 1,000 to normalize the value; "α" is a value (ranging 1–10) attributed by the researcher, representing the scholars' importance to the year of publication criterion. The closer the value is to 10, the higher the relevance of the year criterion. The "α" coefficient has been fixed to 5; "ResearchYear" represents the year in which the research was performed; "PublishYear" is the year in which the paper was published; and "Σ Cit" is the number of citations obtained by the article.

Based on the InOrdinatio index, this analysis avoided some limitations related to bibliometric analyses, such as the number of citations or the number of citations *per* year, which do not consider the articles' relevance according to the editorial collocation of each paper.

The second part, following previous studies on the CE (i.e., De Pascale et al., 2021; Esposito et al., 2020) based on thematic issues, was structured as follows: (a) research methods; (b) geographical location; (c) 3R dimension; (d) level of analysis; (e) type of SC; and (f) investigated technology.

Table 9.1 provides a detailed description of the classification system adopted according to the analytical framework.

The next sections will briefly present and discuss the descriptive and thematic analysis results based on the previously described coding framework.

Table 9.1. Classification System for Analyzing Articles.

A. Research Methods
A1. Case/field study/interview
A2. Empirical
A3. Commentary/normative/policy
A4. Theoretical
B. Geographical location
B1. North America
B2. South America
B3. Africa
B4. Europe
B5. Asia
B6. Australia
C. 3R Dimension
C1. Reduce
C2. Reuse
C3. Recycle
D. Level of Analysis
D1. Micro
D2. Meso
D3. Macro
E. Type of SC
E1. Agriculture
E2. Dairy
E3. Livestock farming
E4. Fish breeding
E5. Various
F. Investigated Technology
F1. Internet of things (IoT)
F2. Big data analytics
F3. Blockchain
F4. Machine learning and robots
F5. Multiple technologies

Source: Authors.

3. Bibliometric and Descriptive Results

The following section presents the research trend concerning articles focusing on big data and digital technologies for the CE transition in the AFS. The selected articles were analyzed using frequency tables, word clouds and pie charts in order to provide synthetic and usable information to the reader.

Fig. 9.2 provides the publishing trends from 2018 to 2021. It is important to stress that no temporal criterion was selected in the search process. This information suggests that scholars began to investigate the role of digital technologies and big data analytics in the circular transition in the agri-food SC in 2018, highlighting the extreme novelty of this topic (Ofori et al., 2019). Moreover, despite the analysis being limited to articles selected in September 2021 (i.e., when the search process was performed), 2021 emerged as the most prolific year. Overall, an increasing trend can be seen, suggesting the growing interest of scholars in these topics, especially after the crises generated by the COVID-19 outbreak, which has posed a challenge to the AFS.

Fig. 9.3 shows the percentage of articles *per* typology. Of the reviewed articles, 65% provide a theoretical contribution, while 26% are empirical articles. A minority of articles are case studies (i.e., 7%) or commentary contributions (i.e., 2%).

Concerning the geographical location, Fig. 9.4 shows that most of the articles were written in Europe (13 articles), followed by Asia (six articles) and North America (five articles). The geographical location was determined based on the corresponding author's affiliation. This criterion was defined since most papers were written by scholars affiliated with different countries. However, this methodological choice limited the results, providing only partial information on the geographical location.

Fig. 9.5 provides the word cloud of the keywords extrapolated from the metadata of each article. A focus on the SC emerged, confirming previous results reported by Esposito et al. (2020), according to which the transition toward CE models is required at an SC level rather than at an individual company level. Moreover, the IoT emerged as the most disruptive technology investigated according to keyword frequency. This finding should be interpreted in light of the concept of "Society 5.0," which is considered "... human-centered society that balances economic advancement with the resolution of social problems by a system that integrates cyberspace and physical space" (Pu & Yano, 2020, p. 21). Thus, IoT technology can integrate cyberspace with physical space, incorporating all the data collected through disruptive technologies.

Following the definition of CE provided by Kirchherr et al. (2017), the spatial dimension of CE explored in the reviewed papers was investigated. Specifically, CE is linked to

> [...] end-of-life concept with reducing, alternatively reusing, recycling and recovering materials in production/distribution and consumption processes, thus operating at the micro-level (products, companies, consumers), meso-level (eco-industrial parks) and macro-level (city, region, nation and beyond), with the aim to accomplish sustainable development. (Kirchherr et al., 2017, pp. 224–225)

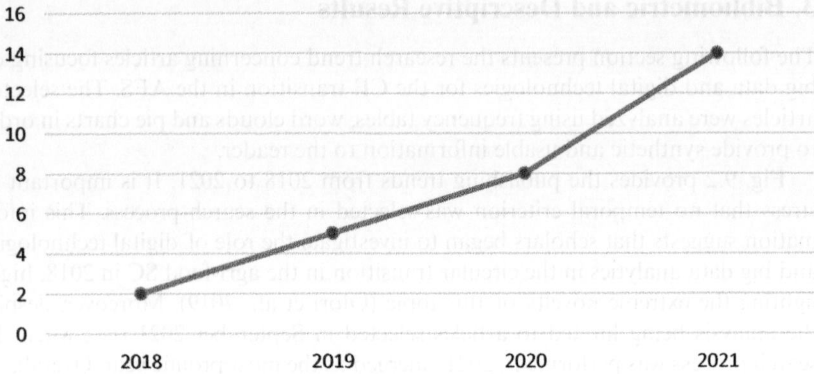

Fig. 9.2. Number of Articles Per Year. *Source*: Authors.

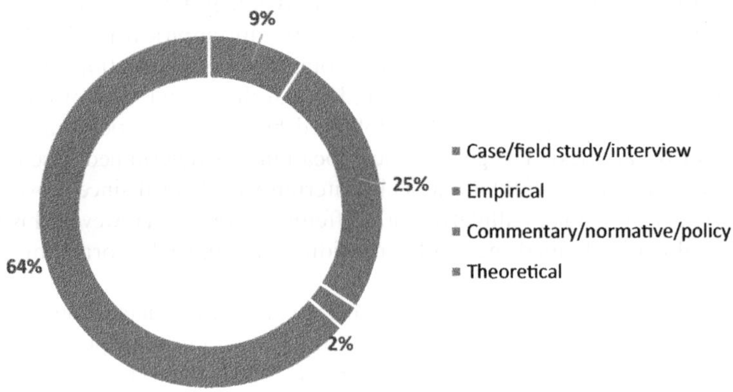

Fig. 9.3. Percentage of Articles Per Type. *Source*: Authors.

Drawing on this definition, Fig. 9.6 shows the percentage of articles that explored the meso- (33%) and macro-dimension (67%). The macro-dimension was the most explored for big data and digital technologies issues. At the same time, the micro-dimension was not investigated in the reviewed articles. This is justified by the fact that the implementation of CE models requires strong cooperation on the part of all actors in the SC, even in different geographical areas, from suppliers to consumers.

The analysis followed with the bibliometric impact assessment, which offered partial information regarding the quality of the articles in terms of citations and editorial collocation. Table 9.2 shows the ranking of the top 10 papers according to the InOrdinatio index, also providing the number of citations *per* paper and some performance indices related to the journals in which the articles were published.

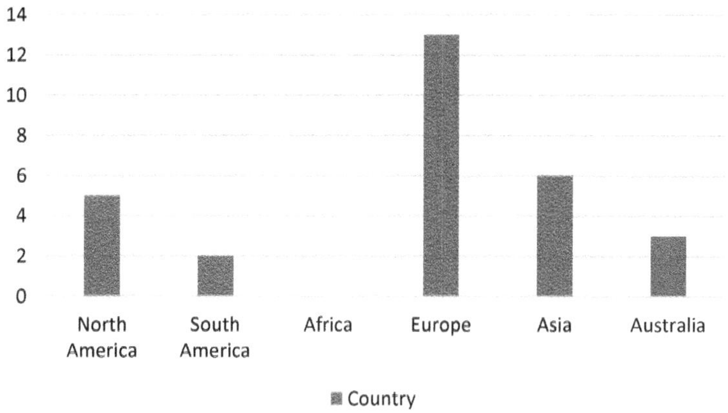

Fig. 9.4. Number of Articles *Per* Geographical Location. *Source*: Authors.

Fig. 9.5. Word Cloud of Keywords. *Source*: Authors.

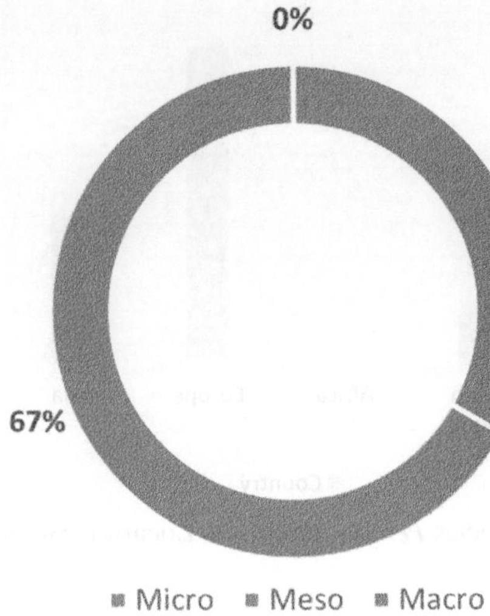

Fig. 9.6. Level of Analysis. *Source*: Authors.

Considering the multidisciplinarity of the SLR topic, an additional analysis was performed based on the subject area investigated by the journal in which the selected papers were published. The *ratio* refers to the journal's interest in scientific contributions focused on big data and digital technologies for the circular transition according to the scientific categories provided by the Scimago Journal Ranking. Table 9.3 shows that both journals based on hard sciences and journals focused on soft sciences are interested in these issues.

4. Thematic Results and Discussion

In this section, the main results of the SLR are briefly discussed according to the analytical framework previously described. The main findings for each reviewed article are provided in Table 9.4.

4.1. Reduce

The first R of the CE stands for reducing resource consumption and waste production. It also refers to the cutting of emissions in the production, distribution and consumption processes. The studies focused on this CE dimension predominantly analyzed the opportunity to exploit the potential of big data and digital technologies to redesign processes from a macro-level perspective (e.g., Ada et al., 2021; Carvalho Fagundes et al., 2020; Kaur, 2019). From this perspective, some authors developed software platforms for agricultural and livestock production impact assessment by analyzing big data and geographical information (e.g.,Arvanitis & Symeonaki, 2020; Kamilaris et al., 2018). Other scholars offered theoretical contributions exploring the AFS from an SC perspective to show how

Table 9.2. Top 10 Papers on Big Data and Digital Technologies for CE Transition in the Agri-food Industry Calculating the InOrdinatio Index (as of September 30, 2021).

Ranking Number	References	Citations	Journal	Journal Impact Factor	H-Index	Scimago Journal Ranking	In Ordinatio
1	Kamble et al. (2020)	192	*International Journal of Production Economics*	7.885	185	2.41	242.007
2	Sharma et al. (2020)	102	*Computers and Operations Research*	4.008	152	1.51	147.004
3	Astill et al. (2019)	84	*Trends in Food Science & Technology*	12.563	188	2.68	124.012
4	Alonso et al. (2020)	71	*Ad Hoc Networks*	3.643	94	0.78	116.003
5	Belaud et al. (2019)	72	*Computers in Industry*	7.635	100	1.43	112.007
6	Režek Jambrak et al. (2021)	10	*Applied Sciences*	2.679	52	0.44	60.002
7	Kaur (2019)	19	*Benchmarking: An International Journal*	2.600	15	0.32	59.002
8	Yadav et al. (2021)	9	*Environmental Science and Pollution Research*	2.741	113	0.85	59.002
9	Vernier et al. (2021)	8	*Sustainability*	3.251	85	0.61	58.003
10	Neethirajan and Kemp (2021a)	7	*Sensing and Bio-Sensing Research*	4.12	28	0.77	57.004

Source: Authors.

digital technologies could facilitate information flows and cooperation among the actors to reduce emissions and harmful effluents in the environment (Tommasetti et al., 2015). Moreover, considering the strict link between sustainability and security in the AFS, some scholars also emphasized how blockchain technology, sensors and the IoT could enhance traceability and monitoring of the critical control point in all processes and phases of agri-food SC (Gawanmeh et al., 2019).

Other articles explored the meso-dimension of CE (e.g., de Souza et al., 2021; Sharma et al., 2020). However, no article investigated CE reduction practices from a micro-perspective. These contributions were all review papers that

Table 9.3. Subject Area and Category of the First 10 Journals According to Table 9.2.

Journal	Subject Area and Category
International Journal of Production Economics	(a) Business/Management and Accounting; (b) Decision Sciences; (c) Economics, Econometrics and Finance; and (d) Engineering
Computers and Operations Research	(a) Computer Science; (b) Decision Sciences; and (c) Mathematics
Trends in Food Science & Technology	(a) Agricultural and Biological Sciences and (b) Biochemistry, Genetics and Molecular Biology
Ad Hoc Networks	(a) Computer Science
Computers in Industry	(a) Computer Science and (b) Engineering
Applied Sciences	(a) Chemical Engineering; (b) Computer Science; (c) Engineering; (d) Materials Science; and (e) Physics and Astronomy
Benchmarking: An International Journal	(a) Business, Management and Accounting and (b) Decision Sciences
Environmental Science and Pollution Research	(a) Environmental Science and (b) Medicine
Sustainability	(a) Energy; (b) Environmental Science; and (c) Social Sciences
Sensing and Bio-sensing Research	(a) Biochemistry, Genetics and Molecular Biology; (b) Computer Science; (c) Engineering; and (d) Materials Science

Source: Authors' elaboration of data retrieved from *Scimago Journal & Country Rank* (https://www.scimagojr.com/).

addressed the state of the art in the following research fields: (a) artificial intelligence and machine learning in the agri-food industry for sustainable operations (i.e., Kakani et al., 2020); (b) big data analytics and modern agriculture technologies in the sustainable coffee SC (i.e., Kittichotsatsawat et al., 2021); (c) agricultural sustainability via remote sensing (i.e., Martos et al., 2021); (d) the limits and potential of SC sustainability through digital technologies; and (e) digital livestock farming (i.e., Neethirajan & Kemp, 2021b). In all these contributions, some common insights emerged. In particular, through the use of agriculture 4.0 technologies (e.g., robotics, the IoT and sensors), agri-food operators and managers could, on the one hand, reduce land, water and air pollution, and on the other hand, achieve better crop performance. More specifically, robotics could provide a greater level of automation, and the declining cost of sensors allows operators to monitor parameters such as climate and soil properties in real time. This timely, affordable and systematic information collection would support managers in their decision-making processes.

Table 9.4. Main Findings of the SLR.

Authors	Type of SC	Technology	Dimension
Reduce			
Kamilaris et al. (2018)	Agriculture	Big data analytics, geospatial analysis and web technologies	Macro
Kaur (2019)	Not defined	Internet of things	Macro
Bronson (2018)	Agriculture	Big data, machine learning	Macro
de Souza et al. (2021)	Not defined	Digital technologies and big data	Meso
Delgado et al. (2019)	Agriculture	Artificial intelligence, big data and internet of things	Macro
Astill et al. (2019)	Not defined	Internet of things, blockchain and big data	Macro
Ada et al. (2021)	Not defined	Internet of things, cloud technologies, blockchain and machine learning	Macro
Kakani et al. (2020)	Agriculture	Artificial intelligence, big Data, robotics, machine learning and deep learning	Meso
Bergier et al. (2021)	Livestock	Cloud computing and big data	Macro
Singh et al. (2019)	Agriculture	Web technology	Macro
Sharma et al. (2020)	Agriculture	Machine learning	Meso
Carvalho Fagundes et al. (2020)	Not defined	Stochastic and computational model	Macro
Martos et al. (2021)	Agriculture	Remote sensing, internet of things and big data	Meso
Kittichotsatsawat et al. (2021)	Agriculture	Internet of things, image processing, convolutional neural networks and remote sensing	Meso
Chapman et al. (2022)	Not defined	Big data and internet of things	Macro
Režek Jambrak et al. (2021)	Not defined	Smart sensors, artificial intelligence, big data and additive technologies with non-thermal technologies	Meso

(*Continued*)

Table 9.4. (*Continued*)

Authors	Type of SC	Technology	Dimension
Jellason et al. (2021)	Agriculture	artificial intelligence, biotechnology, the Internet of things, big data and robotics	Macro
Neethirajan and Kemp (2021)	Agriculture	Sensor technology, big data and blockchain	Meso
Vernier et al. (2021)	Agriculture	Information and communication technologies	Meso
Mondejar et al. (2021)	Agriculture	Geographic information system, precision agriculture, artificial intelligence and robotics	Macro
Reuse			
Belaud et al. (2019)	By-products	Big data	Micro
Annosi et al. (2020)	Not defined	Digital technologies and big data	Macro
Recycle			
Sheldon (2020)	Not defined	Big data	Micro
Redesign			
Alonso et al. (2020)	Livestock	Internet of things, edge computing, distributed ledger technologies and big data	Macro
Arvanitis and Symeonaki (2020)	Agriculture	Computational intelligence, Robotics, big data and cloud computing	Macro
Yadav et al. (2021)	Agriculture	Internet of things, blockchain, robotics, big data analysis and cloud computing	Macro
Fleming et al. (2021)	Agriculture	Digital technologies in general	Macro
Kanzanconglu et al. (2021)	Not defined	Big data	Macro
Kamble et al. (2020)	Agriculture	Big data, blockchain and data analytics	Macro

Source: The authors.

4.2. Reuse

The second R stands for reuse of waste and products, perhaps after repair, or directly, in whole or in part, as components of other products. Only two articles investigated the role of digital technologies and big data in implementing reuse practices. Annosi et al. (2020) analyzed the main challenges agri-food firms encounter in adopting digital technologies for sustainable development. They found that the dominant barriers are the lack of appropriate incentives, the high costs of digital technology implementation and the age and education of farmers and agri-food operators. Accordingly, within agri-food SCs, the use of digital technology for sustainable development can be related to different perceptions of incentives by different actors because benefits and costs do not always accrue equitably (Thorlakson, de Zegher & Lambin, 2018).

Moreover, rural areas may be disadvantaged in shifting toward disruptive environmental, social and economic sustainability technologies. Belaud et al. (2019) developed an approach to exploit big data to enhance sustainability management to valorize agricultural waste. Specifically, they applied this approach to the rice SC in agricultural waste valorization to pre-treatment lignocellulosic biomass.

4.3. Recycle

The third R is based on recycling. This CE practice requires waste to be recycled to use as secondary raw material. Among the reviewed articles, only Sheldon (2020) explored disruptive technologies for recycling practices. He highlighted that the development in genomics combined with big data analytics has completely changed the discovery of new enzymes, leading to the birth of a bio-based CE through biomass conversion.

4.4. Redesign

In addition to the three dimensions of the CE, the literature study highlighted a fourth R related to the use of digital technologies and big data in design processes. In particular, the insights obtained from the study on the data acquired through smart sensors, robots, blockchain technologies, etc., can contribute to redesigning the production processes to orient the SCs toward circular models. These models aim to reduce environmental impacts, improve resource efficiency and optimize production to ensure sustainable competitiveness. From this perspective, the last R envelops all the CE practices of reducing, reuse and recycling and – at the same time – is the final purpose of completely changing the economic paradigm from micro- to meso- and macro-perspective. Some scholars focused their attention on the livestock SC, providing a platform based on the IoT, artificial intelligence and blockchain technology in a smart farming scenario to monitor the state of dairy cattle and feed grain in real time, to redesign the processes promptly and to guarantee sustainability and traceability in all process stages (Alonso et al., 2019; Jung et al., 2021). Other scholars investigated the use of big data and digital technologies in the agriculture SC (i.e., Arvanitis & Symeonaki, 2020; Fleming et al., 2021; Kamble et al., 2020; Yadav et al., 2020). For example,

Kamble et al. (2020) explored how to achieve sustainable performance in the agri-food SC using insights from big data analytics. Accordingly, they developed a framework for practitioners based on SC visibility and SC resources to redesign all the involved processes. Meanwhile, Fleming et al. (2021) proposed a big data infrastructure to exploit the advantages of the digital revolution in the Australian context. Arvanitis and Symeonaki (2020) assessed the use of agricultural cyber-physical systems to monitor various fundamental cultivation parameters, such as temperature, humidity, soil moisture and plant health, to design a sustainable farm SC. Lastly, Yadav et al. (2020) applied interpretative structural modeling to establish the interrelationships among the enablers of IoT adoption in the agri-food system.

5. Conclusions

This chapter provides a conceptual contribution on the role of data analysis and digital technologies in redesigning business strategies. Moreover, the impact of data on the decision-making processes in the AFS for the CE transition has been explored. This chapter has investigated the state of the art research on this relevant topic through a SLR. In particular, the study has revealed that scholars have mainly provided theoretical contributions. Moreover, the findings also show that – although each study focused on one dimension of the CE paradigm – most of the examined papers have analyzed the role of digital technologies in collection, storage and analytical processes and not in the specific reuse–reduce–recycle practices. Furthermore, the macro-dimension emerged as the primary spatial dimension of analysis adopted by the researchers. Accordingly, big data analytics should be considered a facilitator for circular decision-making and utilized to generate insights for processes integration and resource allocation. Indeed, big data and digital technologies can vastly enhance agri-food business operations via data-driven decision-making. The possibility to develop data-driven decision support systems is pivotal in a growing business concept such as CE and more in the agri-food systems in which several parties are involved, and peculiarities characterize each SC according to the food type that is produced sold or administered. However, the effectiveness of such a data-driven CE depends on the quality of data generated and collected along the SCs. This point should be considered a critical issue on which scholars, managers and data scientists must work to support the AFS in an effective and efficient transition toward the "reduce–reuse–recycle" paradigm.

Furthermore, the findings should be interpreted from a practical perspective providing the following insights. The identification of different technologies for each R of the CE paradigm (reduce, reuse and recycle) can entail significant implications for data-driven decision-makers. More specifically, managers of the AFS can rely on the results to support the definition of CE strategies and identify the most appropriate technology for the implementation of reducing, reusing or recycling practices. Moreover, if the agri-food company is already digitalized, the results should support the managers in defining, compliant with the technology already owned, what circular practice should be implemented according to the type of agri-food SC. This – in turn – should reduce the investment for CE practices while maximizing the technological resources already owned by the agri-food company. Moreover, considering that the food SC differs profoundly by type of product sector, the classification of results according to the type of SC can provide further information to identify adequate technologies for each product chain. Another important issue concerns the fourth R of the CE (redesign), which is emerged from the literature study. The scientific contributions analyzed have highlighted the strong interrelationship among the various circular practices that must strongly consider data produced by digital technologies. These data should support managers in redesigning the SCs, processes and systems according to the predictive and prescriptive analysis developed through big data analytics. This process – in turn – will lead to the development of a data-driven CE. Scholars can use the results as a foundation to investigate aspects not sufficiently explored in the extant literature. These findings may support managers in identifying technologies that are more suitable for the implementation of CE practices. Practitioners could explore the disruptive technologies that will enhance environmental SC efficiency.

The authors recognize that the present research has several limitations. The first is related to the subjective definition of the search string, which impacted the results. Moreover, the exclusion and inclusion criteria defined *ex ante* and the selected databases influenced the findings, narrowing the analysis field. The developed analytical framework also shaped the results, potentially excluding other relevant insights that might have been extrapolated from the selected papers.

Starting from these limitations, future research could explore the effective use of big data for the AFS, including empirical analyses and case studies to provide more practical insights for practitioners, managers and policy-makers to orient the global pathway toward sustainable development and global resilience (Kashef et al., 2021).

References

Ada, N., Kazancoglu, Y., Sezer, M. D., Ede-Senturk, C., Ozer, I., & Ram, M. (2021). Analyzing barriers of circular food supply chains and proposing Industry 4.0 solutions. *Sustainability*, *13*(12), 6812.

Alonso, R. S., Sittón-Candanedo, I., García, Ó., Prieto, J., & Rodríguez-González, S. (2020). An intelligent edge-IoT platform for monitoring livestock and crops in a dairy farming scenario. *Ad Hoc Networks*, *98*, 102047.

Annosi, M. C., Brunetta, F., Capo, F., & Heideveld, L. (2020). Digitalization in the agri-food industry: the relationship between technology and sustainable development. *Management Decision*.

Arvanitis, K. G., & Symeonaki, E. G. (2020). Agriculture 4.0: The role of innovative smart technologies towards sustainable farm management. *The Open Agriculture Journal*, *14*(1), 130–135.

Astill, J., Dara, R. A., Campbell, M., Farber, J. M., Fraser, E. D., Sharif, S., & Yada, R. Y. (2019). Transparency in food supply chains: A review of enabling technology solutions. *Trends in Food Science & Technology*, *91*, 240–247.

Barile, S., Ciasullo, M. V., Troisi, O., & Sarno, D. (2017). The role of technology and institutions in tourism service ecosystems: Findings from a case study. *The TQM Journal, 29*(6), 811–833. https://doi.org/10.1108/TQM-06-2017-0068

Belaud, J. P., Prioux, N., Vialle, C., & Sablayrolles, C. (2019). Big data for agri-food 4.0: Application to sustainability management for by-products supply chain. *Computers in Industry*, *111*, 41–50.

Bergier, I., Papa, M., Silva, R., & Santos, P. M. (2021). Cloud/edge computing for compliance in the Brazilian livestock supply chain. *Science of the Total Environment*, *761*, 143276.

Bronson, K. (2018). Smart farming: including rights holders for responsible agricultural innovation. *Technology Innovation Management Review*, *8*(2), 7–14.

Chapman, J., Power, A., Netzel, M. E., Sultanbawa, Y., Smyth, H. E., Truong, V. K., & Cozzolino, D. (2022). Challenges and opportunities of the fourth revolution: A brief insight into the future of food. *Critical Reviews in Food Science and Nutrition, 62*(10), 2845–2853.

Chui, K. T., Lytras, M. D., & Visvizi, A. (2018). Energy sustainability in Smart Cities: Artificial intelligence, smart monitoring, and optimization of energy consumption. *Energies*, *11*(11), 2869. https://doi.org/10.3390/en11112869

Cosimato, S., & Troisi, O. (2015). Green supply chain management: Practices and tools for logistics competitiveness and sustainability. The DHL case study. *The TQM Journal, 27*(2), 256–276. https://doi.org/10.1108/TQM-01-2015-0007

de Souza, M., Pereira, G. M., de Sousa Jabbour, A. B. L., Jabbour, C. J. C., Trento, L. R., Borchardt, M., & Zvirtes, L. (2021). A digitally enabled circular economy for mitigating food waste: Understanding innovative marketing strategies in the context of an emerging economy. *Technological Forecasting and Social Change*, *173*, 121062.

del Hoyo, R. P., Visvizi, A., & Mora, H. (2021). Inclusiveness, safety, resilience, and sustainability in the smart city context. In A. Visvizi, R. P. del Hoyo (Eds.), *Smart Cities and the un SDGs* (pp. 15–28). Elsevier.

De Pascale, A., Arbolino, R., Szopik-Depczyńska, K., Limosani, M., & Ioppolo, G. (2021). A systematic review for measuring circular economy: The 61 indicators. *Journal of Cleaner Production*, *281*, 124942.

Delgado, J. A., Short, N. M., Jr, Roberts, D. P., & Vandenberg, B. (2019). Big data analysis for sustainable agriculture on a geospatial cloud framework. *Frontiers in Sustainable Food Systems*, *3*, 54.

Esposito, B., Sessa, M. R., Sica, D., & Malandrino, O. (2020). Towards circular economy in the agri-food sector. A systematic literature review. *Sustainability*, *12*(18), 7401.

Esposito, B., Sessa, M. R., Sica, D., & Malandrino, O. (2021). Exploring corporate social responsibility in the Italian wine sector through websites. *The TQM Journal*, *33*(7), 222–252.

Fagundes, M. V. C., Teles, E. O., de Melo, S. A. V., & Freires, F. G. M. (2020). Decision-making models and support systems for supply chain risk: Literature mapping and future research agenda. *European Research on Management and Business Economics*, *26*(2), 63–70.

Food and Agriculture Organization of the United Nations. (2019). *The state of food and agriculture, moving forward on food loss and waste reduction*. Food and Agriculture Organization of the United Nations.

Fleming, A., Jakku, E., Fielke, S., Taylor, B. M., Lacey, J., Terhorst, A., & Stitzlein, C. (2021). Foresighting Australian digital agricultural futures: Applying responsible innovation thinking to anticipate research and development impact under different scenarios. *Agricultural Systems*, *190*, 103120.

Gawanmeh, A., Parvin, S., Venkatraman, S., de Souza-Daw, T., Kang, J., Kaspi, S., & Jackson, J. (2019, April). A framework for integrating big data security into agricultural supply chain. In *IEEE fifth international conference on big data computing service and applications (BigDataService)* (pp. 191–194) Newark, CA.

Jellason, N. P., Robinson, E. J., & Ogbaga, C. C. (2021). Agriculture 4.0: Is Sub-Saharan Africa Ready? *Applied Sciences*, *11*(12), 5750.

Jung, J., Maeda, M., Chang, A., Bhandari, M., Ashapure, A., & Landivar-Bowles, J. (2021). The potential of remote sensing and artificial intelligence as tools to improve the resilience of agriculture production systems. *Current Opinion in Biotechnology*, *70*, 15–22.

Kakani, V., Nguyen, V. H., Kumar, B. P., Kim, H., & Pasupuleti, V. R. (2020). A critical review on computer vision and artificial intelligence in food industry. *Journal of Agriculture and Food Research*, *2*, 100033.

Kamble, S. S., Gunasekaran, A., & Gawankar, S. A. (2020). Achieving sustainable performance in a data-driven agriculture supply chain: A review for research and applications. *International Journal of Production Economics*, *219*, 179–194.

Kamilaris, A., Anton, A., Blasi, A. B., & Prenafeta-Boldú, F. X. (2018). Assessing and mitigating the impact of livestock agriculture on the environment through geospatial and big data analysis. *International Journal of Sustainable Agricultural Management and Informatics*, *4*(2), 98–122.

Kashef, M., Visvizi A., & Troisi O. (2021). Smart city as a smart service system: Human–computer interaction and smart city surveillance systems. *Computers in Human Behavior*, *124*, 2021. ISSN 0747-5632. https://doi.org/10.1016/j.chb.2021.106923

Kaur, H. (2019). Modelling internet of things driven sustainable food security system. *Benchmarking: An International Journal, 28*(5), 1740–1760.

Kazancoglu, Y., Pala, M. O., Sezer, M. D., Luthra, S., & Kumar, A. (2021). Drivers of implementing Big Data Analytics in food supply chains for transition to a circular economy and sustainable operations management. *Journal of Enterprise Information Management*. https://doi.org/10.1108/JEIM-12-2020-0521

Kirchherr, J., Reike, D., & Hekkert, M. (2017). Conceptualizing the circular economy: An analysis of 114 definitions. *Resources, Conservation & Recycling*, *127*, 221–232. https://doi.org/10.1016/j.resconrec.2017.09.005

Kittichotsatsawat, Y., Jangkrajarng, V., & Tippayawong, K. Y. (2021). Enhancing coffee supply chain towards sustainable growth with big data and modern agricultural technologies. *Sustainability*, *13*(8), 4593.

Lytras, M. D., & Visvizi, A. (2019). Big data and their social impact: Preliminary study. *Sustainability*, *11*(18), 5067. https://doi.org/10.3390/su11185067

Lytras, M. D., & Visvizi, A. (2020). Big data research for social science and social impact. *Sustainability*, *12*(1), 180. https://doi.org/10.3390/su12010180

Malik, R., Visvizi, A., & Skrzek-Lubasi⊠ska, M. (2021). The gig economy: Current issues, the debate, and the new avenues of research. *Sustainability*, *13*(9), 5023.

Martos, V., Ahmad, A., Cartujo, P., & Ordoñez, J. (2021). Ensuring agricultural sustainability through remote sensing in the Era of Agriculture 5.0. *Applied Sciences*, *11*(13), 5911.

Merli, R., Preziosi, M., & Acampora, A. (2017). How do scholars approach the circular economy? A systematic literature review. *Journal of Cleaner Production*, *178*, 703–722.

Mondejar, M. E., Avtar, R., Diaz, H. L. B., Dubey, R. K., Esteban, J., Gómez-Morales, A., ... & Garcia-Segura, S. (2021). Digitalization to achieve sustainable development goals: Steps towards a Smart Green Planet. *Science of the Total Environment*, *794*, 148539

Moher, D., Liberati, A., Tetzlaff, J., Altman, D. G., & TP Group. (2009). Linee guida per il reporting di revisioni sistematiche e meta-analisi: il PRISMA Statement. *PLoS Med,* 6(7), e1000097

Neethirajan, S., & Kemp, B. (2021a). Digital livestock farming. *Sensing and Bio-Sensing Research*, *32*, 100408.

Neethirajan, S., & Kemp, B. (2021b). Digital twins in livestock farming. *Animals*, *11*(4), 1008.

Ofori, M., & El-Gayar, O. (2019, December). The state and future of smart agriculture: Insights from mining social media. In *IEEE international conference on big data (big data)* (pp. 5152–5161).

Pagani, R. N., Kovaleski, J. L., & Resende, L. M. (2015). Methodi Ordinatio: a proposed methodology to select and rank relevant scientific papers encompassing the impact factor, number of citation, and year of publication. *Scientometrics*, *105*(3), 2109–2135.

Petticrew, M., & Roberts, H. (2008). *Systematic reviews in the social sciences: A practical guide*. John Wiley & Sons.

Pizzi, S., Caputo, A., Corvino, A., & Venturelli, A. (2020). Management research and the UN sustainable development goals (SDGs): A bibliometric investigation and systematic review. *Journal of Cleaner Production*, *276*, 124033.

Polese, F., Troisi, O., Grimaldi, M., & Romeo, E. (2019). A big data-oriented approach to decision-making: A systematic literature review. In 22nd International *conference proceedings* (pp. 472–496).

Polese, F., Troisi, O., Torre, C., & Maione, G. (2017). Performance evaluation and measurement in public organizations: A systematic literature review. *International Journal of Business Administration*, *8*(1), 106–117.

Pu, S., & Yano, M. (2020). Market quality approach to IoT data on blockchain big data. In *Blockchain and crypt currency* (pp. 21–40). Springer.

Režek Jambrak, A., Nutrizio, M., Djekić, I., Pleslić, S., & Chemat, F. (2021). Internet of Nonthermal Food Processing Technologies (IoNTP): Food Industry 4.0 and sustainability. *Applied Sciences*, *11*(2), 686.

Segura, S. (2021). Digitalization to achieve sustainable development goals: Steps towards a Smart Green Planet. *Science of the Total Environment*, *794*, 148539.

Sharma, R., Kamble, S. S., Gunasekaran, A., Kumar, V., & Kumar, A. (2020). A systematic literature review on machine learning applications for sustainable agriculture supply chain performance. *Computers & Operations Research*, *119*, 104926.

Sheldon, R. A., & Norton, M. (2020). Green chemistry and the plastic pollution challenge: towards a circular economy. *Green Chemistry*, *22*(19), 6310–6322.

Sica, D., Malandrino, O., Esposito, B., Supino, S., & Sessa, M. R. (2019). The pathway towards social responsibility in Italian Wine Sector: The Feudi di San Gregorio SpA experience. *Journal of Health Science*, *7*, 273–281.

Singh, R., Kumar, J., & Nayak, A. (2019). AGROY: Creating value through smart farming. *Emerald Emerging Markets Case Studies*.

Su, B., Heshmati, A., Geng, Y., & Yu, X. (2013). A review of the circular economy in China: Moving from rhetoric to implementation. *Journal of Cleaner Production*, *42*, 215–227.

Thorlakson, T., de Zegher, J. F., & Lambin, E. F. (2018). Companies' contribution to sustainability through global supply chains. *Proceedings of the National Academy of Sciences*, *115*(9), 2072–2077.

Tommasetti, A., Vesci, M., & Troisi, O. (2015). The internet of things and value co-creation in a service-dominant logic perspective. In F. Colace, M. De Santo, V. Moscato, A. Picariello, F. Schreiber, & L. Tanca (Eds.), *Data management in pervasive systems. Data-centric systems and applications* (pp. 3–19). Springer. https://doi.org/10.1007/978-3-319-20062-0_1

Troisi, O., D'Arco, M., Loia, F., & Maione, G. (2018, January). Big data management: The case of Mulino Bianco's engagement platform for value co-creation. *International Journal of Engineering Business Management, 10,* 1–8. https://doi.org/10.1177/1847979018767776

Tranfield, D., Denyer, D., & Smart, P. (2003). Towards a methodology for developing evidence-informed management knowledge by means of systematic review. *British Journal of Management*, *14*(3), 207–222.

Troisi, O., Fenza, G., Grimaldi, M., & Loia, F. (2022). Covid-19 sentiments in smart cities: The role of technology anxiety before and during the pandemic. *Computers in Human Behavior, 126,* 1–16. ISSN 0747-5632. https://doi.org/10.1016/j.chb.2021.106986

Troisi, O., Grimaldi, M., & Loia, F. (2020). Redesigning business models for data-driven innovation: A three-layered framework. In *The international research & innovation forum* (pp. 421–435). Springer.

Troisi, O., Visvizi, A., & Grimaldi, M. (2021). The different shades of innovation emergence in smart service systems: The case of Italian Cluster for Aerospace Technology. *Journal of Business and Industrial Marketing*. https://doi.org/10.1108/JBIM-02-2020-0091

Vernier, C., Loeillet, D., Thomopoulos, R., & Macombe, C. (2021). Adoption of ICTs in agri-food logistics: Potential and limitations for supply chain sustainability. *Sustainability*, *13*(12), 6702.

Visvizi, A., Lytras, M. D., Damiani, E., & Mathkour, H. (2018). Policy making for smart cities: Innovation and social inclusive economic growth for sustainability. *Journal of Science and Technology Policy Management*, *9*(2), 126–133. https://doi.org/10.1108/JSTPM-07-2018-079

Yadav, S., Luthra, S., & Garg, D. (2021). Modelling internet of things (IoT)-driven global sustainability in multi-tier agri-food supply chain under natural epidemic outbreaks. *Environmental Science and Pollution Research*, *28*(13), 16633–16654.

Yadav, V. S., Singh, A. R., Raut, R. D., & Govindarajan, U. H. (2020). Blockchain technology adoption barriers in the Indian agricultural supply chain: an integrated approach. Resources, *Conservation and Recycling, 161*, 104877.

Part 3

Business and Policy-making Process Empowered by Big Data

Chapter 10

Business Processes Powered by Big Data: Current Issues and New Research Directions

Radosław Malik and Katarzyna Rybkowska

Abstract

This chapter uses multiple research methods, including quantitative science mapping analysis (SciMat) and a qualitative literature review, to provide insight into the academic debate unfolding at the intersection of big data and business processes. SciMat analysis based on keyword co-occurrence enabled identifying 12 of the most productive research themes, as reflected in a poll of 301 articles about big data and business processes. The three most important themes are: firm performance, Industry 4.0, and innovation. The traditional literature review on firm performance indicated that big data analytics (BDA) positively influence business process performance and have a beneficial impact on a firm's performance, that is, the role of big data is viewed as critical in the context of Industry 4.0 because it enhances productivity and improves business processes. The benefits of BDA can be achieved only if the organizational obstacles related to planning, workforce attitude, and alignment with strategy are overcome. Moreover, big data is perceived as a significant source of innovation in an organization and can be conceptualized with the use of a resource-based view (RBV) of the firm. BDA positively influence business processes, which is strengthened by adequate implementation and openness to innovation.

Keywords: Big data; business processes; Industry 4.0; firm performance; innovation; science mapping analysis

Big Data and Decision-Making: Applications and Uses in the Public and Private Sector, 145–161

Published under exclusive licence by Emerald Publishing Limited
doi:10.1108/978-1-80382-551-920231010

1. Introduction

Big data has long been viewed as a potential game changer in business and management (Fosso Wamba et al., 2015). However, despite its documented and perceived high operational and strategic impact, empirically verified mechanisms of business value creation with the use of big data have been contested (Günther et al., 2017). Nevertheless, today consensus has been reached that big data offers organizations unprecedented opportunities to gain and maintain competitive advantage through a variety of big data business models (Troisi et al., 2021; Visvizi et al., 2021; Wiener et al., 2020). The importance of data-driven decisions in every management field has led to the emergence of new sub-management areas supported by big data (Khisro et al., 2021; Kushwaha et al., 2021). However, the link between big data and business processes remains a seldomly researched area (Brinch et al., 2021) and its value creation potential continues to be largely unexplored (Al-Anqoudi et al., 2021; Masoumi et al., 2021)

Thus, the increased data-driven business orientation intensifies the use of big data in various business processes posing a challenge for business practitioners and creates an urgent call for scientific research into this rapidly proliferating research field. The substantial research value and considerable potential for business application justifies a review of nascent research into the use of big data in business processes to highlight major research domains and delineate potential research opportunities. This chapter addresses the absence of literature reviews concerning the application of big data to business processes by mapping major research themes and reviewing their research contribution.

Applying SciMat analysis based on keyword co-occurrence bibliometric data improves the understanding of the research structure on the conceptual intersection of big data and business process research. The application of this research method sets the foundation for subsequent literature reviews of the most prolific themes in the reviewed research field, which facilitates the provision of answers to the following research questions:

Q1: What are the key research themes in the literature connecting the concepts of big data and business processes?
Q2: What insight can be gleaned from the articles discussing the most developed themes in big data and business process literature?

The remainder of this chapter is structured as follows. The research method, analytical tools applied and their limitations are discussed in Section 2. The SciMat results are shown in Section 3. Section 4 elaborates on the insight from the articles on the most significant themes identified with the use SciMat analysis and presented in the previous section. Conclusions follow in Section 5.

2. Science Mapping: Method and Research Limitations

This study uses SciMat analysis, a type of bibliometric method, as a primary research method. Bibliometric methods are commonly accepted strategies for analyzing the output of scientific research and are valued as tools for measuring scientific productivity and impact (Gutiérrez-Salcedo et al., 2018). SciMat analysis enables researchers and others to identify and visualize the research themes and their connections, providing quantitative insight into the structure of the research field represented by the pool of research articles (Chen, 2017). SciMat analysis used in this research utilizes article keywords and identifies the frequency of their co-occurrence (number of articles in which two given keywords occur together) to provide insight into the content of the research field (Callon et al., 1983) as the keywords reflect the contents of an article (Weismayer & Pezenka, 2017). The SciMat analysis is a largely automatic, algorithm-based process supported by various specialized software (Moral-Munoz et al., 2019). In this research, SciMat software (Cobo et al., 2012) is used for its flexibility and quality.

SciMat analysis based on keywords co-occurrence with the application of SciMat software already has been applied to related subjects, such as a large study on big data (López-Robles et al., 2019) and to research on process modeling for Industry 4.0 (Sott et al., 2021), as well as to a number of other business and economics reviews, including the links between sustainable development and human resource management (Santana & Lopez-Cabrales, 2019), the gig economy (Malik et al., 2021), and the future of work (Santana & Cobo, 2020).

The analysis carried out in this research aims to identify the important research themes and their thematic networks in a five-step process that consists of (I) data collection; (II) pre-processing; (III) detection of research themes; (IV) visualization of themes and thematic connections; and (V) interpretation.

In the data collection step (I), a set of articles about the analyzed research field is retrieved from a database, typically Web of Science (WoS) and/or Scopus, together with the full set of bibliometric data. In the pre-processing step (II), duplications are removed from the dataset and keywords grouped based on various criteria such as plural and singular nouns, American and British spelling, abbreviations and full names (Sott et al., 2021). With the use of SciMat software, the detection of research themes (step III) is performed based on keywords co-occurrence with the use of an equivalence index to calculate the similarity between the themes and a simple center algorithm to create a network of links between themes (Cobo et al., 2011).

In step IV, the visualization of themes and their thematic connections is per formed to produce an individual thematic network of each theme and strategic diagram where the identified themes are presented. Interpretation (step V) of the graphic representation of the themes and their thematic networks is the last step in the process.

The thematic network of each theme is visualized as a network structure with the major keyword (the theme name) positioned in the center of the network (step IV). The subsequent interpretation (step V) indicates through the thickness of the lines the bond strength between the keywords in the thematic network and which is derivative of keywords co-occurrence frequency. The size of the spheres is proportional to the number of publications with the given keyword (Santana & Cobo, 2020). An example of thematic network of theme "M" is shown in Fig. 10.1.

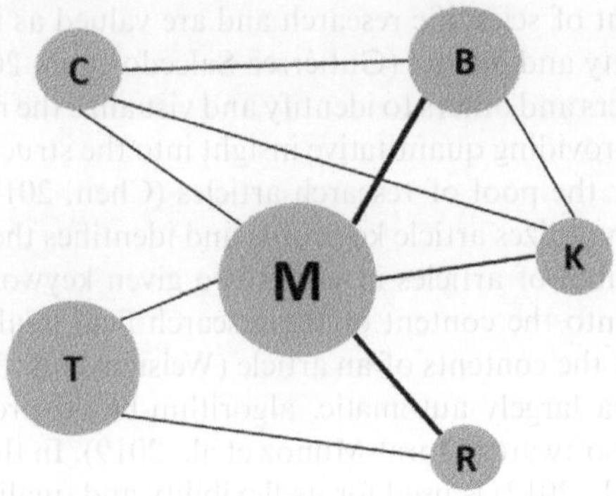

Fig. 10.1. Thematic Network (Example). *Source*: Authors' example.

In the visualization step, the themes are also plotted on a strategic diagram in which the density (vertical axis) indicates the internal strength of a connection within a thematic network of a theme and the centrality (horizontal axis) shows the intensity of the links between one theme's thematic network and others in the strategic diagram (Callon et al., 1991). The four quadrants (Q1–Q4) of the strategic diagram represent themes with various density and centrality conditions as shown in Fig. 10.2.

In the last step of SciMat analysis (step V), the interpretation is provided based on the location of the themes in the four quadrants of the strategic diagram. *Motor themes (Q1)* have high centrality and density covering the most developed themes in the analyzed research field. *Basic and transversal themes (Q2)* include themes with high centrality and low density indicating their high level of connectivity with other themes in the diagram but relative lack of internal development. *Emerging or declining themes (Q3)* are ones characterized by a low level of centrality and density and can be viewed as having limited importance for the research field. *Highly developed and isolated themes (Q4)* feature themes with high density and low centrality and can be viewed as well-developed internally but with limited connectivity with the rest of the themes in the diagram (Sott et al., 2021). Thus, the interpretation step provides an opportunity to identify crucial features of the research landscape in the investigated field, indicating the

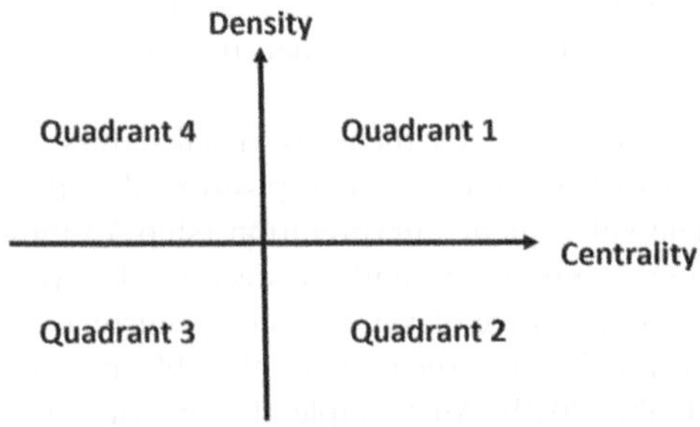

Fig. 10.2. Strategic Diagram (Example). *Source*: Authors' example.

most explored research avenues as well as hinting at less frequently explored paths that may constitute research gaps (Chen, 2017).

The use of bibliometric research methods, and science mapping in particular, is not deprived of research limitations.

1. The outcome of the analysis relies on the input data quality, for example, on the accuracy of the choice of keywords to adequately represent the content of the text. This limitation cannot be easily addressed, as the authors of the articles are free to choose their own keywords.
2. The choice of databases in the data collection step influences the pool of texts that are included in the analysis and may distort the quality of the outcome. This limitation can be addressed with the use of reputable scientific databases and by employing multiple databases to provide the most comprehensive scope of analysis.
3. In the majority of studies that employ science mapping, the researchers must limit the scope of discussion to a range of themes, as the typical research article length does not allow for exhaustive analysis. This limitation can be addressed with a clearly defined research goal and precise phrasing of research questions that indicate the types of themes that are to be discussed in detail in the research article.
4. SciMat analysis provides insight into the structure of the research based exclusively on a quantitative approach, which necessarily limits the potential insight from the research. To address this research limitation and enhance the research quality, this research method should be supplemented with a qualitative research approach, such as a systematic literature review or discussion of the content of the articles.

3. Big Data and Business Processes: Results of The Scimat Analysis

The data collection for the purpose of this research was performed on January 28, 2022 and covered research texts indexed in the WoS to ensure high-quality, solely peer-reviewed research as input data. In order to identify the pool of texts relevant to the goal of this study, the search query was run based on the phrase " 'big data' AND 'business process*' " in all fields of the database. In the data collection step, the scope of the texts was limited to research articles and book chapters to ensure high-quality input data. The search returned 301 texts with 1,497 keywords and the whole dataset was downloaded to the SciMat software and further steps of SciMat analysis were performed. In the pre-processing step, the dataset was refined with the removal of duplications and keywords grouping as specified in the previous section. In the outcome of this process, 301 texts with 1,436 keywords were qualified to the theme-detection step of SciMat analysis. In this part of the research, an equivalence index was used as a network normalization measure and simple center algorithm was used for clustering with the cluster

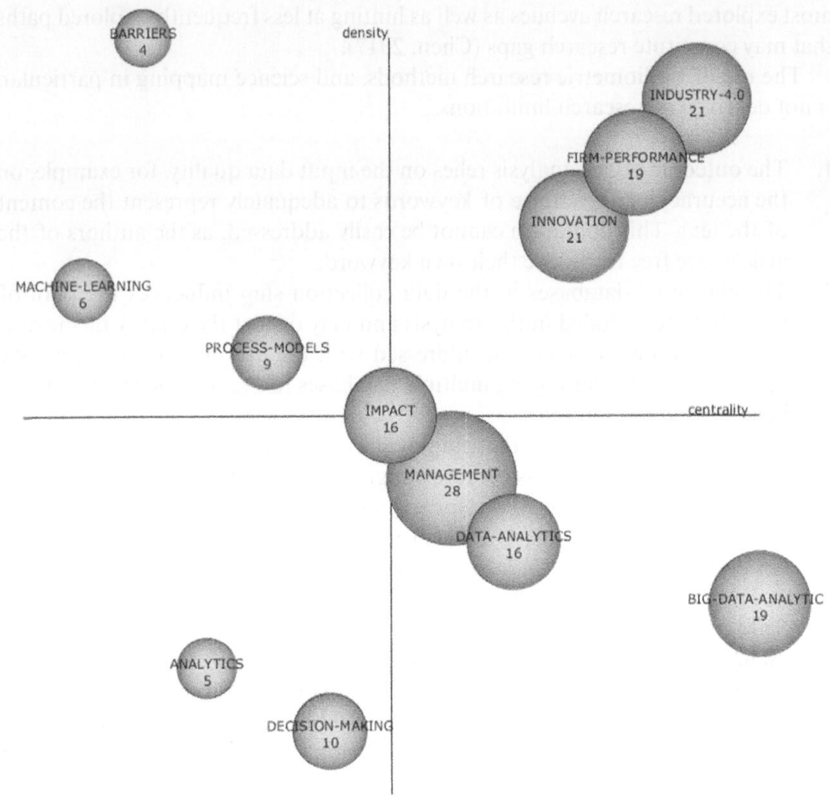

Fig. 10.3. Strategic Diagram of Big Data and Business Process Research Themes (Number of Documents). *Source*: Own research.

size (thematic network size) set between six and three keywords to ensure adequate granularity of the results. In the visualization step of the SciMat analysis performed in SciMat software, the strategic diagram of big data and the business research field was generated together with the thematic network of each theme. The strategic diagram is shown in Fig. 10.3.

The visualization of themes in the strategic diagram of the big data and business process research shows 12 themes allocated according to their centrality and density. The interpretation of the results of the strategic diagram analysis allow the identification of three motor themes (*Quadrant 1*) that combine high centrality with high density, and therefore can be considered the most well-developed themes in the analyzed field of study, which are firm performance, Industry 4.0, and innovation.

Further interpretation of the strategic diagram indicates three basic and transversal themes (*Quadrant 2*), which are management, data analytics, and BDA. These themes are not highly developed internally (low density) but are well-connected with other themes in the diagram (high centrality). Moreover, emerging or declining themes (*Quadrant 3*) are represented by two themes: analytics and decision-making. These themes are characterized by relatively low density and low centrality, which implies their proportionate insignificance in the big data and business process research field. Furthermore, three themes (barriers, machine learning and process models) were qualified as highly developed and isolated themes, which connotes a high level of their internal development but also implies these themes have been seldom researched in connection with other themes in the strategic diagram of the big data and business process research field. In an unusual coincidence, one theme (impact) is positioned exactly in the center of the strategic diagram. This location indicates equally moderate density and centrality, which prevents unambiguous allocation of it to any of the discussed theme types.

Each theme in the strategic diagram of big data and business process research can be further examined with the insight from their thematic network. The visualization and interpretation of the thematic networks of the three motor themes are presented to address the first research question of this chapter.

The thematic network of "firm-performance" in big data and business process research is shown in Fig. 10.4.

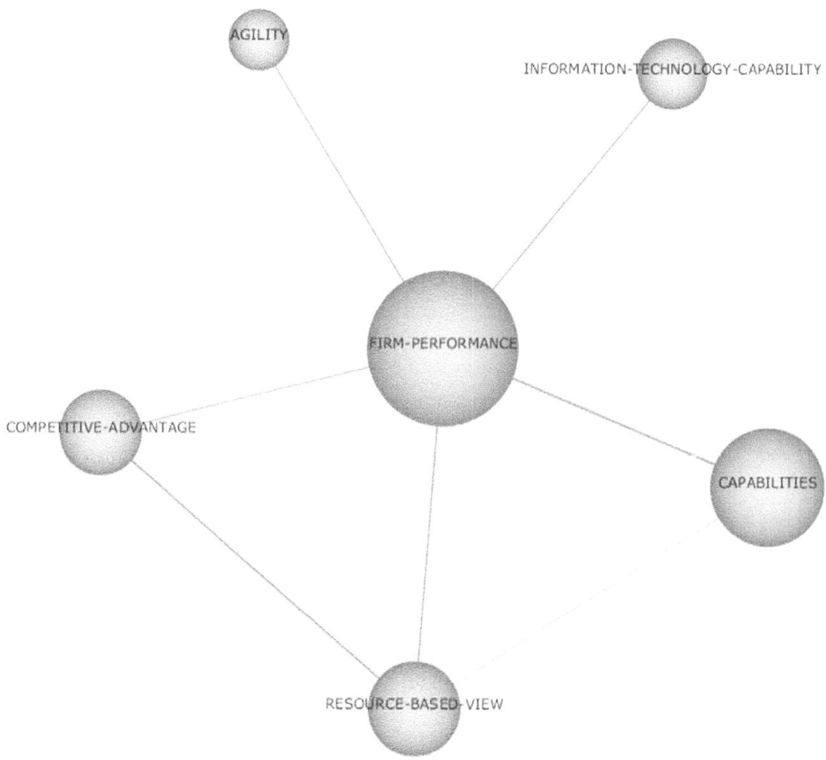

Fig. 10.4. Thematic Network ("Firm-Performance") in Big Data and Business Process Research. *Source*: Own research.

"Firm-performance" in big data and business process research is frequently discussed in connection with "competitive-advantage," "resource-based-view," "capabilities," "information-technology-capability," and "agility." A particularly dense network of connected research encompasses a conceptual network linking the research of "firm-performance" with "competitive advantage," "resource-based-view," and "capabilities."

The thematic network of "Industry-4.0" is the second motor theme, with slightly lower values of centrality and density than "firm-performance" as indicated on the strategic diagram. The thematic network of "Industry-4.0" in big data and business process research is shown in Fig. 10.5.

The interpretation of the thematic network of "Industry-4.0" implies that it is frequently jointly discussed with "internet-of-things," "cyber-physical-systems," "supply-chain-management," "manufacturing," "smart" in big data and business process research. Notably, there are two conceptual triads that emerge from the "Industry-4.0" thematic network. A particularly strong conceptual connection has been forged in the research between "Industry-4.0," "internet-of-things," and

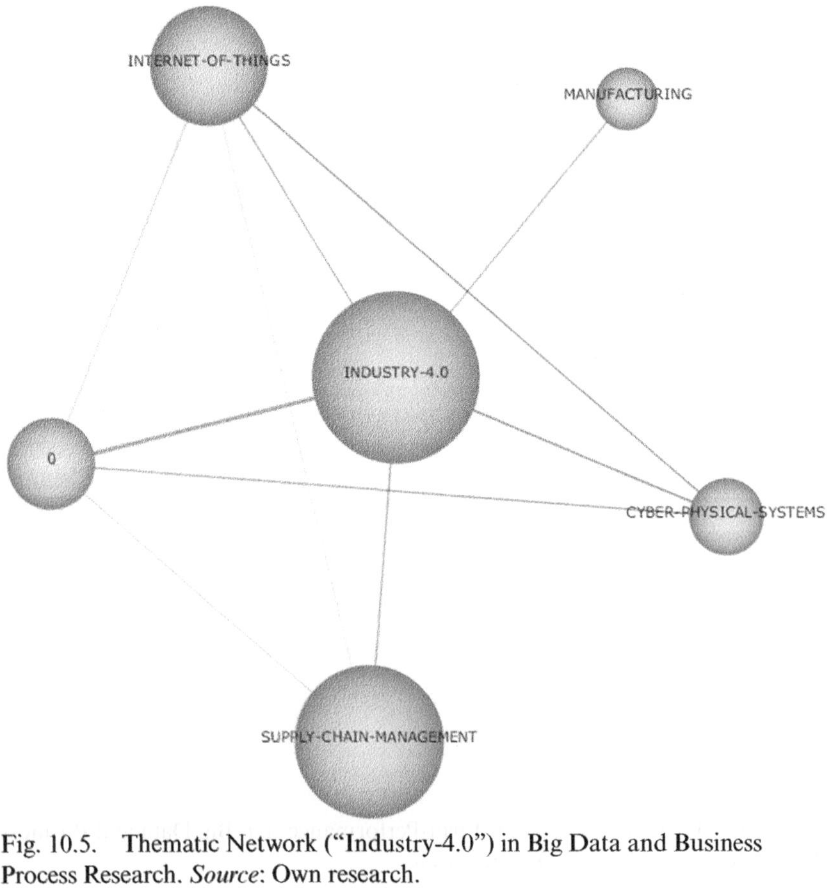

Fig. 10.5. Thematic Network ("Industry-4.0") in Big Data and Business Process Research. *Source*: Own research.

"cyber-physical-systems." Moreover, the three concepts of "Industry-4.0," "internet-of-things," and "supply chain management" are also well interlinked in the body of research on big data and business processes.

The third motor theme visualized in the strategic diagram of big data and business process research is "innovation," and its thematic network is presented in Fig. 10.6.

Within the big data and business process research field, the keyword "innovation" is frequently discussed in connection with "knowledge-management," "performance," "framework," "exploration," and "ambidexterity." In this thematic network, there are three subsets of highly connected research areas that include the following research axes: "innovation-framework-performance," "innovation-exploration-performance," and "innovation-'knowledge-management'-performance." "Innovation" is a theme that can be recognized as one with a relatively small number of documents, as indicated by the size of the sphere, compared to "performance" and "framework" in its thematic network, which may be a derivative of its superior network of co-occurrence with other keywords.

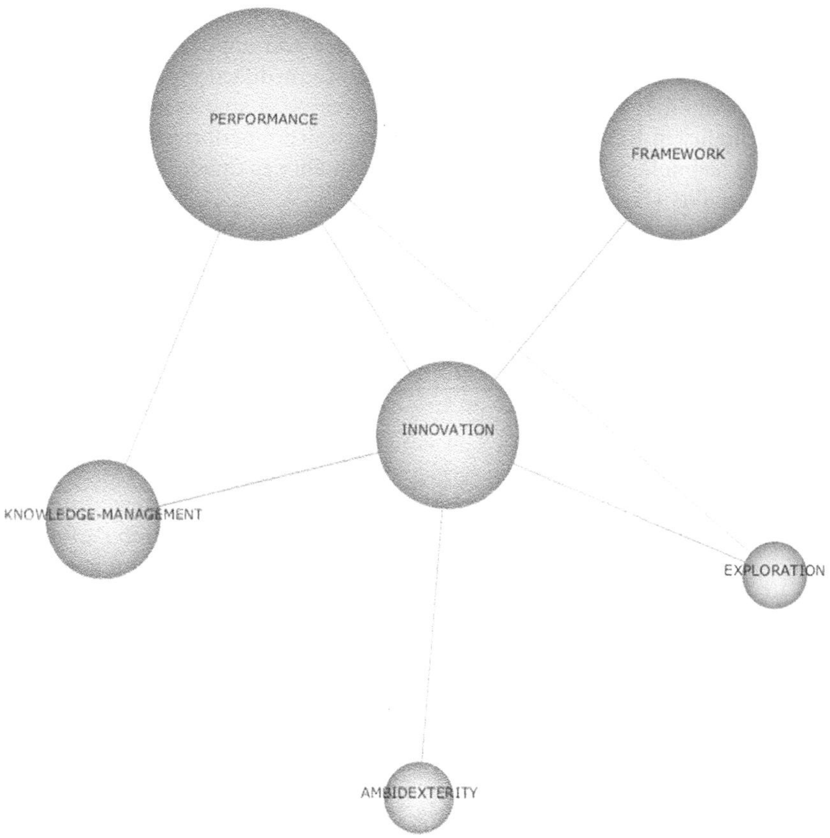

Fig. 10.6. Thematic Network ("Innovation") in Big Data and Business Process Research. *Source*: Own research.

4. Discussion

The outcome of the SciMat analysis of big data in business processes in the scientific literature revealed 12 significant themes with their leading motor themes that have the largest contribution to the research field due to their degree of development and connectivity with other themes. In this section, the content of these texts will be reviewed to add qualitative insight, augment the quality of the answers to the research questions formulated in the introduction, and enhance the chapter's contribution.

Firm performance has been highlighted as a motor theme in the SciMat analysis of the big data in business processes field of study. The high degree of centrality and density indicates that this theme constitutes a major area of interest among the research community.

This empirical study indicates that the adoption of business analytics, which includes big data, positively influences business process performance (Aydiner et al., 2019) and firm performance (Cao & Duan, 2017). Moreover, it has been argued for the existence of a positive relationship between business process performance and firm performance (Aydiner et al., 2019). Similar results were drawn from an empirical study on business intelligence and analytics that revealed a positive influence on organizational performance mediated by business process change capabilities (Torres et al., 2018). However, other studies indicated the key role of quality in BDA as a factor influencing a firm's performance, vindicating perceived technology, talent, and information quality as significant determinants of BDA quality (Fosso Wamba et al., 2019).

However, converting big data investments into firm performance may be a complex undertaking that may encompass four processes that require various areas of focus are: the asset-creation process with a focus on data and technology; the capability-creation process with a focus on skills and capabilities; the transformation process with a focus on organization management; and the competition process with a focus on the industry and ecosystem (Cao & Duan, 2017).

BDA are viewed to have considerable potential in enabling improvements in business processes. Through the conceptualization of BDA based on the RBV of a firm, it has been empirically verified that the significance of BDA resources varies but in some configurations may lead to significant incremental or radical process innovation capabilities. This is the case especially for top performing companies which by adopting a harmonized approach and investing in a broad range of resources are shown to largely benefit from their big data investments (Mikalef & Krogstie, 2020).

However, improvement of knowledge-intensive business process through BDA may require a more fine-grained approach that should consist of three distinctive phases in which BDA is used to support various areas: supporting individual knowledge-intensive tasks; supporting individual decision-makers and their ability to gain analytical insights and turn them into action; and sharing the acquired knowledge among decision-makers (Marjanovic, 2022).

Industry 4.0 has been identified as a motor theme in big data and business process-related studies. Its business application potential is viewed as of paramount importance, which is confirmed by a patent analysis conducted on The United States Patent and Trademark Office database shows that big data in Industry 4.0 is a significant patented technology field in the United States, second only to cloud computing (Ardito et al., 2019).

The conceptual study on the improvement of business processes and Smart Production Systems (SPS) as part of Industry 4.0 showed that SPS affects business process management (BPM) improvements and are based on three pillars: BDA, Cyber-Physical Systems (CPS) and Internet of things (IoT). The authors identified in total 26 drivers that have an impact on improved BPM clearly indicating the complexity of the research problem (Queiroz et al., 2020). Other exploratory research argues that the application of Industry 4.0 via technologies such as BDA, IoT, and CPS is expected to enhance productivity in supply chain management. The benefit is achieved due to the implicit integration and transparency of the supply chain as well as fast information exchange. These technologies are perceived as boosting the efficiency in supply chain processes such as inventory management, procurement, automation, and process integration (Fatorachian & Kazemi, 2020).

Industry 4.0 enabled by technological progress and fueled by improved data analytics can bring significant business benefits, as shown in a case study conducted on a large logistics-oriented organization that indicated its positive impact on a decrease in productivity losses, fuel consumption, air pollution, and noise (Hopkins & Hawking, 2018). Another case study that investigated supply chain process management in the construction industry showed that implementing BDA using machine learning and artificial intelligence (AI) to process diverse datasets could improve the rate and depth of decisions made by machines without human intervention. The authors also demonstrated that the consistent introduction of augmented reality, cloud computing, IoT, smart tracking sensors, and BDA could largely improve the quality of the supply chain and enhance participants' satisfaction (Patrucco et al., 2020).

Research on Industry 4.0 in the field of big data in business processes has also been conducted in developing countries. The empirical research based on a survey of Indian professionals showed that smart manufacturing supported by BDA is viewed as advancing economic performance by reducing the environmental cost, supply chain costs, and improving the return on assets (Raut et al., 2019). The result of another empirical study argues that the lack of motivation from customers/on adopting Industry 4.0 technologies, a deficit of long-term planning on the adoption of Industry 4.0 technologies,, and a lack of awareness about Industry 4.0's contributions to ethical and sustainable production constitute critical challenges (Kumar et al., 2020).

In the body of knowledge about big data and business processes, *innovation* is viewed as interlinked with performance in a variety of industries, organizations, and research fields. However, numerous attempts have been made to review the structures, mechanisms, and interdependencies to provide an adequate framework to improve the understanding of how the application of big data in business processes contributes to innovation.

In looking into AI-integrated data-driven customer-relations management systems as part of knowledge management in organizations, a framework of

16 success factors have been identified to support the improvement of business processes, with the support of top management viewed as critical for successful implementation (Chatterjee et al., 2020). Further studies showed that big data, with its prerequisites of management support, infrastructure, people, a data-driven culture, and absorptive capacity, can boost innovation and consequently enhance a company's competitive advantage. However, the company's success in this respect is conditional on adequate management processes, which includes goal setting, team building, metrics selection, and implementation planning (Kabir & Carayannis, 2013; Visvizi et al., 2021).

Moreover, it has been argued that BDA boost dynamism and greatly influence organizational agility, which contribute to dynamic BPM and the successful adoption of innovative information systems. It has been indicated that, owing to BDA, it is possible to collect diverse data and analyze multiple processes in real-time. Therefore, it has been advocated that BDA-capable business process management systems promote efficiency, effectiveness, and innovation (Rialti et al., 2018).

The application of BDA to the real estate industry can be considered an innovation that falls on fertile soil, as the real estate market relies heavily on databases, especially in terms of topographic information, micro- and macro-economic data, demographic data, historical series of transactions, and increasingly, streams of data generated by social networks. Consequently, BDA in the real estate industry is considered necessary to optimize decision-making processes and encourage better risk management, with significant consequences, in particular, for BPM (Battisti et al., 2020).

A rare example of an empirical study on innovation in big data and business processes literature was based on semi-structured interviews with managers in the oil and gas industry. The study shows that big data is viewed as a crucial factor for value creation through innovations in new products, processes, and services. The study argues that it has a positive impact on both tangible (organizational performance) and intangible (societal) aspects, but the application process could be challenging and time-consuming and largely depends on experts' tacit knowledge. However, if the application process is successfully managed, BDA can support managers in establishing an adequate strategy for the firm. Additionally, the authors affirm that big data is crucial for the oil and gas industry and encourage managers to invest in these initiatives (Sumbal et al., 2019).

The research conducted on small and medium enterprises from the manufacturing sector showed that intellectual capital (defined for the purpose of the study as human, structural, and relational capital) has a massive influence on balancing the innovation and exploitation activities of an organization (Troisi et al., 2021). The authors of this specific study reckon that the successful digital transformation to Industry 4.0 requires capabilities such as organizational ambidexterity (ability to be efficient in the management of current business demands and adaptive to changes in the external environment), which can be best accomplished by improving the firm's intellectual capital and enhancing the capacity to absorb technology-related knowledge. The study concludes that well-developed and ambidextrous organizations are more willing to implement innovation and optimize existing processes (Mahmood & Mubarik, 2020).

The findings of the research provide managerial implications, as it highlights that the implementation of big data in the organization positively impacts business processes, organization management, and economic performance. However, firms are required to build a bundle of related resources and competencies to effect the appropriate implementation of big data. Two of the key aspects are the substantive preparation of managers to implement big data and planning a long-term strategy. Thanks to optimized decision-making processes, efficient risk management, and innovation, a company can gain a competitive advantage and strengthen its position on the market. Nonetheless, the process of implementing big data into an organization should be considered a long-term undertaking that requires resources, knowledge, and often, a redesign of existing processes.

5. Conclusions

The use of SciMat analysis allows for quantitative insight into the growing body of research on the conceptual intersection of big data and business processes. The review of articles discussing the three key themes identified by the SciMat analysis has provided qualitative insight into the state of the art practice in this research field and enabled the authors to address the two research questions specified in the introduction.

The application of the strategic diagram tool in the SciMat analysis indicated 12 major themes in the research on big data and business processes. "Firm-performance," "Industry-4.0," and "innovation" were considered motor themes, which shows they are the most productive themes in the research interlinking big data and business processes.

The empirical studies on firm performance related to big data and business processes indicate that the adoption of big data business analytics generally positively influences firm performance; however, the positive impact largely hinges upon the quality of the business analytics. Moreover, to successfully leverage the potential benefits from BDA, managerial focus on data and technology, as well as on skills and capabilities, is deemed essential. Business analytics based on big data improve business process performance, which in turn could further strengthen their positive impact on firm performance.

In the research on Industry 4.0 in big data and business process literature, there is an increasingly common view that the implementation of big data within organizations could enhance productivity and improve existing processes. However, preparation of an organization to use big data is highlighted as crucial before data-driven changes can be implemented. The large variety of obstacles may interfere with the process, such as a lack of funds for investment in Industry 4.0 technologies, a deficit of IT-based infrastructure, workforce resistance due to fears of job losses after implementation, and/or an inadequate strategy.

It seems that there is an emerging consensus in the research on innovation in big data and business processes literature that big data is a relevant source of innovation in organizations. Moreover, it is broadly recognized that BDA have a positive impact on the improvement of business processes in companies. However, essential aspects that allow a firm to realize these benefits are proper implementation, an adequate strategy, and openness to innovation.

The findings of the research provide managerial implications, as it highlights that the implementation of big data in an organization positively impacts business processes, organization management, and economic performance. However, firms are required to build a bundle of related resources and competencies to appropriately implement big data. Two of the key aspects are the substantive preparation of managers to implement big data and a long-term strategy. Thanks to optimized decision-making processes, efficient risk management, and the use of innovation, a company could gain a competitive advantage and strengthen its position on the market. Nonetheless, the process of implementing big data into an organization should be considered a long-term undertaking, requiring sufficient resources, knowledge, and often a redesign of existing processes.

The contribution of the research conducted for this chapter is threefold.

1. The chapter uses SciMat analysis, which is an innovative research method seldom utilized to review an early stage research field, although it provides an initial review of a research field that has not been examined previously with the use of literature review methods.
2. The chapter provides an early assessment of the state of the art practice in the growing body of literature on big data and business processes and identifies themes that up to the present have generated the major focus of researchers.
3. The chapter provides a review and synthesis of the research on the three themes related to the conceptual field of big data and business processes, indicating its substantial business applications.

6. References

Al-Anqoudi, Y., Al-Hamdani, A., Al-Badawi, M., & Hedjam, R. (2021). Using machine learning in business process re-engineering. *Big Data and Cognitive Computing*, *5*(4), 61. https://doi.org/10.3390/BDCC5040061

Ardito, L., Petruzzelli, A. M., Panniello, U., & Garavelli, A. C. (2019). Towards Industry 4.0: Mapping digital technologies for supply chain management–marketing integration. *Business Process Management Journal*, *25*(2), 323–346. https://doi.org/10.1108/BPMJ-04-2017-0088/FULL/PDF

Aydiner, A. S., Tatoglu, E., Bayraktar, E., Zaim, S., & Delen, D. (2019). Business analytics and firm performance: The mediating role of business process performance. *Journal of Business Research*, *96*, 228–237. https://doi.org/10.1016/J.JBUSRES.2018.11.028

Battisti, E., Shams, S. M. R., Sakka, G., & Miglietta, N. (2020). Big data and risk management in business processes: Implications for corporate real estate. *Business Process Management Journal*, *26*(5), 1141–1155. https://doi.org/10.1108/BPMJ-03-2019-0125/FULL/PDF

Brinch, M., Gunasekaran, A., & Fosso Wamba, S. (2021). Firm-level capabilities towards big data value creation. *Journal of Business Research*, *131*, 539–548. https://doi.org/10.1016/J.JBUSRES.2020.07.036

Callon, M., Courtial, J. P., & Laville, F. (1991). Co-word analysis as a tool for describing the network of interactions between basic and technological research: The case of polymer chemsitry. *Scientometrics*, *22*(1), 155–205.

Callon, M., Courtial, J. P., Turner, W. A., & Bauin, S. (1983). From translations to problematic networks: An introduction to co-word analysis. *Social Science Information*, *22*(2), 191–235.

Cao, G., & Duan, Y. (2017). How do top- and bottom-performing companies differ in using business analytics? *Journal of Enterprise Information Management*, *30*(6), 874–892. https://doi.org/10.1108/JEIM-04-2016-0080/FULL/PDF

Chatterjee, S., Ghosh, S. K., & Chaudhuri, R. (2020). Knowledge management in improving business process: An interpretative framework for successful implementation of AI–CRM–KM system in organizations. *Business Process Management Journal*, *26*(6), 1261–1281. https://doi.org/10.1108/BPMJ-05-2019-0183/FULL/PDF

Cobo, M. J., López-Herrera, A. G., Herrera-Viedma, E., & Herrera, F. (2011). Science mapping software tools: Review, analysis, and cooperative study among tools. *Journal of the American Society for Information Science and Technology*, *62*(7), 1382–1402. https://doi.org/10.1002/ASI.21525

Cobo, M. J., Lõpez-Herrera, A. G., Herrera-Viedma, E., & Herrera, F. (2012). SciMAT: A new science mapping analysis software tool. *Journal of the American Society for Information Science and Technology*, *63*(8), 1609–1630. https://doi.org/10.1002/ASI.22688

Fatorachian, H., & Kazemi, H. (2020). Impact of Industry 4.0 on supply chain performance. *Production Planning & Control*, *32*(1), 63–81. https://doi.org/10.1080/09537287.2020.1712487

Fosso Wamba, S., Akter, S., & de Bourmont, M. (2019). Quality dominant logic in big data analytics and firm performance. *Business Process Management Journal*, *25*(3), 512–532. https://doi.org/10.1108/BPMJ-08-2017-0218/FULL/PDF

Fosso Wamba, S., Akter, S., Edwards, A., Chopin, G., & Gnanzou, D. (2015). How "big data" can make big impact: Findings from a systematic review and a longitudinal case study. *International Journal of Production Economics*, *165*, 234–246. https://doi.org/10.1016/j.ijpe.2014.12.031

Günther, W. A., Rezazade Mehrizi, M. H., Huysman, M., & Feldberg, F. (2017). Debating big data: A literature review on realizing value from big data. *The Journal of Strategic Information Systems*, *26*(3), 191–209. https://doi.org/10.1016/J.JSIS.2017.07.003

Gutiérrez-Salcedo, M., Martínez, M. Á., Moral-Munoz, J. A., Herrera-Viedma, E., & Cobo, M. J. (2018). Some bibliometric procedures for analyzing and evaluating research fields. *Applied Intelligence*, *48*(5), 1275–1287. https://doi.org/10.1007/S10489-017-1105-Y/FIGURES/5

Hopkins, J., & Hawking, P. (2018). Big data analytics and IoT in logistics: A case study. *International Journal of Logistics Management*, *29*(2), 575–591. https://doi.org/10.1108/IJLM-05-2017-0109/FULL/PDF

Kabir, N., & Carayannis, E. (2013). Big data, tacit knowledge and organizational competitiveness. *Journal of Intelligence Studies in Business*, *3*, 54–62. https://doi.org/10.13140/RG.2.1.4183.6960

Khisro, J., Lindroth, T., & Magnusson, J. (2021). Mechanisms of constraint: A clinical inquiry of digital infrastructuring in municipalities. *Transforming Government: People, Process and Policy*, *16*(1), 81–96. https://doi.org/10.1108/TG-01-2021-0014

Kumar, R., Singh, R. K., & Dwivedi, Y. K. (2020). Application of Industry 4.0 technologies in SMEs for ethical and sustainable operations: Analysis of challenges. *Journal of Cleaner Production*, *275*, 124063. https://doi.org/10.1016/J.JCLEPRO.2020.124063

Kushwaha, A. K., Kar, A. K., & Dwivedi, Y. K. (2021). Applications of big data in emerging management disciplines: A literature review using text mining. *International Journal of Information Management Data Insights*, *1*(2), 100017. https://doi.org/10.1016/J.JJIMEI.2021.100017

López-Robles, J. R., Rodríguez-Salvador, M., Gamboa-Rosales, N. K., Ramirez-Rosales, S., & Cobo, M. J. (2019). The last five years of Big Data Research in Economics, Econometrics and Finance: Identification and conceptual analysis. Procedia *Computer Science*, *162*, 729–736. https://doi.org/10.1016/j.procs.2019.12.044

Mahmood, T., & Mubarik, M. S. (2020). Balancing innovation and exploitation in the fourth industrial revolution: Role of intellectual capital and technology absorptive capacity. *Technological Forecasting and Social Change*, *160*, 120248. https://doi.org/10.1016/J.TECHFORE.2020.120248

Malik, R., Visvizi, A., & Skrzek-Lubasińska, M. (2021). The gig economy: Current issues, the debate, and the new avenues of research. *Sustainability*, *13*(9), 5023.

Marjanovic, O. (2022). A novel mechanism for business analytics value creation: Improvement of knowledge-intensive business processes. *Journal of Knowledge Management*, *26*(1), 17–44. https://doi.org/10.1108/JKM-09-2020-0669/FULL/PDF

Masoumi, H., Farahani, B., & Shams Aliee, F. (2021). Systematic and ontology-based approach to interoperable cross-domain open government data services. *Transforming Government: People, Process and Policy*, *16*(1), 110–127. https://doi.org/10.1108/TG-08-2021-0132

Mikalef, P., & Krogstie, J. (2020). Examining the interplay between big data analytics and contextual factors in driving process innovation capabilities. *European Journal of Information Systems*, *29*(3), 260–287. https://doi.org/10.1080/0960085X.2020.1740618

Moral-Munoz, J. A., López-Herrera, A. G., Herrera-Viedma, E., & Cobo, M. J. (2019). Science mapping analysis software tools: A review. *Springer Handbooks*, *1*, 159–185. https://doi.org/10.1007/978-3-030-02511-3_7

Patrucco, A., Ciccullo, F., & Pero, M. (2020). Industry 4.0 and supply chain process re-engineering: A coproduction study of materials management in construction. *Business Process Management Journal*, *26*(5), 1093–1119. https://doi.org/10.1108/BPMJ-04-2019-0147/FULL/PDF

Queiroz, M. M., Fosso Wamba, S., Machado, M. C., & Telles, R. (2020). Smart production systems drivers for business process management improvement: An integrative framework. *Business Process Management Journal*, *26*(5), 1075–1092. https://doi.org/10.1108/BPMJ-03-2019-0134/FULL/PDF

Raut, R. D., Mangla, S. K., Narwane, V. S., Gardas, B. B., Priyadarshinee, P., & Narkhede, B. E. (2019). Linking big data analytics and operational sustainability practices for sustainable business management. *Journal of Cleaner Production*, *224*, 10–24. https://doi.org/10.1016/J.JCLEPRO.2019.03.181

Rialti, R., Marzi, G., Silic, M., & Ciappei, C. (2018). Ambidextrous organization and agility in big data era: The role of business process management systems. *Business Process Management Journal*, *24*(5), 1091–1109. https://doi.org/10.1108/BPMJ-07-2017-0210/FULL/PDF

Santana, M., & Lopez-Cabrales, A. (2019). Sustainable development and human resource management: A science mapping approach. *Corporate Social Responsibility and Environmental Management*, *26*(6), 1171–1183. https://doi.org/10.1002/CSR.1765

Santana, M., & Cobo, M. J. (2020). What is the future of work? A science mapping analysis. *European Management Journal*, *38*(6), 846–862. https://doi.org/10.1016/j.emj.2020.04.010

Sott, M. K., Furstenau, L. B., Kipper, L. M., Reckziegel Rodrigues, Y. P., López-Robles, J. R., Giraldo, F. D., & Cobo, M. J. (2021). Process modeling for smart factories: Using science mapping to understand the strategic themes, main challenges and future trends. *Business Process Management Journal*, *27*(5), 1391–1417. https://doi.org/10.1108/BPMJ-05-2020-0181

Sumbal, M. S., Tsui, E., Irfan, I., Shujahat, M., Mosconi, E., & Ali, M. (2019). Value creation through big data application process management: The case of the oil and gas industry. *Journal of Knowledge Management*, *23*(8), 1566–1585. https://doi.org/10.1108/JKM-02-2019-0084/FULL/PDF

Torres, R., Sidorova, A., & Jones, M. C. (2018). Enabling firm performance through business intelligence and analytics: A dynamic capabilities perspective. *Information & Management*, *55*(7), 822–839. https://doi.org/10.1016/J.IM.2018.03.010

Troisi, O., Visvizi, A., & Grimaldi, M. (2021). The different shades of innovation emergence in smart service systems: The case of Italian cluster for aerospace technology. *Journal of Business & Industrial Marketing* (ahead-of-print). https://doi.org/10.1108/JBIM-02-2020-0091

Visvizi, A., Troisi, O., Grimaldi, M., & Loia, F. (2021). Think human, act digital: Activating data-driven orientation in innovative start-ups. *European Journal of Innovation Management* , *25*(6), 452–478. https://doi.org/10.1108/EJIM-04-2021-0206

Weismayer, C., & Pezenka, I. (2017). Identifying emerging research fields: A longitudinal latent semantic keyword analysis. *Scientometrics*, *113*(3), 1757–1785. https://doi.org/10.1007/s11192-017-2555-z

Wiener, M., Saunders, C., & Marabelli, M. (2020). Big-data business models: A critical literature review and multiperspective research framework. *Journal of Information Technology*, *35*(1), 66–91. https://doi.org/10.1177/0268396219896811

Chapter 11

Barriers and Practical Challenges for Data-driven Decision-making in Circular Economy SMEs

Anne-Mari Järvenpää, Jari Jussila and Iivari Kunttu

Abstract

The circular economy (CE) model is seen as an alternative model to the linear economy models, which seem to be reaching their physical limits. The CE business model aims to reuse materials and decrease the need for virgin materials. This requires the implementation of a reverse supply chain, close collaboration between actors, as well as well-organized logistics. For this reason, the CE companies have typically high demand for digitalized processes and the utilization of data on both operational and business development dimensions. Also the utilization of big data collected from the companies' business environment can provide new opportunities for business development in CE. Despite the fact that utilization of data collected from the business environment and operations enables data-driven approaches for various decision-making functions in companies, many companies still struggle to figure out how to use analytics to take advantage of their data. In the small- and medium-sized enterprises (SMEs), in particular, the managers are facing difficulties with ever-increasing amounts of data and sophisticated analytics. Indeed, prior research identified several kinds of barriers to the effective utilization of data in SMEs. Still, research on data-driven decision-making remains scarce in CE context. This chapter presents a case study consisting of seven cases, all representing SMEs operating in the field of CE in Finland. In the case study, the barriers and practical challenges for data-driven decision-making in CE SMEs are investigated. Based on the case study results, this chapter proposes that utilization of data, lack of resources, lack of capabilities, and regulation are the main barriers to data-driven decision-making in CE SMEs.

Big Data and Decision-Making: Applications and Uses in the Public and Private Sector, 163–179

Published under exclusive licence by Emerald Publishing Limited
doi:10.1108/978-1-80382-551-920231011

Keywords: Data-driven decision-making; circular economy; small- and medium-sized enterprises; big data; innovation; sustainability

1. Introduction

Whereas the current linear economic model based on "take–make–dispose" is reaching its physical limits not least due to the unbearable amounts of waste, CE-based economy system is emerging as an alternative to this model (Suchek et al., 2021). The CE incorporates a regenerative system that minimizes the entry and waste of resources, emissions, and expenditure of energy through slowing down, closing, and straightening the energy circuits (Geissdoerfer et al., 2017). CE is based on closed-loop production systems and material flows. It aims to reuse materials and decrease the need for virgin materials, which requires the implementation of a reverse supply chain and cooperation between actors (Urbinati et al., 2017). The principal logic of the CE is to convert waste into resources by applying technical or biological conversion. The outcome of the conversion can be re-used in an industrial process or returned to the biosphere (McDonough & Braungart, 2010). The business concepts related to the area of CE aim at addressing sustainable development needs by minimizing resource input and waste, emissions, and energy leakage without jeopardizing growth and prosperity (Urbinati et al., 2017). Sustainability enriches corporate value with relational meaning and dialogue by making the aims of the corporation more transparent and demonstrating mutual responsibility (Ciasullo & Troisi, 2013) for social, environmental, and economic development.

Technological advancements, especially in the past decade, have revolutionized the way that both every day activities are conducted (Mureddu et al., 2020). To be successful in the rapidly changing CE business environments, the companies operating in this area have typically high demand for utilization of data on both operational and business development dimensions. It is known that exploratory utilization of data collected from business processes, customers, competitors, and other sources enable data-driven approaches for various decision-making functions in companies. In addition to that, ever-increasing big data provides opportunities for innovative companies in new business and process development (Visvizi et al., 2021) in terms of, for example, material flows, customer behavior, or logistics planning. However, many companies still struggle to figure out how to use analytics to take advantage of their data. The managers are facing difficulties with ever-increasing amounts of data and sophisticated analytics (Ransbotham et al., 2016; Susha et al., 2017). This is particularly true for firms operating in the CE business environments, in which a firm may obtain significant competitive advantages by coming up with new innovations and customer solutions. On the other hand, operational requirements related to, for example, supply chain management, production, and material flows are significantly higher in CE business than in many other business areas. For the companies, data-driven decision-making can reduce costs, improve operations efficiency, increase stakeholder loyalty, and increase communication flows within the organization and ecosystem (Pulkkinen et al., 2019; Troisi et al., 2020). For this reason, it is natural that the CE companies show increasing interest in investing in business intelligence and other practical data-based tools that enable them to make systematic planning for the future at both the strategic and operational level (Järvenpää et al., 2020). Business data also provide the companies with a basis for rapid and rational decision-making concerning their key operations, including business and product development. However, due to their relatively small organizations with limited competences and resources, SMEs are often rather streamlined and limited in their financial resources and capabilities. For this reason, developing capabilities to utilize data in their business analytics and operations is particularly important for SMEs (Järvenpää et al., 2020).

This chapter considers the data-driven decision-making and management mechanisms and practices in innovative SMEs operating in the evolving CE-related industries. This study aims at answering the following research question: *What are the barriers and practical challenges in data-driven decision-making in circular economy SMEs?* This question is aimed to be answered at both the strategic and operational level through a qualitative comparative case study consisting of seven cases, each representing a SME operating in CE in Finland. Thus, this study presents a qualitative multiple case analysis using the case companies as a unit of analysis. For this reason, the study contributes to the existing research on data-driven decision-making and management by focusing on the SMEs. The study extends the existing literature concerning barriers to the use of data in a complex but increasingly important business area of CE. The findings of the study may also have significant managerial interest, given that managers, particularly in SMEs are facing difficulties with ever-increasing amounts of data and sophisticated analytics. This chapter is organized as follows. Section 2 outlines the theoretical background of the chapter, and focuses on four main barrier types. Section 3 presents the methodological choices of the chapter. Section 4 focuses on the results obtained from the analysis of the empirical data. Discussion and concluding remarks are presented in Section 5.

2. Challenges for Data-Driven Decision-Making in SMEs

The rapid progress in industrial digitalization has caused a massive increase in the amounts of data. This data, collected from the operational or business processes of the companies provide new sources of value (Ruohomaa, 2020). Data-driven decision-making is an approach to managing big data throughout the entire decision-making cycle of the organization, where the role of the data-driven management is to base business decisions on data analytic thinking to make use of data in prescribing actions, predicting future developments, and driving change (Troisi et al., 2020, p. 538). Thus, the impact of utilization of data on the economy has also been referred to as "the new oil" (Hilbert, 2016). However, large and multinational companies often have capabilities to fully deploy data in their business on both operational and strategic levels, many SMEs are still lacking competence and resources for data-driven decision-making (Iqbal et al., 2018). It has been shown that big data analysis tools and technologies as themselves do not allow the automatic attainment of innovation (Troisi et al., 2021), competitive advantage (Watson, 2016), or increased stakeholder value. This may be particularly problematic for SMEs that typically do not have capabilities or resources to allocate for full-scale deployment of these kinds of tools (Järvenpää et al., 2020).

2.1. Utilization of Data

Järvenpää et al. (2021) discussed what kinds of data is typically used in data analytics in SME context. The data can be (1) machine-generated – when it comes from, for example, machines, sensors, mobile phone applications, or computer networks; (2) human-generated – when it is collected by people, for example, personal information; and data generated in technology-mediated interactions via, for example, documents, emails, and social media services; and (3) business-generated – including transaction data from point-of-sale or enterprise resource planning systems (Olshannikova et al., 2017; Saggi & Jain, 2018). In addition, the data may also originate from company internal or external sources. The external data sources include open data, acquired data, customer-provided data, and freely available data (Hartmann et al., 2016).

Previous studies in the data-driven decision-making in SMEs (Iqbal et al., 2018; Kim et al., 2003; Parra et al., 2019; Ransbotham et al., 2016) have identified several types of obstacles and challenges in harnessing big data in the operations of SMEs. The challenges may include a low level of understanding of big data and classifying emerging developments such as big data analytics as hysteria and not as a viable business opportunity. Other challenges are lack of adequate infrastructure to analyze data, lack of in-house data analytic experts, lack of representative case studies, and success stories in big data analytics in SMEs. Lack of expertise in selecting suitable solutions and effort needed in order to understand the available data, as well as dirty data and other data quality issues may challenge the data-driven decision-making in SMEs. The SMEs operating in CE are likely to face these kinds of challenges in their business operations and planning. However, the CE SMEs also have their own, specific challenges that are related to their business area. Their key challenges are often related to materials that they are re-using. Material quality issues as well as the barriers related to the information exchange in material flow supply and demand, infrastructure, and transportation are found to be key obstacles for using data in decision-making (Winans et al., 2017). As stated by Strand and Syberfeldt (2020), external data may be the key asset for data-driven decision-making in organizations, but still most organizations primarily utilize internal data. In the field of CE companies, Strand and Syberfeldt (2020) found that valuable data for waste can be found external data sources: maps, orthophotos, and road data; property and civil data; and traffic and weather data.

2.2. *Lack of Resources*

Typical approaches to utilizing data analytic methods in companies vary from relatively simple statistical and optimization tools in traditional spreadsheet software packages to more sophisticated data visualization and analytics tools including descriptive, predictive, and prescriptive methods (Davenport & Harris, 2017). While large corporations can typically invest in specialist data scientists and in-house technology infrastructure, SMEs often lack both the expertise and the tools to benefit from data analytics (Parra et al., 2019). Ormazabal et al. (2018) and Rizos et al. (2016) have indicated that two main resource-based barriers for CE SMEs include lack of technical and financial resources. What comes to financial resources, it is natural that adopting data analytics tools and technologies require financial resources from the companies in terms of both investments in information managements tools and human resources operating these systems. In fact, inadequate information management systems have been recognized as one of the major barriers for CE activities in SME context (Rizos et al., 2016).

2.3. *Lack of Capabilities*

Rizos et al. (2016) indicate that the lack of internal technical skills is one of the key obstacles preventing SMEs from taking advantage of the opportunities provided by CE. The SMEs do not have the technical capacity to identify, assess, and implement more advanced technical opportunities that would enable them fully take advantage of CE-related business models. Consequently, these firms often prioritize technologies and tools which they are already operating. Furthermore, the SMEs may not have enough understanding on what kinds of technological solutions (such as analytical methods) are available in the first place and which of these methods could be feasible in their context (Järvenpää et al., 2021).

2.4. *Regulation*

Flash Eurobarometer Survey number 441 (*Flash Eurobarometer 441. European SMEs and the Circular Economy*, 2016) investigated what issues firms encountered when undertaking CE activities, and which of the following five barriers were significant: (1) lack of human resources; (2) lack of expertise to implement these activities; (3) complex administrative or legal procedures; (4) cost of meeting regulations or standards; and (5) difficulties in accessing finance (Garcés-Ayerbe et al., 2019). According to Garcés-Ayerbe et al. (2019), of those firms ($N = 7{,}843$) that had implemented or were implementing at least one of the CE measures the biggest barrier was complex administrative or legal procedures (perceived by 31% of the respondents) and the second was cost of meeting regulations or standards (28%). Despite the fact, this study was not focused on data-driven decision-making in CE firms, it can be inferred that regulation may also impact data-driven decision-making in CE SMEs. Regulatory barriers frequently mentioned in literature include, for instance, lack of consistent regulatory framework and obstructing laws and regulations (Hart et al., 2019).

3. Methodology

This chapter presents a comparative qualitative case study of seven CE SMEs, all located in Finland. The case companies provide services related to waste management, biogas production, material recycling, the manufacturing of products based on waste materials or consulting, as summarized in Table 11.1. The research data used in this study was collected by two rounds of interviews. First interview round was conducted by two of the authors that interviewed each company representative, mainly CEOs, in May 2021. The interviews lasted about 60 minutes each, and they were recorded and transcribed prior to analysis.

Table 11.1. Summary of the Case Companies Used in This Study.

Case	Interviewed Person	1st Interview Round	2nd Interview Round (Group Interview)	2nd Interview Round (Group Interview)	Industry	Core Business Area
A	COO	X	X	50	Combined facilities support activities	Waste management, recycling services, and solutions for households and companies
B	Service Manager	X	X	60	The treatment and disposal of non-hazardous waste	Waste management and recycling services for households and companies
C	CEO	X	X	80	The treatment and disposal of non-hazardous waste	Waste management and recycling services for households and companies
D	CEO	X	–	<5	Security services	Disposal of confidential material
E	Quality Manager	X	–	20	Hazardous waste management	Waste processing and disposal
F	CEO	X	–	10	The dismantling of wrecks	Recycling services for wrecks
G	CEO	–	X	<5	Management consulting	CE

Source: Authors.

In the interviews, the researchers used a semi-structured interview template that sought insight into how companies are utilizing data in strategic decision-making. Special attention was paid to the barriers and obstacles of data usage in the CE area. After the analysis of the first interview round, the second round was conducted by three of the authors as a group interview of the company representatives in November 2021.

The purpose of the second interview round was to validate preliminary conclusions, clarify some of the ambiguities and to gain a deeper understanding on the topic.

4. Results

In this section, we summarize the results of the analysis made based on the case-specific interviews. Following the research question, the analysis of results is divided into four sections, each of which presents the key results of the interviews in the four challenge categories identified from literature: utilization of data, lack of resources, and lack of capabilities, and regulation. Some key results from the case data are also summarized in Table 11.2.

Table 11.2. Key Results From the Case Data.

Challenge Category	Challenge in Cases
Utilization of data	Data is scattered in various information systems [F] Combining data from various sources is challenging and time-consuming [A] Pre-processing and cleaning of data is challenging and time-consuming [D] Manually inputting of data is needed because data does not automatically transfer between information systems [D]
Lack of resources	Inadequate information management systems [C] [D] [F] Current in-house information systems do not support ad hoc reporting and drilling of essential data [F]
Lack of capabilities	Insufficient competence in using existing information systems [A] [D] [F] Lack of capability in using and refining collected data [A] [D] [F] No in-house competence in developing reporting, automated queries [A] [B] [D] [F]
Regulation	The legislation must be followed, the data must be collected in the form required by legislation [G]

Source: Authors.

4.1. Utilization of Data

The reliability and data quality play a critical role in achieving the desired output. Challenges include missing data, wrong data, and unusable data (Kim et al., 2003), also referred to as "dirty data" and the cleaning of these (dirty) datasets (Iqbal et al., 2018). Many organizations suffer from data quality issues that may lead to bad decisions and a negative data-driven culture (Parra et al., 2019). Based on the interviews, data utilization challenges are mainly caused by various information systems, challenges in data processing, and manual data input.

> At the moment we are in the beginning in developing descriptive analytics, the challenge is that we are still cleaning data and there is a lot to do before we get descriptive analytics in sensible form. (Case E)

> We've never considered our business as data-driven, that we would collect and utilize the data. We have quite a few data collection points that provide fragmented data, which in turn brings challenges to the next steps, namely processing and analysis. Our key challenge is that data is not perceived as fuel for doing business analyses, our expertise has not evolved through data collection and processing. Our situation culminates through many reasons. (Case C)

For waste management company (case A) one critical challenge is that it is not possible to measure fulfillment rates for all waste containers. Therefore, there is missing data on waste container fulfillment rates. This is especially a challenge for optimizing routes of emptying waste containers because there is incomplete information for decision-making. Technologies for measuring waste container fulfillment are not perceived cost effective enough for the company to invest:

> Data is being collected from the fulfillment rates of the waste containers. However, we do not currently have a system that could process and analyze that data. (Case A)

The processing in that case requires real-time processing to be useful for the company. As has been recognized in the literature, the benefit for the company necessitates in addition to real-time data processing also relatively fast responses from the operational management (Watson, 2016):

> We found that processing information must be more real-time to be able to make the right decisions in the right moment. (Case A)

> We have the same system as other companies, and it doesn't meet today's demands. We collect a lot of data from everything, the

> biggest problem is how to put it together, automate processing and visualization. The resources allocated for doing this is scarce, as it has not been needed before. There will be more reporting requirements and the best solution would be reporting models. According to the provided models it would be possible to compile required reports from the data. (Case A)

The information systems used by the companies provide several challenges for the utilization of data. Many of the challenges that the companies face is not related to data analytics software or services by themselves, but to those information systems that generate or originate the data used for data analysis.

> We store information in several systems that do not discuss with each other. It is a challenge to make use of information from different systems. We partially lack data collection automation, some of the information is still stored manually. In general, the waste sector has a single ERP system in use. Software development has been a challenge, and it hasn't developed quite so quickly over the past few years. Knowledge management is not commonplace in any organization in this industry. We need basic knowledge and insight into how this is worth doing – and we need help with that. (Case B)

> Interoperability is a word I hope you write strongly down, it's a challenge in the big picture. It is not worth making solutions for just one company, region, or industry. Information must also serve statistics and reporting to the EU. This has been underthought from a waste management perspective – local and regional measures are made, and the connection is not open through interfaces forward. (Case G)

4.2. Lack of Resources

Based on the interview data, the main resource related challenges are lack of platform and lack of time. Rizos et al. (2016) has suggested that inadequate information management systems include one of the main barriers to CE activities in SME context.

> The challenge is that we have no data platform. (Case C)

> The main challenge is that we are not exploiting data to the extent that could be. We collect a lot of data, but we are a small company, and we do not have the resources (to exploit data). (Case D)

> There is no time to form essential (data) packages. (Case F)

> The same owner has several plants with same technology. There are weekly reports available that could be compared, but they are not used (because lack of time). (Case F)

Based on the interview data, it seems that the companies may possess remarkable amounts of data, but the problem is that there are no dedicated resources in the company that have skill, capabilities, and tools to collect, process, analyze, and interpret the relevant information to support managerial decision-making and operational management in the company.

> We have a lot of data, but compiling information into the necessary form and visualizing it is a stumbling block. For example, if I could get the information necessary for myself from the accounting, it would be relevant. (Case F)

According to the work of Ransbotham et al. (2016) despite the increased access to useful data, companies' ability has decreased to apply analytics insight into strategy and the challenge is to get useful insight for decision-making. They stated that companies are not effective to disseminate and use insight strategically.

4.3. Lack of Capabilities

When asked about the lack of capabilities as a potential barrier for data utilization in CE SMEs, the interviewed company representatives mentioned lack of expertise and infrastructure. Our interview data was quite coherent in this, and most of the interviews supported this finding:

> We don't understand analytics in a way we would be able to design a data platform. (Case C)

The interviewees' insights were in line with many studies. For example, Iqbal et al. (2018) stated that SMEs are still lacking competences and resources for data-driven decision-making and Rizos et al. (2016) indicated that lack of technical skills is one of the key obstacles preventing SMEs from taking advantage of the opportunities provided by CE. As SME's usually concentrate on their core business and competencies, they might miss opportunities to take advantage of data (Iqbal et al., 2018):

> We lead by emotion, not by information. (Case C)

Data utilization in SMEs is hindered by the fact that they are incapable to analyze data by themselves because of the shortage of data analytics expert and high set-up costs (Iqbal et al., 2018). Parra et al. (2019) found that the use of data depends on the senior management technological familiarity and that data analysis are mainly used rather at management level not operational. Nevertheless, managers data analysis expertise relates to tracking indicators, dashboards, and tailored spreadsheets (Parra et al., 2019).

> The biggest challenge is that the staff do not have sufficient competence to use systems. Activities focus on standardized programs and systems such as enterprise resource planning and customer management, staff do not have sufficient skills to exploit, and process collected data in Excel or PowerBI. (Case A)

> If the new system is easy to use, it will be easier to deploy it. Due to resistance to change, we need to invest in introducing a new system so that everyone adopts it, and no one is left to use the old one. (Case B)

Ransbotham et al. (2016) categorized companies at three levels of analytical maturity: analytical challenged, analytical practitioners, and analytical innovators. They suggested that analytical innovators are likely to have formal strategy for analytics focusing on skills development, data management, and cultural norms. To further clarify this topic within our case study companies, we specifically inquired about this on the second interview round (group interview) by asking the interviewees: "What kind of bottleneck is competence in utilizing data and what could help you to overcome the competence-based barriers?" Many of the company representatives named the lack of experience on data utilization as the main bottleneck. One central reason for that is the fact that the core business of the companies is not related to data, and the SMEs are reluctant to focus their limited resources outside of their core business area:

> Since we have not been engaged in data processing and utilization, our know-how has not evolved. (Case A)

> In the customer's experience and the end-user perspective, the challenge is to combine the substance into the digital field: to translate the hopes into digital so that an easy-to-use perspective could be made. Developing a customer perspective on the side of waste management companies is of interest to big firms. But it is often the case that is understood coding but there is no understanding of what it is in the field. (Case G)

> Waste management operators are looking too much inward. They should benchmark services from more advanced fields. In many areas, new services have emerged through the use of open data. (Case C)

The interview data also shows that the mindset and culture in the companies focuses on much on technologies and engineering thinking at the operational level. In this context, the considerations on data utilization or service-oriented business development may sound distant managerial topics:

> The waste industry is often focused on engineering thinking. We should emphasize the importance of customer experience, not just making smooth and efficient systems for ourselves, but that the customer could benefit and thus increase recycling activity. We could develop better service solutions for customers if we have a good understanding of customer experience and the ability to take advantage of service design. (Case B)

> It would be interesting to look at the exploitation of data across corporate boundaries. There are channels to which companies should export information, but we need solutions that go beyond companies and benefit the sector as a whole. (Case C)

In both interview rounds, the company representatives mentioned co-operation with students. Interviewees think that the students have better skills than their staff, and they think that co-operation with students provides valuable ideas for companies. As there is a shortage of data analytics experts in the labor market, co-operation with students could provide new opportunities for companies as well as missing case studies and examples of data analytics in SMEs. This could be one potential way of filling the capability in the companies.

> We can train staff, but we are getting ideas from students' projects that helps us significantly. (Case A)

> It seems like the student knows how to use these instruments (analytic tools) better than us. (Case B)

> A lot of competence comes along through students' work, but conversely, each company has its own systems for which students do not find competence. However, it is knowledge sharing and training, getting from students' know-how to the company and from company to students. I see cooperation with students as important. (Case A)

> Students are a potential resource; we have done several collaborative data analytics projects that have been surprisingly good. Students have such competence, e.g. the features of Excel, which we don't. (Case B)

4.4. Regulation

In the first round of interviews regulation and legislation was mentioned by several companies while discussing data-driven decision-making. Therefore, in the second interview round we directly inquired: Is the legislation barrier or challenge for data utilization? Based on the interviewees 'opinions, it seemed that regulation may cause barriers, but on the other hand, some of these barriers can be overcome by increasing knowledge and skills within the companies:

> Legislation generally speaking is a lagging force. (Case C)

> GDPR is often misunderstood (in companies) and the development might be stopped just in case. Legislation is important, you can take a great risk if you don't understand it. We need more understanding and a critical analysis of what the GDPR is and what are its requirements for data utilization. It hinders development because it is not exactly known what it actually prevents. (Case C)

We wanted to further understand, whether the industry is data-driven or "legislation driven" and to what degree does legislation impact at decision-making. Hence, we inquired in the group interview: Is the activity controlled by data or delivered under the coercion of legislation?

> The legislation must be followed, the data must be collected in the form required by legislation. For example, the EU Implementing Regulation defines that reporting of reusable building parts and materials must be done in tons, even if no such information can be found. What is asked can contradict what exists. (Case G)

> The idea in all legislation should be permissiveness for development, not to make a regulation that is locked up at this moment. Regulation should enable new innovations, new systems, and their exploitation. (Case G)

> If there is material, which is treated in tons, but the reporting requirement is cubic meters, measuring and monitoring may not go hand in hand. This will bring challenges and errors in the statistics. (Case A)

> Uncertainty where legislation is going to guide, meaning where we should focus on and allocate resources, or do we have any more interests in the first place – it is a legislative problem that cannot be influenced by ourselves, but to live with it. (Case A)

5. Discussion

The objective of this chapter was to increase understanding on the practical challenges and barriers to data-driven decision-making perceived by CE SMEs. In this manner, the chapter increases understanding of how data in its different forms influences the processes of decision-making, and management on operational and strategic levels. In this chapter, four major challenge themes were identified: utilization of data, lack of resources, lack of capabilities, and regulation. The CE SMEs had several data utilization challenges for decision-making. The data is fragmented in several information systems that do not communicate with each other. Operations rely to some extent on manually inputted data, and there are challenges in automated data collection and developing automated queries to support the discovery of essential information. Concerning lack of resources, the Finnish CE SMEs mostly highlighted lack of platforms and lack of time for hindering data-driven decision-making. The platforms that the CE SMEs use are mostly adequate for reporting but fall short on discovering and visualizing essential information.

Based on the interviews the lack of capabilities for data-driven decision-making in CE included some usual suspects. For example, lack of competence (Iqbal et al., 2018; Rizos et al., 2016) in data and performance management (Aho, 2012; Parra et al., 2019; Ransbotham et al., 2016). These results add to the previous studies on dynamic capabilities of CE firms (Khan et al., 2020a, 2020b) from the perspective of SMEs. Some novel insights pointed out by the managers include the need for a mindset shift from engineering thinking to design thinking: "not just making smooth and efficient systems for our selves, but that the customer could benefit and thus increase recycling activity." It was also pointed out that large firms are more customer oriented, whereas the CE SMEs customer perspective on the waste management is underdeveloped. This may indicate challenge the competitive advantage for CE SMEs if bigger national or international companies enter the same market. Interestingly, several of the SMEs noted that students, who they have collaborated with, have more advanced data analytics skills than they do and that the students can offer valuable help in capability development, and thus fill the competency gaps in the companies.

In CE and waste management industry the regulation and legislation enforce what companies must do, and regulation has been found as a barrier in earlier studies as well (Garcés-Ayerbe et al., 2019). It can be interpreted based on the interviews that in this sense the CE SMEs are more legislative-driven than data-driven. Reflecting on the MoSCoW method of what can be considered as "must have," "should have," "could have," and "won't have" for the design of data-driven decision-making (cf. Kollwitz et al., 2018), the regulation defines what must be done. "Should have" and "could have" in data-driven decision-making are something extra that most SMEs don't have dedicated resources or capabilities to perform.

The CE SMEs also recognized that they could benefit from open data, and application programming interfaces (APIs) for local and regional waste management data, which has been also recognized important in other industries (Jussila et al., 2019). One implication for policy-making in Smart Cities is that SMEs especially need support in terms of open data repositories and APIs to support their reporting and business development (see also Watson & Ryan, 2021). Most SMEs do not have resources themselves to develop needed interfaces for data flow and management. Instead, they need to rely on third-party information system providers that may not have the same incentives or need to meet the legislative requirements as the CE SMEs. Regional actors could pool together resources to develop information resources and systems to better support CE SMEs business. Increasing funding for CE SMEs development could significantly support meeting the European Union (European Commission, 2018) net-zero greenhouse emissions by 2050 and the national carbon neutrality goals.

Acknowledgment

This research was supported by the European Regional Development Fund Project Green Smart Services in Developing Circular Economy SMEs (A77472).

References

Aho, M. (2012). What is your PMI? A model for assessing the maturity of performance management in organisations. Proceedings of the International Conference on Performance Management: From Strategy to Delivery. PMA Cambridge11-13 July.

Ciasullo, M. V., & Troisi, O. (2013). Sustainable value creation in SMEs: A case study. *The TQM Journal*, *25*(1), 44–61.

Davenport, T., & Harris, J. (2017). *Competing on analytics: Updated, with a new introduction: The new science of winning*. Harvard Business Press.

European Commission. (2018). A clean planet for all. A European long-term strategic vision for a prosperous, modern, competitive and climate neutral economy. *Com(2018)*, *773*, 25. https://eur-lex.europa.eu/legal-content/EN/TXT/PDF/?uri=CELEX:52018DC0773&from=EN

Flash Eurobarometer 441. European SMEs and the Circular Economy. (2016). https://doi.org/10.4232/1.12668

Garcés-Ayerbe, C., Rivera-Torres, P., Suárez-Perales, I., & Leyva-De La Hiz, D. (2019). Is it possible to change from a linear to a circular economy? An overview of opportunities and barriers for European small and medium-sized enterprise companies. *International Journal of Environmental Research and Public Health*, *16*(5), 851.

Geissdoerfer, M., Savaget, P., Bocken, N. M. P., & Hultink, E. J. (2017). The circular economy – A new sustainability paradigm? *Journal of Cleaner Production*, *143*, 757–768. https://doi.org/10.1016/j.jclepro.2016.12.048

Hart, J., Adams, K., Giesekam, J., Tingley, D., & Pomponi, F. (2019). Barriers and drivers in a circular economy: The case of the built environment. *Procedia Cirp*, *80*, 619–624.

Hartmann, P. M., Zaki, M., Feldmann, N., & Neely, A. (2016). Capturing value from big data – a taxonomy of data-driven business models used by start-up firms. *International Journal of Operations and Production Management*, 36(10), 1382–1406. https://doi.org/10.1108/IJOPM-02-2014-0098/FULL/PDF

Hilbert, M. (2016). Big data for development: A review of promises and challenges. *Development Policy Review*, *34*(1), 135–174.

Iqbal, M., Kazmi, S. H. A., Manzoor, A., Soomrani, A. R., Butt, S. H., & Shaikh, K. A. (2018). A study of big data for business growth in SMEs: Opportunities & challenges. 2018 International Conference on Computing, Mathematics and Engineering Technologies: Invent, Innovate and Integrate for Socioeconomic Development, ICoMET 2018 - Proceedings, 2018-January, 1–7. https://doi.org/10.1109/ICOMET.2018.8346368

Järvenpää, A.-M., Kunttu, I., Jussila, J., & Mäntyneva, M. (2021). Data-driven decision-making in circular economy SMEs in Finland. *Springer* proceedings *in complexity* (pp. 371–382). https://doi.org/10.1007/978-3-030-84311-3_34

Järvenpää, A.-M., Kunttu, I., & Mäntyneva, M. (2020). Using foresight to shape future expectations in circular economy SMEs. *Technology Innovation Management Review*, *10*(7), 41–50. https://doi.org/http://doi.org/10.22215/timreview/1374

Jussila, J., Kukkamäki, J., & Mäntyneva, M. (2019). Open data and open source enabling smart city development: A case study in Häme region. *Technology Innovation Management Review*, *9*(9), 25–34.

Khan, O., Daddi, T., & Iraldo, F. (2020a). Microfoundations of dynamic capabilities: Insights from circular economy business cases. *Business Strategy and the Environment*, *29*(3), 1479–1493.

Khan, O., Daddi, T., & Iraldo, F. (2020b). The role of dynamic capabilities in circular economy implementation and performance of companies. *Corporate Social Responsibility and Environmental Management*, *27*(6), 3018–3033.

Kim, W., Choi, B. J., Hong, E. K., Kim, S. K., & Lee, D. (2003). A taxonomy of dirty data. *Data Mining and Knowledge Discovery*, *7*(1), 81–99.

Kollwitz, C., Mengual, M., & Dinter, B. (2018). Cross-disciplinary collaboration for designing data-driven products and service. In *Pre-ICIS SIGDSA symposium on decision analytics connecting people, data & things* (pp. 1–15).

McDonough, W., & Braungart, M. (2010). *Cradle to cradle: Remaking the way we make things*. North Point Press.

Mureddu, F., Schmeling, J., & Kanellou, E. (2020). Research challenges for the use of big data in policy-making. *Transforming Government: People, Process and Polic*, *14*(4), 593–604.

Olshannikova, E., Olsson, T., Huhtamäki, J., & Kärkkäinen, H. (2017). Conceptualizing big social data. *Journal of Big Data*, *4*(1). https://doi.org/10.1186/s40537-017-0063-x

Ormazabal, M., Prieto-Sandoval, V., Puga-Leal, R., & Jaca, C. (2018). Circular economy in Spanish SMEs: Challenges and opportunities. *Journal of Cleaner Production*, *185*, 157–167. https://doi.org/10.1016/j.jclepro.2018.03.031

Parra, X., Tort-Martorell Llabrés, X., Ruiz Viñals, C., & Álvarez Gómez, F. (2019). A maturity model for the information-driven SME. *Journal of Industrial Engineering and Management*, *12*(1), 154–175.

Pulkkinen, J., Jussila, J., Partanen, A., & Trotskii, I. (2019). Data strategy framework in servitization: Case study of service development for a vehicle fleet. *Springer Proceedings in Complexity*, 377–389. https://doi.org/10.1007/978-3-030-30809-4_34

Ransbotham, S., Kiron, D., & Prentice, P. K. (2016). Beyond the hype: The hard work behind analytics success. *MIT Sloan Management Review*, *57*(3).

Rizos, V., Behrens, A., van der Gaast, W., Hofman, E., Ioannou, A., Kafyeke, T., Flamos, A., Rinaldi, R., Papadelis, S., Hirschnitz-Garbers, M., & Topi, C. (2016). Implementation of circular economy business models by small and medium-sized enterprises (SMEs): Barriers and enablers. *Sustainability (Switzerland)*, *8*(11). Retrieved from https://www.mdpi.com/about/announcements/784

Ruohomaa, H. (2020). *Ecosystem-based development in the transition of fourth industrial revolution* (Acta Wasae). University of Vaasa. http://urn.fi/URN:ISBN:978-952-476-931-0

Saggi, M. K., & Jain, S. (2018). A survey towards an integration of big data analytics to big insights for value-creation. *Information Processing & Management*, *54*(5), 758–790.

Strand, M., & Syberfeldt, A. (2020). Using external data in a BI solution to optimise waste management. *Journal of Decision Systems*, *29*(1), 53–68. https://doi.org/10.1080/12460125.2020.1732174

Suchek, N., Fernandes, C. I., Kraus, S., Filser, M., & Sjögrén, H. (2021). Innovation and the circular economy: A systematic literature review. *Business Strategy and the Environment*, *April*, 1–17. https://doi.org/10.1002/bse.2834

Susha, I., Janssen, M., & Verhulst, S. (2017). Data collaboratives as "bazaars"?: A review of coordination problems and mechanisms to match demand for data with supply. *Transforming Government: People, Process and Policy*, *11*(1), 157–172. https://doi.org/10.1108/TG-01-2017-0007

Troisi, O., Maione, G., Grimaldi, M., & Loia, F. (2020). Insights on data-driven decision-making from three firms. *Industrial Marketing Management*, *90*(October), 538–557.

Troisi, O., Visvizi, A., & Grimaldi, M. (2021). The different shades of innovation emergence in smart service systems: The case of Italian cluster for aerospace technology. *Journal of Business & Industrial Marketing*. https://doi.org/10.1108/JBIM-02-2020-0091

Urbinati, A., Chiaroni, D., & Chiesa, V. (2017). Towards a new taxonomy of circular economy business models. *Journal of Cleaner Production*, *168*, 487–498. https://doi.org/10.1016/j.jclepro.2017.09.047

Visvizi, A., Troisi, O., Grimaldi, M., & Loia, F. (2021). Think human, act digital: activating data-driven orientation in innovative start-ups. *European Journal of Innovation Management*, *25*(6), 452–478. https://doi.org/10.1108/EJIM-04-2021-0206

Watson, H. J. (2016). Creating a fact-based decision-making culture. *Business Intelligence Journal*, *21*(2), 5–9.

Watson, R. B., & Ryan, P. J. (2021). Visualization and Waste Collection Route Heuristics of Smart Bins Data using Python Big Data Analytics. The 4th International Conference on Software Engineering and Information Management, 124–130.

Winans, K., Kendall, A., & Deng, H. (2017). The history and current applications of the circular economy concept. *Renewable and Sustainable Energy Reviews*, 68(October 2015), 825–833. https://doi.org/10.1016/j.rser.2016.09.123

Chapter 12

A Co-evolutionary Perspective on Data-driven Organization: Highlights from Smart Cities in the Covid-19 Era

Francesca Loia

Abstract

The growing turbulence of the external environment has progressively led to the necessity by organizations of exploiting new opportunities provided by data-driven approaches for supporting the even more complex decision-making processes. The new digital environment has led to the development and adoption of innovative approaches; also in the urban context which has always been characterized by different, interconnected, and dynamic dimensions. Urban governance models have been enhanced by smart technologies, which act as enablers of advanced services and foster connections between citizens, public and private organizations, and decision-makers. In this context, the objective of this chapter is to examine the role of data-driven approaches in the urban context during the chaotic and high variable circumstances related to the diffusion of the Coronavirus disease 2019 (Covid-19). Thanks to the adoption of the co-evolutionary perspective, a cycle in urban governance decision-making approach based on digital technologies is depicted and its contribution for managing the ongoing Covid-19 is traced. The results of the analysis highlight how the data-driven approach supports urban decision-making process and shed light on the co-evolutionary perspective as heuristic device to map the interactions settled in the networks between local governments, data-driven technologies, and citizens. In this sense, this chapter offers interesting insights, potentially capable of generating useful implications for both researchers and professionals in the public sector.

Keywords: Data-driven organization; big data; urban governance; smart cities; co-evolutionary perspective; Covid-19

Big Data and Decision-Making: Applications and Uses in the Public and Private Sector, 181–201

Published under exclusive licence by Emerald Publishing Limited
doi:10.1108/978-1-80382-551-920231012

1. Introduction

The last decades have seen increasing attention on social systems characterized always more by growing complexity. Starting from the problem of the limited information in the decision-making process, the higher and quicker development of always better data management technologies has recently contributed to making easier and faster the activity of gathering and processing large amounts of data with reference to specific process and performance indicators within organizations (Lytras & Visvizi, 2019; Lytras et al., 2020a; Troisi et al., 2018). Data-driven approaches permit to extract useful information from large datasets or streams of data. They can reveal insights by effectively supporting decision-making, also in the urban context which has always been characterized by different, interconnected, and dynamic dimensions (2021; Visvizi & Lytras, 2019), in which the decision-making processes are enhanced by smart technologies. The new digital environment fosters connections between citizens, public and private organizations, and urban local governance. Digital technology enhances strategic relationships by increasing transparency and involvement of stakeholders and reducing the informational asymmetry of decision-makers (Troisi, Grimaldi et al., 2021; Troisi, Maione et al., 2020). Thereby, ICT infrastructures and innovative regulatory framework can encourage a renewal of public administrations' approaches favoring more social accountable-oriented practices. The goal is to strengthen community-based initiatives and improve transparency and liability by guaranteeing access to information by holding stakeholders (Gaventa & McGee, 2010; Lytras & Visvizi, 2020; Visvizi & Lytras, 2019). The technological evolution makes it possible to gather and analyze data across machines, enabling faster, more flexible, and more efficient processes to produce higher quality urban services (Lytras et al., 2019; Lytras & Visvizi, 2018). In this scenario, due to the increasing information fluxes of data surrounding organizations' life, cities are required to collect, analyze, and interpret data to translate them into information to be used to enhance decision-making. While new technological tools have been developed, on the other side the major challenges regarding environmental, energy, and demographic issues require a change in urban governance models aimed at creating value and achieving a long-term sustainable advantage (Chui et al., 2018; Kearns & Paddison, 2000). However, the diffusion of the Covid-19 has more and more highlighted the chaotic and high variable circumstances related to the current social, political, and economic scenario in the urban context.

Based on these considerations, the objective of this chapter is to investigate the urban governance approaches based on digital technologies adopted during the pandemic by adopting a co-evolutionary perspective. Through this view, which is constantly used in social sciences (Abatecola, Breslin et al., 2020; Abatecola, Mari et al., 2020; Sandhu & Kulik, 2019), it is possible to describe the urban context through a multilevel approach (Benson, 1977). As a result, a cycle in urban governance decision-making approaches based on digital technologies is depicted and its contribution for managing the ongoing Covid-19 is traced. The objective of this chapter is to showcase how the data-driven approach influences urban governance and contemporary societies. That is, it examines how the decision-making process and strategy design process benefit from data-driven approaches and how it impacts the overall performance of a city.

In the remainder of this chapter, we present a brief introduction to data-driven organizations and urban governance approaches in the digital era. Then, the co-evolutionary perspective is applied to the urban context. Against this backdrop, the co-evolutionary cycle in urban governance decision-making approaches, based on digital technologies for managing the ongoing Covid-19 outbreak, is presented. Then, the proposed model is discussed. Conclusions and future lines of research are outlined.

2. Theoretical Background

2.1. Data-driven Organizations: New Shades in the Decision-making Process

Becoming a data-driven organization is currently a vision for several organizations. It has been frequently mentioned in the literature that data-driven organizations are likely to be more successful than organizations that mostly make decisions on gut feelings. Several organizations aim to become data-driven (Davenport & Bean, 2018; Halper & Stodder, 2017; Kayabay et al., 2022), since those types of organizations are likely to capitalize on business insights more frequently than organizations that are not data-driven (Kruschwitz et al., 2016). An organization has been defined as data-driven "when it uses data and analysis to help drive action – even if that action is a deliberate inaction" (Halper & Stodder, 2017). The use of big data analysis within organizations does not imply (only) the application of analytics. It requires the embracing of a total data perspective based on the careful selection of the right methodological mindset to extract significant information and meanings from data and gain competitive advantage from their employment (Gandomi & Haider, 2015). The data-driven approach, indeed, implies a broader orientation that envelops strategically data collection, analysis, and interpretation in all the phases. The willingness to collect useful data, which should be turned into relevant information for competitive advantage, should start from strategy and should continue in resource selection, technology use, capabilities application, and fit alignment, and should be spread across the different moments of value creation, from design to renewal (co-creation strategies) (Troisi et al., 2018; Troisi, Maione et al., 2020). The data-driven approach allows at combining constantly research and data collection activities with their proper interpretation leading to the transformation of data into information and, through incremental processes of exchange, to the renewal of the knowledge acquired (Troisi, Grimaldi et al., 2021; Troisi, Maione et al., 2020). The recognized need to change management based on the adoption of new technologies has been addressed in literature through the proposition of a new orientation based on a data mindset and on strategies aimed at improving decision-making (Lytras et al., 2020; Visvizi et al., 2021).

Troisi, Grimaldi et al. (2021) and Troisi, Maione et al. (2020) identify the key dimensions of data-driven approach:

- *Data-driven culture* is linked to the strategic need to establish – and, then, spread inside and outside the organization – an orientation in which data represents a key strategic lever for the enhancement of choices and decisions at each organizational level (Kruschwitz et al., 2016). By embracing data-driven culture, the ability to undertake efficient decisions can be improved thanks to the extraction of insights from data and to the continuous and dynamic adaptation to environmental changes (Medina-Borja, 2015).
- *Integrated infrastructure of smart technologies* allows at gathering, extrapolating, and managing information by increasing data accessibility and reducing complexity (Chaffey & Patron, 2012).
- *Data analysis skills* (Chen et al., 2013; Gupta & George, 2016) can transform data into (oriented) information, (finalized) knowledge, and new value. Users and providers should be able to gain benefits from data according to their own objectives. If, on the one hand, the main organizational purpose is to align decisions with strategies, users aim at gaining benefits from the purchase of services, by increasing their knowledge and experience.
- *Process management* between heterogeneous data sources which are processed and optimized within the different organizational contexts (micro-organizational sphere, macro-external sphere, and environment) in a recursive logic. Data analysis should be supported with the development of the right analysis and methodological skills (or through the recruitment of big data analysts) and with the management's ability to catch innovative features from data. At the end of the process, feedback, opinions, and insights (from users but also from managers and employees) are collected to produce new knowledge that can be stored and reused as accumulated experience for the restarting of the cycle.
- *Continuous improvement* obtained by the circularity of the data-driven process shows that, to manage the insight extracted, technical and management skills and people creativity can lead to undertake more effective decisions. This effectiveness can improve consistently over time by pursuing sustainable competitive advantage, co-evolution, and continuous improvement.

Data-driven organization, thus, requires a variety of analyst roles, typically organized into multiple teams, such as based on data analysts, data and analytics engineers, business analysts, data scientists, statisticians, quants, accountants and financial analysts, and data visualization specialists. In general terms, new skills and qualities are required within organizations, for instance based on the detail and methodological orientation as well as patience and curiosity (Anderson, 2015). Along this line, a data-driven organization requires the transformation from command and control hierarchies to post-bureaucratic organizational structures wherein employees at all levels can be empowered while simultaneously being controlled (Berner et al., 2014). The data-driven approach also impacts the decision-making process. Extant studies on information and knowledge management conceptualize an approach that leads managers to base their decisions on analytical and critical thinking, the data-driven decision-making (LaValle et al., 2011; McAfee et al., 2012). The aim is to ensure that the growing amount of data collected by organizations is translated into innovative actions. This can improve organizations' performance and lead to development and continuous learning. Data-driven organizations can apply data-driven decisions for all types of analytics (descriptive, predictive, and prescriptive), and all types of decisions (operational, tactical, and strategical). In practice, we assume that most organizations aim for a subset of combinations of analytics and decisions. Actually, several managers have taken several steps to initiate transformations to a data-driven organization, by introducing mantras such as "business insights are based on data and not opinions," holding large kick-off events, educating employees in Self-Service Business Intelligence tools, and hiring data scientists and artificial intelligence programers. Despite these good intentions, most of the organizations still struggle and few of them seem to reach their vision. In two recent surveys (Bean & Davenport, 2019; Halper & Stodder, 2017) roughly 30% of the organizations had made a successful shift to be data-driven. The other organizations struggled with their barriers or had not started to move toward a data-driven culture. According to Halper and Stodder (2017), the biggest barrier to being data-driven was "lack of business executive support/corporate strategy" (42% of 264 respondents), and the most frequently mentioned step managers took to develop a data-driven culture was "make the case to corporate leadership to invest in business intelligence and analytics" (57% of 230 respondents). In response to the low share of organizations that make a successful shift to become data-driven, Davenport and Bean (2018) suggested that organizations "... need more concerted programs to achieve data-related cultural change."

2.2 Urban Governance in the Digital Era: Opportunities and Challenges From Data-driven Approaches

Nowadays, cities are embedded in global systems and there is a growing need to ensure competitiveness in the urban context in terms of economic, human, social, and political capitals through innovative governance models (Zygiaris, 2013). Thus, cities should optimize public and private interests, local and central states, by working to develop common policies and strategies also by exploiting the innovative digital environment (Lytras et al., 2021). In our digital era, urban territories should implement a systems governance that aims at pursuing: (1) economic, cultural, and eco-sustainable development; (2) social inclusion and equity; (3) enhancement of territorial competitiveness; (4) improvement of overall quality of life (Lytras, Visvizi, Torres-Ruiz et al., 2020; Visvizi et al., 2018; Visvizi & del Hoyo, 2021; Visvizi & Lytras, 2020). The increasing diffusion of ICTs, big data approaches, and automatized techniques such as machine learning, has led to the development of smart cities (Nam & Pardo, 2011; Visvizi et al., 2021; Visvizi & Lytras, 2019), in which decision process are enhanced by smart technologies. Accordingly, the merging of computing, Internet technology, and telecommunications has supported the development of numerous integrated sensory devices that work together across larger infrastructures, focusing on data processing, exchange, storage, and security (Lytras, Visvizi, Zhang et al., 2020). Actually, ICTs infrastructure is related to numerous emerging and optimized technologies (e.g., Internet of things (IoT) and big data, along with cognitive computing, advanced analytics, business intelligence, 5G networks, anticipatory context-sensitive computing, and advanced data platforms warehouse) which act as enablers of advanced smart city services (Lytras & Visvizi, 2018; Visvizi et al., 2018; Visvizi & Lytras, 2018). The new digital environment fosters connections between citizens, public and private organizations, and urban local governance. It enhances strategic relationships by increasing transparency and involvement of stakeholders and reducing the informational asymmetry of decision-makers (Ciasullo et al., 2020; Troisi et al., 2019). Thereby, ICT infrastructures and innovative regulatory framework can encourage a renewal of public administrations' approaches in favor of more social accountable-oriented practices. The goal is to strengthen community-based initiatives and improve transparency and liability by guaranteeing access to information by holding stakeholders (Gaventa & McGee, 2010; Visvizi & Lytras, 2019, 2020). The technological evolution makes it possible to gather and analyze data across machines, enabling faster, more flexible, and more efficient processes to produce higher quality urban services (Lytras et al., 2019; Lytras & Visvizi, 2018). The varied set of new technologies that contemporary organizations can adopt, belong to two main categories of tools:

- Engagement platforms such as websites, communities, mobile applications, social networks to keep in touch with citizens and with a varied set of stakeholders, and engagement platforms (Breidbach et al., 2014) to allow the sharing of ideas, values, and proposition with users.
- Research analytics tools allow data collection and analysis through automatized instruments thanks to the application of methods and techniques such as decision support systems (DSS), cognitive computing, and fuzzy logic.

All these technologies and tools enable strong interconnections between technology, people, and institutions, three main dimensions behind the definition of a smart city (Nam & Pardo, 2011). As depicted in Fig. 12.1, thanks to the technological dimension, it is possible to enable the interconnection between the social and institutional levels (Ciasullo et al., 2020). In this scenario, due to the increasing information fluxes of data surrounding organizations' life, cities are required to collect, analyze, and interpret data to translate them into information to be

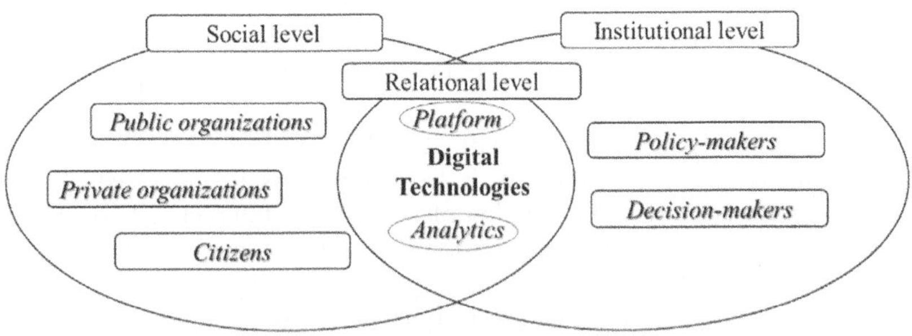

Fig. 12.1. The Role of Digital Technologies in the Urban Governance. *Source*: Author's elaboration based on Ciasullo et al. (2020).

used to enhance decision-making. While new technological tools have been developed, on the other side the major challenges regarding environmental, energy, and demographic issues require a change in urban governance models aimed at creating value and achieving a long-term sustainable advantage (Chui et al., 2018; Kearns & Paddison, 2000).

If governance mediated by ICTs fosters cities development (da Cruz et al., 2019; Kashef et al., 2021), nevertheless the application of technology does not involve the automatic attainment of competitive and sustainable advantage. The use of technology in urban governance should be integrated by urban entrepreneurship (Meijer & Thaens, 2018), which exploits the possibilities of innovation offered by technology through the adoption of a proactive mindset. Besides, the top-down approach should be integrated with the bottom-up approach, and there should be cooperation between public and private actors. The combination of top-down and bottom-up, and of cooperation and competition give birth to the concept of meta-governance (defined vertically and spread horizontally) (da Cruz et al., 2019). An effective meta-governance strategy should harmonize all stakeholders' needs to renew and regenerate cities thanks to the active involvement of private and public companies, citizens and civil society in the development of co-created decision-making (Alkhammash et al., 2019; Lytras, Visvizi, Torres-Ruiz et al., 2020). The main features of this new urban governance model are: (1) new power distribution (at the policy and institutional level; (2) decentralized and diffused decision-making that enables empowered knowledge exchange thanks to technology-mediated relationships; and (3) new technology-mediated interactions and new possibilities to collect data from users automatically and rapidly.

Infrastructure integration, technology-mediated services, social learning to strengthen human infrastructures, governance systems for institutional improvement, and citizen engagement are just some of the components on which new governance models should be based according to a smart city vision. An intelligent governance vision aims, above all, to exploit and coordinate citizens' enthusiasm and skills to represent their interests more effectively and efficiently. The awareness of the advantages deriving from the adoption of a smart city model leads to the emergence of social creative innovations, which in turn can ensure an increase in citizen confidence. Some scholars (Eriksson-Zetterquist et al., 2011) have highlighted how smart cities, understood as true learning organizations, are able not only to create, develop, and acquire knowledge but also to influence the behavior of people and organizations through the exploitation of new knowledge and skills. In this regard, collaborative relationships within a smart city allow overtaking traditional partnerships between public sector organizations, leaving space for the spread of government models that can generate greater value than the sum of the individual parties involved in the processes. Technological platforms designed to ensure high-tech performances must be properly integrated into social platforms, thus enabling all the actors involved to become an active part of value creation mechanisms (Anttiroiko, 2012). This shift of perspective gives a different role to the technological and social platforms, increasingly defined as facilitators for the activation of collaborative networks among social stakeholders (Wachhaus, 2011).

3. A Co-Evolutionary Perspective on Data-Driven Organization in the Smart City Context

The increasing complexity of external environment has progressively led to the emersion of the organizational co-evolution metaphor that has its roots in the biological concept of two species or populations which evolve, each adapting to the other. In the 1990s, co-evolutionary lenses were applied in social sciences and have positioned themselves in the scientific debate concerning opportunities and threats of applying Darwinism to the study of the organization/environment relationship (Cafferata, 2016; Grandinetti, 2018; Hodgson & Knudsen, 2010). Co-evolution has been commonly conceived as the joint and dynamic outcome of strategic objectives and environmental/institutional/external pressures (Lewin & Volberda, 1999). Every co-evolutionary process is also featured by the properties of interdependence and reciprocal feedback between and among different units of analysis (e.g., intra-organizational, firms, networks, or populations). A co-evolutionary perspective can be considered virtuous for the organizations when it creates social and economic value for all the parties involved (Cafferata, 2016), by combining the effect of the intertwined relationship between environmental determinism and strategic voluntarism. The use of co-evolution in social sciences is constantly growing (Abatecola, Breslin et al., 2020; Abatecola, Mari et al., 2020; Sandhu & Kulik, 2019) and an increasing number of scholars maintain that the current complexity of social systems can no longer be exhaustively explained through considering firms, and their environment, as single, static, and separate units of analysis (Abatecola, Breslin et al., 2020; Abatecola, Mari et al., 2020; Adinolfi, 2021; Bassano et al., 2019; McCarthy et al., 2017; Paniccia & Leoni, 2019). In contrast, the interdependent behavior of these units can be properly interpreted and, somehow, also anticipated, only through adopting a multilevel, dialectical approach (Benson, 1977), characterized by dynamic thinking in circles (Weick, 1969) and reciprocity.

Through this point of view, organizational decisions can be considered the fruits of the interaction of the decision-maker with the environment in a sort of learning path nourished by environmental feedback (in evolutionary terms, decisions could be called inter-actors). These decisions emerge from the combination of irreducible units of information (in evolutionary terms, replicators) made up of cognitive level heuristics and behavioral level routines (Breslin, 2008). Cognitive level heuristics include schemas, beliefs, and assumptions that provide perspectives through which individuals view the world (Breslin, 2008), while behavioral level routines include patterns of behavior that act as procedural memory (Breslin, 2008). These units of information evolve over time according to the threefold cycle of variation/selection/retention (Breslin, 2011).

Variations in heuristics/routines are recurrently produced in the brains as decision-makers interact with the external environment (Breslin, 2008); such variations can be unintentional when they emerge as the result of unconscious self-organization processes of the information units (intuition) or intentional when they are the result of the decision-makers conscious application of rational cognitive processes (deliberation). Here digital technologies can play an important role by allowing the collection of information units and their rational organization through the application of algorithms. These variations are selected by the decision-makers and become enacted, so the concrete decision is "a subset of a much larger 'pre-practice' variation mechanism" of the information units (Breslin, 2011).

Selection occurs on at least two levels: internal decision-maker selection and external environmental selection of routines/heuristics. The internal level is strictly nested within the external, occurring at a different hierarchical level. As Breslin (2008) notes concerning entrepreneurship that internal selection occurs at the decision-maker level while external selection pressures are more likely to occur at the organizational level. Individuals carry out an internal selection (vicarious selection) to anticipate selection by the environment: "The better adapted the vicarious selector, the closer the match between external and internal selection processes" (Breslin, 2011). Vicarious selection may be affected by noise in the feedback signal or by cognitive biases. These biases may reinforce positive feedback from the environment, leading to overconfidence. This in turn may influence the decision-making processes and internal selection mechanisms.

> Following success, this overconfidence can be self-reinforcing, with entrepreneurs exploiting current activities rather than exploring new ones [...], which in turn results in fewer variations [...]. The greater the effect of cognitive biases, the less strong the match between internal and external selection processes. (Breslin, 2011, p. 226)

Along these lines, digital technologies can offer support for the decision-making process, by containing the cognitive biases and processing the growing amount of data collected by organizations which can be translated into innovative actions critical for organizations' performance.

This Darwinist perspective emphasizes the consideration of novelty as the engine of any evolutionary system and highlights the need for variation alongside selective retention to address the complex decisional challenges of a changing, unpredictable world.

In this regard, the data-driven organization makes decisions by effectively and consistently utilizing data and combining irreducible units of information (in evolutionary terms, replicators) which evolve over time according to the threefold cycle of variation/selection/retention (Breslin, 2008, 2011). In line with a co-evolutionary framework (Adinolfi, 2021), such a kind of participatory multilevel governance can start from the diffusion and co-development of a cohesive culture to develop and implement policies according to a participatory approach. Each phase of policy creation and realization, from design to implementation and evaluation, is the fruit of the interaction between urban decision-makers and the stakeholders.

The iterative and co-evolutionary process with reference to decision-making in urban governance is illustrated in Fig. 12.2. This participatory process can be conceived as a cycle that starts with an exploratory phase and can follow incremental steps toward innovative hypotheses such as smart service development. Once selected an intervention, a process is implemented and managed during its execution phase in order to compare its performance with some indicators and evaluate the results. Positive evaluations lead to the consolidation of decisions and the establishment of organizational routines (retention).

The main steps of this model of participatory governance can be included in a decision-making cycle composed of the following stages: (1) exploration and alignment between objectives and community goal (variation); (2) choice of interventions and implementation (selection); (3) evaluation of interventions and consolidation (retention); and (4) potential continuous improvement cycling back to the exploratory phase.

The co-evolutionary cycle can be renewed over time (as indicated by the arrow in the figure). The participatory and multilevel governance regenerates the smart culture produced through the constant renewal of values and knowledge. The entrepreneurial attitude to innovation and the continuous development of educational, learning, and engagement activities can allow reinforcing the cohesive culture shared by actors. In this way, community members can reproduce the smart culture over time by adapting it to environmental changes and co-designing gradually the foundations for a smart future.

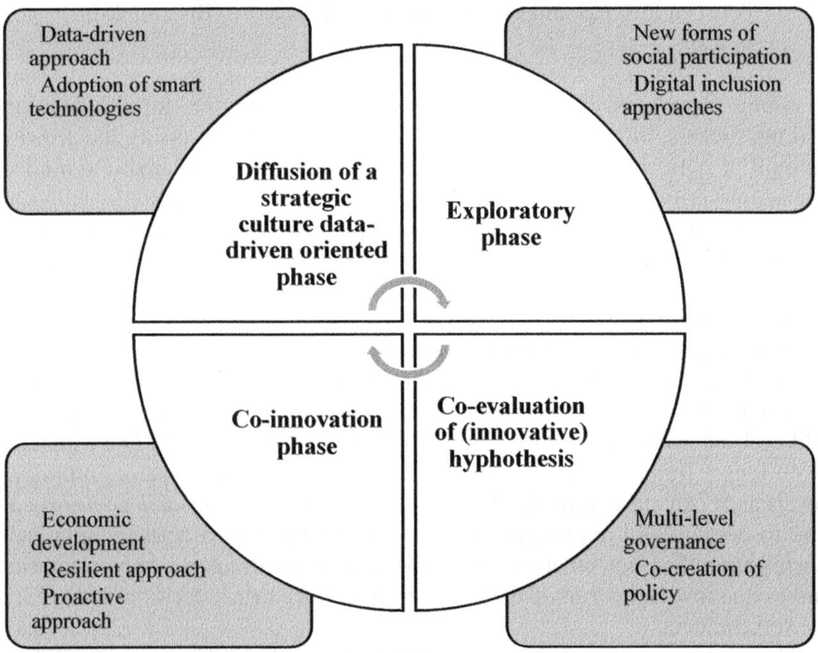

Fig. 12.2. Co-evolutionary Cycle in Urban Governance Decision-making Approaches. *Source*: The author.

4. A Co-Evolutionary Perspective on Data-Driven Urban Organization During the Covid-19

Covid-19 pandemic, also known as the coronavirus pandemic, dominated 2020 and 2021, and probably in the 2021 it still continuing to be a relevant topic from a social, health, political, and economic perspective. Covid-19 was first identified in December 2019 in Wuhan, China. During the annual Lunar New Year holiday, the infectious disease Covid-19 has started to spread in China. Considering that in this period people returned to their family homes and several billion people have traveled on crowded planes, trains, and buses, each infected person had numerous close contacts over a protracted time and across long distances. Thus, the Chinese government needed to quickly act: China focused on traditional public health outbreak response tactics – isolation, quarantine, social distancing, and community containment (Wu & McGoogan, 2020). However, other approaches based on sophisticated digital technologies have been applied by the Chinese government. In fact, Chinese government used data from enabled GPS in order to offer telecom providers a precise record of the user's itinerary. The authorities used this information to manage limited medical resources more efficiently by, for example, directing tests for the virus to high-risk subjects identified by the artificial intelligence algorithm. China, also, used electronic records of medicine purchases to identify sick individuals who may have attempted to flee quarantine (Iandolo et al., 2021). Therefore, data analytics helped Chinese authorities to establish the chain of transmission of the virus. On March 2, 2020, China reported only 126 new cases, compared to 851 in South Korea and 835 in Iran, out of a total of 1,969 new cases worldwide (Goldman, 2020). From here, several countries have started to use these techniques for the treatment, medication, screening, prediction, forecasting, contact tracing, and drug/vaccine development process during the Covid-19 pandemic in order to reduce the human intervention in medical practice (Lalmuanawma et al., 2020).

As synthetized in the Table 12.1, the co-evolutionary cycle in urban decision-making processes based on digital technologies for managing the Covid-19 outbreak has been theorized, based on several empirical evidences collected during the pandemic years.

In the first stage of the diffusion of the pandemic, data-driven applications have been immediately recognized as essential by several governments to ensure effective decision-making processes by urban governance. Since the emergence of Covid-19, the necessity of deploying technology to improve community well-being and maintain urban functions has increased (Sharifi, 2021; Sharifi & Khavarian-Garmsir, 2020). Cities have been recognized as the epicenter of Covid-19 (Zangari et al., 2020), mainly because high population density and mobility can increase the infection rate rapidly (Salway et al., 2020). The necessity of using technology and innovative solutions to deal with the pandemic has been emphasized by all health-related organizations (Salway et al., 2020). Data-driven smart solutions based on an urban platforms have been defined in order to deal with the spread of the virus and to guarantee citizen well-being (Petrović et al., 2021). For instance, in the UK, Newcastle, the largest city in the North East of

Table 12.1. Co-evolutionary Cycle in Urban Governance Decision-making Approaches Based on Digital Technologies for Managing the Ongoing Covid-19 Outbreak.

Temporal Impact	Phases of Co-evolutionary Cycle	Description	Examples in Urban Governance
Short term	*Diffusion of a strategic culture data-driven oriented phase*	Adoption of data-driven approaches and implementation of smart technologies to curb the spread of Covid-19	Readaptation of urban data platform for monitoring the implementation of policies to prevent the spread of Covid-19 and social well-being
Medium term	*Exploratory phase*	Exploration and alignment between governance objectives and community goal (*variation*)	Exploration of technologies already defined for the real-time epidemiologic data collection and analysis, risk assessment, support in the decision-making processes, and design/implementation of public health initiatives
Medium term	*Co-evaluation of (innovative) hypothesis*	Choice of interventions and implementation (*selection*)	Evaluation of new urban governance approaches such as based on mobile applications, smart technologies have guaranteed a quick Covid-19 patient assessment based on user-provided symptoms integrated with contact tracing, volunteer help during quarantine; unmanned aerial vehicle-based Covid-19 outdoor safety surveillance, test scheduling, and augmented reality-based pharmacy shop assistant
Long term	*Co-innovation phase*	Interventions' evaluation and consolidation (*retention*)	Design new standardized protocols for sharing data and information during emergencies; definition of standardization and interoperability of data; enhancement of data security; and improvement of digital skills

Source: Author's elaboration.

England established a comprehensive observation platform to capture and monitor complex interactions as a result of planned and unplanned interventions in the city. The Newcastle Urban Observatory (UO) program was developed on the ethos of open data for social well-being and a large-scale, real-time, data capture infrastructure has been developed over several years with the aim of monitoring many aspects of urban landscapes. The data elaboration offers a wide range of city metrics including mobility (traffic flows, congestion, car park occupancy, and bus GPS tracks), pedestrian flows, environmental indicators of air quality (e.g., NO_2, NO, Ozone, PM2.5, and PM10), climatic variables (wind, rainfall, temperature, and humidity), infrastructure (energy usage, water flows, water quality, etc.), and many more. With the spread of Covid-19, a team of data scientists and programers used sensor data to create data visualizations collated in the form of a dashboard. On the week prior to the full lockdown announcement in the UK, elaborations suggested that the roads were quieter and there were fewer people on city streets. Following the initial findings, the UO research team realized that there was an opportunity to highlight the value of high-temporal resolution city data as a means of understanding the efficacy of policy interventions and the wider social response in real time for researchers and urban governments. While the automated collection and curation of smart city data was already in place in Newcastle, and mechanisms existed for accessing and downloading the data via Application Programming Interfaces, improving usability for the specific lens of Covid-19 impacts required further data integration, analysis, and visualization. To provide a more valuable service to track the impact of the Covid-19 policy response, a dashboard was developed by repurposing the live data feeds. The first version was developed in 48 hours using information from pedestrian, traffic, car park, and air quality sensors. The system updates in real time showing the status across multiple indicators. Visualization in graphical form, data download, and basic change against baselines were provided (James et al., 2020).

In the exploratory phase, during the first times of diffusion, data-driven approaches have helped in handling the huge, unprecedented amount of data derived from public health surveillance, real-time epidemic outbreaks monitoring, trend nowcasting/forecasting, regular situation briefing and updating from governmental institutions and organisms, and health facility utilization information (Bragazzi et al., 2020). Several digital solutions have been developed during the pandemic to implement a strategy to contain the virus spread, monitor human stress, and collective well-being, and collect complex space-time events related to Covid-19 safety measures (Basmi et al., 2021). As happened in several smart cities, the proper combination of a contact-tracing app, robots, and digital thermal-gantries put in place by the government to trace, track, and mitigate the early first wave of the pandemic along with the civil society involvements to manage the spread of the virus proved essential for containing the pandemic crisis (Söderström et al., 2020). Several countries – such as Ecuador, Brazil, Mexico, USA, and Europe – have invested in their capacity to gather, analyze, act around, and communicate data (Bloomberg Cities Network, 2020; Fernández-Naranjo et al., 2021; Pereira et al., 2020). By utilizing already existing smart city systems, IoT sensors, and machine learning techniques, data-driven approaches were rapidly implemented to provide timely support in real time for policy decisions as complex events played out. Digital structure was already in place with sensors and data infrastructures which had already been established/installed by several cities over the last five years with the aim to collect long-term data baselines and obtain city metrics which are critical to capture the interdependencies and linkages in complex systems as urban context. In this sense Covid-19 has demonstrated there is a genuine demand for real-time data and analytics in a city context (James et al., 2020).

During the co-evaluation of innovative hypothesis, data-driven approaches have been widely disseminated in urban governance as well as innovative services such as mobile applications were developed, for instance using AppSheet and Google Apps Script technologies, in order to prevent the spread of Covid-19 and provide support to (potentially) infected citizens. In this sense, smart technologies have guaranteed a quick Covid-19 patient assessment based on user-provided symptoms integrated with contact tracing, volunteer help during quarantine, drones for outdoor safety surveillance, and test scheduling and augmented reality-based pharmacy shop assistant (Petrović et al., 2021).

In the co-innovation phase, the interventions defined have been consolidated in the decision-making urban governance approaches based on designing new standardized protocols for sharing data and information during emergencies (Bragazzi et al., 2020). Further efforts should be done by urban governments in order to deeply implement such approaches in their strategies. For instance, some actions need to be prioritized:

- Ensure standardization and interoperability of data and smart city systems by formulating city-based technology management policies (Troisi, Fenza et al., 2022).
- Enhance data security and protection through the development of data policies in compliance with national laws and guidelines (Wylde et al., 2022).
- Establishment of new mechanisms for information sharing among city and state governments (Gavurova et al., 2022).
- Establishment of adequately data management organization which includes a chief city data officer (World Economic Forum, 2020).
- Definition of objective indicators for monitoring service delivery by developing assessment frameworks (World Economic Forum, 2020).
- Improvement of citizens, governments, and organizations digital skills for increasing the propensity of urban government to adopt new technologies (Azoulay & Jones, 2020; Troisi, Kashef et al., 2022).

5. Toward a Co-Evolutionary Cycle in Urban Governance: New Challenges and Opportunities for Decision-Making Based on Data-Driven Approach

Based on the innovative adoption of a co-evolutionary perspective for re-reading the urban governance approaches, several reflections could be drawn considering the contribution of digital technologies in containing the Covid-19 pandemic spreads.

An urban data-driven approach, indeed, can allow for combining constantly research and data collection activities with their proper interpretation leading to the transformation of data into information and, through incremental processes of exchange, to the renewal of the knowledge acquired. Thus, there is the necessity to redefine and reframe the urban governance framework in order to include emerging technologies effectively in the territorial strategies.

By embracing this Darwinist perspective, novelty is considered as the engine of any evolutionary system, including also the urban context. The exploration, choice, and evaluation of innovative approaches based on digital technologies have become increasingly central to addressing the complex decisional challenges of a changing, dynamic, and always more unpredictable urban environment.

This work, in an original way, outlines the iterative and co-evolutionary process with reference to decision-making in urban governance defining the participatory process as a cycle that starts with an exploratory phase and can follow incremental steps toward innovative hypotheses. As has happened in recent years, urban governance has been driven to innovate in order to contain the spread of the virus and mitigate the economic, political, and social crisis.

Once selected and implemented several interventions, the positive evaluations obtained from local and national governments have led to the consolidation of innovative hypotheses and the establishment of new organizational routines within urban governance based on a data-driven approach. The participatory governance model, as defined in Section 3, is based on the main steps that can be included in a decision-making cycle. In the step of exploration and alignment between objectives and community goal (variation), the urban data platforms have been readapted during the pandemic in order to prevent the diffusion of the Covid-19. During the choice of interventions, new approaches have been defined by the urban governance such as based on real-time epidemiologic data collection and analysis. In the third step, the interventions based on smart technologies have been evaluated and consolidated. Finally, potential continuous improvement cycling pushes to define new standardized protocols.

In this regard, participatory multilevel governance appears to be the most appropriate approach through which supporting the diffusion and co-development of a cohesive culture among stakeholders. Each phase of policy creation and realization, from design to implementation and evaluation is the fruit of the interaction between urban decision-makers and stakeholders. Users are utilizing digital and social platforms to prevent the spread of Covid-19 as well they are improving their digital skills for sharing information and services with the institutions. The participatory and multilevel governance regenerates the smart culture produced through the constant renewal of values and knowledge. The entrepreneurial attitude to innovation and the continuous development of educational, learning, and engagement activities can allow reinforcing the cohesive culture shared by actors. In this way, community members can reproduce the smart culture over time by adapting it to environmental changes and co-designing gradually the foundations for a smart future.

In such a direction, new rules are emerging and multiple changes are required to both individuals and urban governments engaged in dynamic paths for unlocking the unlimited and growing potential of digital technologies (Lytras et al., 2021; Troisi, Fenza et al., 2022; Troisi, Kashef et al., 2022; Visvizi et al., 2018). In such a direction, several efforts from the urban governments are required for helping to mitigate the sudden changes due to health and economic crisis, for offering takeaways on managing Covid-19's urban impact, and for enhancing implications for multilevel governance, as well as developing considerations for policy-makers for building more resilient cities.

6. Implications, Conclusions, and Future Lines of Research

Covid-19 shed light on a major challenge, not only in terms of global health, but also in the way the possibly contagious cities are managed in the wake of a pandemic and also beyond. Besides the health, economic, and social challenges due to the spread of Covid-19, empirical evidence highlighted the highly heterogenous crisis from the urban point of view which requires significant implications in terms of governance approaches.

From a theoretical point of view, this work highlights, for the first time, the relevant contribution of the co-evolutionary perspective in the urban governance context. A co-evolutionary perspective, indeed, can be considered virtuous for analyzing the organizations, including urban systems, as it can emphasize the effect of the intertwined relationship between environmental determinism and strategic voluntarism. As demonstrated by the use of co-evolution in social sciences (Abatecola, Breslin et al., 2020; Abatecola, Mari et al., 2020; Sandhu & Kulik, 2019), the current complexity of social systems can no longer be exhaustively explained by considering urban governance, and their environment, as single, static, and separate units of analysis (Abatecola, Breslin et al., 2020; Abatecola, Mari et al., 2020; Adinolfi, 2021; Bassano et al., 2019; McCarthy et al., 2017; Paniccia & Leoni, 2019). On the contrary, the interdependent behavior between decision-makers and external environment can be properly interpreted and, somehow, also anticipated, only through adopting a multilevel approach.

On the other hand, from a managerial perspective, this work, in an innovative way, offers interesting insights by highlighting the co-evolutionary cycle in urban governance decision-making approaches based on four main steps. Urban managers, through the definition of exploration, choice, and evaluation steps, can be supported to address the complex decisional challenges of a changing, dynamic, and always more unpredictable urban environment. Furthermore, this work underlines how the data-driven approach affects urban decision-making. An urban data-driven approach, how revealed by the empirical evidence, can allow for combining constantly research and data collection activities with their proper interpretation leading to the transformation of data into information and, through incremental processes of exchange, to the renewal of the knowledge acquired by decision-makers. The data-driven approach, thus, deeply influences contemporary societies, by supporting the decision-making process and impacting the strategy setting and overall performance in several domains, including the urban government's sector. Thus, there is the necessity to redefine and reframe the urban governance framework in order to include emerging technologies effectively in the territorial strategies.

However, although the pandemic has strongly pushed the adoption of digital technologies into governance approaches, several barriers should be addressed to make future urban governments more effective. Overall, future research efforts could investigate new approaches aimed at supporting the standardization, interoperability, security, and protection of urban data through the development of appropriate data policies. Future research could focus on privacy issues which could be balanced with the communication of the potential value of big data analytics and with the governance openness and transparency. Furthermore, new mechanisms for information sharing among city and state governments should be defined in order to improve the connections between stakeholders and urban decision-makers, and policy-makers. Along these lines, an adequately urban data management organization and the role of the chief city data officer should be defined in a widespread manner with the aim to support this new orientation based on a data mindset and on strategies aimed at improving decision-making. Also, the lack of digital skills of citizens, governments, and organizations should be addressed in order to increase the propensity of urban government to adopt new technologies.

By concluding, in the urban environments, new ecosystems of innovative urban governance have been emerging with the potential to re-shape the approaches adopted by policy-makers and parameters of urban decision-making, by offering new institutional settings and reconstituting cities' multiscalar relations. This new approach refers not only to the current situation characterized by the chaotic and high variable circumstances related to the pandemic but also to a long period, with the aim to build a more sustainable and safe future in the urban context.

References

Abatecola, G., Breslin, D., & Kask, J. (2020). Do organizations really co-evolve? Problematizing co-evolutionary change in management and organization studies. *Technological Forecasting and Social Change*, *155*, 119964.

Abatecola, G., Mari, M., & Poggesi, S. (2020). How can virtuous real estate public–private partnerships be developed? Towards a co-evolutionary perspective. *Cities*, *107*, 102896.

Adinolfi, P. (2021). A journey around decision-making: Searching for the "big picture" across disciplines. *European Management Journal*, *39*(1), 9–21.

Alkhammash, E. H., Jussila, J., Lytras, M. D., & Visvizi, A. (2019). Annotation of smart cities Twitter micro-contents for enhanced citizen's engagement. *IEEE Access*, *7*, 116267–116276.

Anderson, C. (2015). *Creating a data-driven organization: Practical advice from the trenches*. O'Reilly Media, Inc.

Anttiroiko, A. V. (2012). Urban Planning 2.0. *International Journal of E-Planning Research*, *1*(1), 16–30.

Azoulay, P., & Jones, B. (2020). Beat COVID-19 through innovation. *Science*, *368*(6491), 553–553.

Basmi, W., Boulmakoul, A., Karim, L., & Lbath, A. (2021). Distributed and scalable platform architecture for smart cities complex events data collection: Covid19 pandemic use case. *Journal of Ambient Intelligence and Humanized Computing*, *12*(1), 75–83.

Bassano, C., Barile, S., Piciocchi, P., Spohrer, J. C., Iandolo, F., & Fisk, R. (2019). Storytelling about places: Tourism marketing in the digital age. *Cities*, *87*, 10–20.

Bean, R., & Davenport, T. H. (2019). Companies are failing in their efforts to become data-driven. *Harvard Business Review*, Retrieved from https://hbr.org/2019/02/companies-are-failing-in-their-efforts-to-become-datadriven. Accessed on September 13, 2022.

Benson, J. K. (1977). Organizations: A dialectical view. *Administrative Science Quarterly*, *22*, 1–21.

Berner, M., Graupner, E., & Maedche, A. (2014). The information panopticon in the big data era. *Journal of Organization Design*, *3*(1), 14–19.

Bloomberg Cities Network. (2020). How data-driven innovation is fueling cities' COVID response. https://bloombergcities.jhu.edu/news/how-data-driven-innovation-fueling-cities-covid-response

Bragazzi, N. L., Dai, H., Damiani, G., Behzadifar, M., Martini, M., & Wu, J. (2020). How big data and artificial intelligence can help better manage the COVID-19 pandemic. *International Journal of Environmental Research and Public Health*, *17*(9), 3176.

Breidbach, C. F., Brodie, R., & Hollebeek, L. (2014). Beyond virtuality: From engagement platforms to engagement ecosystems. *Managing Service Quality*, *24*(6), 592–611.

Breslin, D. (2008). A review of the evolutionary approach to the study of entrepreneurship. *International Journal of Management Reviews*, *10*(4), 399–423.

Breslin, D. (2011). Reviewing a generalized Darwinist approach to studying socio-economic change. *International Journal of Management Reviews*, *13*(2), 218–235.

Cafferata, R. (2016). Darwinist connections between the systemness of social organizations and their evolution. *Journal of Management & Governance*, *20*(1), 19–44.

Chaffey, D., & Patron, M. (2012). From web analytics to digital marketing optimization: Increasing the commercial value of digital analytics. *Journal of Direct, Data and Digital Marketing Practice*, *14*(1), 30–45.

Chen, J., Chen, Y., Du, X., Li, C., Lu, J., Zhao, S., & Zhou, X. (2013). Big data challenge: A data management perspective. *Frontiers of computer Science*, *7*(2), 157–164.

Chui, K. T., Lytras, M. D., & Visvizi, A. (2018). Energy sustainability in smart cities: Artificial intelligence, smart monitoring, and optimization of energy consumption. *Energies*, *11*(11), 2869.

Ciasullo, M. V., Troisi, O., Grimaldi, M., & Leone, D. (2020). Multi-level governance for sustainable innovation in smart communities: An ecosystems approach. *International Entrepreneurship and Management Journal*, *16*(4), 1167–1195.

da Cruz, N. F., Rode, P., & McQuarrie, M. (2019). New urban governance: A review of current themes and future priorities. *Journal of Urban Affairs*, *41*(1), 1–19.

Davenport, T. H., & Bean, R. (2018). Big companies are embracing analytics, but most still don't have a data-driven culture. *Harvard Business Review*, *6*, 1–4.

Eriksson-Zetterquist, U., Kalling, T., & Styhre, A. (2011). *Organizing technologies*. Copenhagen Business School Press DK.

Fernández-Naranjo, R. P., Vásconez-González, E., Simbaña-Rivera, K., Gómez-Barreno, L., Izquierdo-Condoy, J. S., Cevallos-Robalino, D., & Ortiz-Prado, E. (2021). Statistical data driven approach of COVID-19 in Ecuador: R0 and Rt estimation via new method. *Infectious Disease Modelling*, *6*, 232–243.

Gandomi, A., & Haider, M. (2015). Beyond the hype: Big data concepts, methods, and analysis. *International Journal of Information Management*, *35*(2), 137–44.

Gaventa, J., & McGee, R. (2010). Introduction: Making change happen-citizen action and national policy reform. In J. Gaventa & R. McGee (Eds.), *Citizen action and national policy reform: Making change happen* (pp. 1–43). New York: Zed.

Gavurova, B., Kelemen, M., & Polishchuk, V. (2022). Expert model of risk assessment for the selected components of smart city concept: From safe time to pandemics as COVID-19. *Socio-economic Planning Sciences*, *82*, 101253.

Goldman, E. (2020). Exaggerated risk of transmission of COVID-19 by fomites. *The Lancet Infectious Diseases*, *20*(8), 892–893.

Grandinetti, R. (2018). Is organizational evolution Darwinian and/or Lamarckian? *International Journal of Organizational Analysis*, *26*(5), 858–874.

Gupta, M., & George, J. F. (2016). Toward the development of a big data analytics capability. *Information & Management*, *53*(8), 1049–1064.

Halper, F., & Stodder, D. (2017). What it takes to be data-driven. *TDWI Best Practices Report*, December, 1–40.

Hodgson, G. M., & Knudsen, T. (2010). Generative replication and the evolution of complexity. *Journal of Economic Behavior & Organization*, *75*(1), 12–24.

Iandolo, F., Loia, F., Fulco, I., Nespoli, C., & Caputo, F. (2021). Combining big data and artificial intelligence for managing collective knowledge in unpredictable environment—Insights from the Chinese case in facing COVID-19. *Journal of the Knowledge Economy*, *12*(4), 1982–1996.

James, P., Das, R., Jalosinska, A., & Smith, L. (2020). Smart cities and a data-driven response to COVID-19. *Dialogues in Human Geography*, *10*(2), 255–259.

Kashef, M., Visvizi, A., & Troisi, O. (2021). Smart city as a smart service system: Human–computer interaction and smart city surveillance systems. *Computers in Human Behavior*, *124*, 106923.

Kayabay, K., Gökalp, M. O., Gökalp, E., Eren, P. E., & Koçyiğit, A. (2022). Data science roadmapping: An architectural framework for facilitating transformation towards a data-driven organization. *Technological Forecasting and Social Change*, *174*, 121264.

Kearns, A., & Paddison, R. (2000). New challenges for urban governance. *Urban Studies*, *37*(5–6), 845–850.

Kruschwitz, N., LaValle, S., Lesser, E., Shockley, R., & Hopkins, M. S. (2016). Big data, analytics and the path from insights to value. *MIT Sloan Management Review*, *52*(2), 21–32.

Lalmuanawma, S., Hussain, J., & Chhakchhuak, L. (2020). Applications of machine learning and artificial intelligence for Covid-19 (SARS-CoV-2) pandemic: A review. *Chaos, Solitons & Fractals*, *139*, 110059.

LaValle, S., Lesser, E., Shockley, R., Hopkins, M. S., & Kruschwitz, N. (2011). Big data, analytics and the path from insights to value. *MIT Sloan Management Review*, *52*(2), 21–32.

Lewin, A. Y., & Volberda, H. W. (1999). Prolegomena on coevolution: A framework for research on strategy and new organizational forms. *Organization Science*, *10*(5), 519–534.

Lytras, M., Visvizi, A., Zhang, X., & Aljohani, N. R. (2020c). Cognitive computing, big data analytics and data driven industrial marketing. *Industrial Marketing Management*, *90*, 663–666.

Lytras, M. D., & Visvizi, A. (2018). Who uses smart city services and what to make of it: Toward interdisciplinary smart cities research. *Sustainability*, *10*(6), 1998.

Lytras, M. D., & Visvizi, A. (2019). Big data research for social science and social impact. *Sustainability*, *12*(1), 180.

Lytras, M. D., Visvizi, A., Chopdar, P. K., Sarirete, A., & Alhalabi, W. (2021). Information management in smart cities: Turning end users' views into multi-item scale development, validation, and policy-making recommendations. *International Journal of Information Management*, *56*, 102146.

Lytras, M. D., Visvizi, A., & Jussila, J. (2020). Social media mining for smart cities and smart villages research. *Soft Computing*, *24*(15), 10983–10987.

Lytras, M. D., Visvizi, A., & Sarirete, A. (2019). Clustering smart city services: Perceptions, expectations, responses. *Sustainability*, *11*(6), 1669.

Lytras, M. D., Visvizi, A., Torres-Ruiz, M., Damiani, E., & Jin, P. (2020b). IEEE access special section editorial: Urban computing and well-being in smart cities: Services, applications, policymaking considerations. *IEEE Access*, *8*, 72340–72346.

McAfee, A., Brynjolfsson, E., Davenport, T. H., Patil, D. J., & Barton, D. (2012). Big data: The management revolution. *Harvard Business Review*, *90*(10), 60–68.

McCarthy, I. P., Collard, M., & Johnson, M. (2017). Adaptive organizational resilience: An evolutionary perspective. *Current Opinion in Environmental Sustainability*, *28*, 33–40.

Medina-Borja, A. (2015). Editorial column—Smart things as service providers: A call for convergence of disciplines to build a research agenda for the service systems of the future. *Service Science*, *7*(1), ii–v.

Meijer, A., & Thaens, M. (2018). Urban technological innovation: Developing and testing a sociotechnical framework for studying smart city projects. *Urban Affairs Review*, *54*(2), 363–387.

Nam, T., & Pardo, T. A. (2011, June). Conceptualizing smart city with dimensions of technology, people, and institutions. In *Proceedings of the 12th annual international digital government research conference: Digital government innovation in challenging times*, College Park, MD, June 12–15 (pp. 282–291).

Paniccia, P. M. A., & Leoni, L. (2019). Co-evolution in tourism: The case of Albergo Diffuso. *Current Issues in Tourism*, *22*(10), 1216–1243.

Pereira, I. G., Guerin, J. M., Silva Júnior, A. G., Garcia, G. S., Piscitelli, P., Miani, A., Distante, C., & Gonçalves, L. M. G. (2020). Forecasting Covid-19 dynamics in Brazil: A data driven approach. *International Journal of Environmental Research and Public Health*, *17*(14), 5115.

Petrovic, N. N., Dimovski, V., Peterlin, J., Meško, M., & Roblek, V. (2021). Data-driven solutions in smart cities: The case of Covid-19 Apps. In *Proceeding of the WWW '21: Companion Proceedings of the Web Conference* 2021, Ljubljana, Slovenia, 19–23 April 2021 (pp. 648–656).

Salway, R. J., Silvestri, D., Wei, E. K., & Bouton, M. (2020). Using information technology to improve COVID-19 care at New York City Health+ Hospitals: Commentary describes New York City Health+ Hospitals use of innovative technological solutions to respond to the COVID-19 pandemic. *Health Affairs*, *39*(9), 1601–1604.

Sandhu, S., & Kulik, C. T. (2019). Shaping and being shaped: How organizational structure and managerial discretion co-evolve in new managerial roles. *Administrative Science Quarterly*, *64*(3), 619–658.

Sharifi, A. (2021). The COVID-19 pandemic: Lessons for urban resilience. In I. Linkov, J. M. Keenan, B. D. Trump (Eds.), *COVID-19: Systemic risk and resilience* (pp. 285–297). Cham, Switzerland: Springer.

Sharifi, A., & Khavarian-Garmsir, A. R. (2020). The COVID-19 pandemic: Impacts on cities and major lessons for urban planning, design, and management. *Science of the Total Environment*, *749*, 142391.

Söderström, O., Paasche, T., & Klauser, F. (2020). Smart cities as corporate storytelling. In *The Routledge companion to smart cities* (pp. 283–300). Routledge.

Troisi, O., Ciasullo, M. V., Carrubbo, L., Sarno, D., & Grimaldi, M. (2019). Meta-management for sustainability in territorial ecosystems: The case of Libera's social reuse of territory. *Land Use Policy*, *84*, 138–153.

Troisi, O., D'Arco, M., Loia, F., & Maione, G. (2018). Big data management: The case of Mulino Bianco's engagement platform for value co-creation. *International Journal of Engineering Business Management*, *10*, 1847979018767776.

Troisi, O., Fenza, G., Grimaldi, M., & Loia, F. (2022). Covid-19 sentiments in smart cities: The role of technology anxiety before and during the pandemic. *Computers in Human Behavior*, *126*, 106986.

Troisi, O., Grimaldi, M., & Loia, F. (2021). Redesigning business models for data-driven innovation: A three-layered framework. In A. Visvizi, M. D. Lytras & N. R. Aljohani (Eds.), *The International Research & Innovation Forum* (pp. 421–435). Cham: Springer.

Troisi, O., Kashef, M., & Visvizi, A. (2022). Managing safety and security in the smart city: Covid-19, emergencies and smart surveillance. In A. Visvizi & O. Troisi (Eds.), *Managing smart cities* (pp. 73–88). Cham: Springer.

Troisi, O., Maione, G., Grimaldi, M., & Loia, F. (2020). Growth hacking: Insights on data-driven decision-making from three firms. *Industrial Marketing Management*, *90*, 538–557.

Visvizi, A., & del Hoyo, R. P. (Eds.). (2021). *Smart cities and the UN SDGs*. Elsevier.

Visvizi, A., & Lytras, M. (Eds.). (2019). *Smart cities: Issues and challenges: Mapping political, social and economic risks and threats*. New York, NY: Elsevier-US.

Visvizi, A., & Lytras, M. D. (2018). Rescaling and refocusing smart cities research: From mega cities to smart villages. *Journal of Science and Technology Policy Management*, *9*, 134–145.

Visvizi, A., & Lytras, M. D. (2020). Sustainable smart cities and smart villages research: Rethinking security, safety, well-being, and happiness. *Sustainability*, *12*(1), 215.

Visvizi, A., Lytras, M. D., & Aljohani, N. (2021b). Big data research for politics: Human centric big data research for policy making, politics, governance and democracy. *Journal of Ambient Intelligence and Humanized Computing*, *12*(4), 4303–4304.

Visvizi, A., Lytras, M. D., Damiani, E., & Mathkour, H. (2018). Policy making for smart cities: Innovation and social inclusive economic growth for sustainability. *Journal of Science and Technology Policy Management*, *9*(2), 126–133.

Visvizi, A., Troisi, O., Grimaldi, M., & Loia, F. (2021). Think human, act digital: Activating data-driven orientation in innovative start-ups. *European Journal of Innovation Management*, *25*(6), 452–478.

Wachhaus, A. (2011). Governance as a framework to support informatics. *Innovation Journal*, *16*(1), 1–14.

Weick, K. E. (1969). Social psychology in an era of social change. *American Psychologist*, *24*(11), 990.

World Economic Forum. (2020). Data-driven cities have better responses to COVID-19. Retrieved March 10, 2022, from https://www.weforum.org/press/2020/12/data-driven-cities-have-better-responses-to-covid-19/

Wu, Z., & McGoogan, J. M. (2020). Characteristics of and important lessons from the Coronavirus disease 2019 (COVID-19) outbreak in China: Summary of a report of 72 314 cases from the Chinese Center for Disease Control and Prevention. *JAMA*, *323*(13), 1239–1242.

Wylde, V., Prakash, E., Hewage, C., & Platts, J. (2022). Covid-19 Era: Trust, privacy and security. In R. Montasari, F. Carroll, I. Mitchell, S. Hara, & R. Bolton-King (Eds.), *Privacy, security and forensics in the internet of things (IoT)* (pp. 31–49). Cham: Springer.

Zangari, S., Hill, D. T., Charette, A. T., & Mirowsky, J. E. (2020). Air quality changes in New York City during the COVID-19 pandemic. *Science of the Total Environment*, *742*, 140496.

Zygiaris, S. (2013). Smart city reference model: Assisting planners to conceptualize the building of smart city innovation ecosystems. *Journal of the Knowledge Economy*, *4*(2), 217–231.

Chapter 13

What Does It Take to Build a Smart Sustainable City? – Modeling an Algorithm of Smart Cities[1]

Olena Sokhatska and Ruslana Lutsiv

Abstract

Our world is changing. Cities of the twenty-first century are becoming independent actors on the international scene. Due to the decentralization, gradually cities gain more power to independently identify their policies, strategies and related priorities, as well as ways of their implementation. As a result, several initiatives can be implemented at the city level at a much faster pace and more efficiently than ever before. The United Nations' (UN) "Transforming Our World: The 2030 Agenda for Sustainable Development" focuses on issues related to sustainable development. In relation to cities, it aims to make them "inclusive, safe, resilient and sustainable." This chapter investigates the conceptual foundations of the term smart sustainable cities and summarizes strategies that have been undertaken in cities, as a means of making them smart and sustainable. Against this backdrop, by focusing on Ukraine, an implementation algorithm based on selected examples drawn from Europe is proposed.

Keywords: Smart sustainable cities; information and communication technology; urbanization; innovation; big data

[1]This chapter was written and submitted to the Editors in early February 2022, prior to the Russian invasion in Ukraine.

Big Data and Decision-Making: Applications and Uses in the Public and Private Sector, 203–213

Published under exclusive licence by Emerald Publishing Limited
doi:10.1108/978-1-80382-551-920231013

1. Introduction

The world is changing. Cities of the twenty-first century are becoming independent actors on the international arena. Cities are the world's economic platforms for production, innovation and trade (UN Habitat, 2016). Due to decentralization, cities gradually gain more power to independently identify their policy strategies and priorities, and consequently the ways and means of their attainment. Several initiatives can be implemented at the city level at a much faster pace and more efficiently than ever before. Cities grow at an exponential pace as people are moving into cities in search of a better life. As a result, about 75% of world energy reserves are consumed in cities; cities emit about 80% of CO_2. At the same time, cities create about 80% of the global GDP (UN Habitat, 2016). Studies show that well-planned and managed urbanization can help overcome poverty due to higher levels of productivity, employment opportunities, increased standard of living, etc. (Visvizi & Troisi, 2022). In 1996, at the Istanbul Conference (Habitat II), governments of 171 countries recognized the growing role of cities for the development of humanity. In 2015, the UN "Transforming Our World: The 2030 Agenda for Sustainable Development" (United Nations, 2015) highlighted a series of imperatives necessary for sustainable development. In this context, the need to "make cities and human settlements inclusive, safe, resilient and sustainable" (Goal 11) was stressed (Visvizi & Perez del Hoyo, 2021).

Undoubtedly, cities offer greater opportunities with regard to education, employment, access to services, etc. Nevertheless, cities face several challenges, such as pollution, lack of adequate infrastructure to meet inhabitants' needs, aging of the population in developed countries and high population growth rates in developing countries, etc. (Visvizi & Lytras, 2019). The question is how to make cities more human-centered, sustainable and livable? One of the possible tools is the concept of *smart sustainable city* that began to actively develop in the 1990s. One of the reasons for the development of the concept was wide implementation of information and communication technology (ICT), their availability for a growing number of people as almost 95% of the world's population is already covered by mobile networks and about 50% of the population are using the Internet (ITU, 2017). This chapter investigates the conceptual foundations of the concept of smart sustainable cities and summarizes strategies that have been undertaken in cities, and by default also in villages, as a means of making them smart and sustainable. Against this backdrop, by focusing on Ukraine, an implementation algorithm based on the EU experience is proposed.

2. Smart City: From Technology Test Bed to Smart City 3.0

Several definitions of the concept of smart city exist (Giffinger et al., 2007; Kashef et al., 2021; Kitchin et al., 2015; Lytras & Visvizi, 2021; Yigitcanlar et al., 2020). With the support of initiatives run by such actors as the European Commission, the International Communication Union (ITU), the Organization for Economic

Co-operation and Development (OECD), UN Habitat, as well as through the private sector involvement, that is, Ericsson, Huawei, Microsoft, the concept of smart city has evolved. That is, it has moved from serving as a simple market for testing sophisticated ICT solutions (Visvizi et al., 2017) to the human-centered concept of sustainable cities (Visvizi et al., 2021), frequently referred to as Smart City 3.0. There are many approaches to the definition of the concept and its components, which requires some generalization and systematization. Particular attention needs to be paid to the analysis of existing world experience and opportunities for implementing the concept and related policy-making instruments in the Ukrainian context.

Ukrainian cities, such as Kyiv, Lviv, Kharkiv, Vinnytsia, and Dnipro are actively implementing smart cities projects, as this provides innovative solutions to crucial problems caused by rapid urbanization. "Digital Agenda of Ukraine 2020" states that the concept of "smart city" is a model of the city which uses ICT to provide the following benefits for society and economies: smart metering, eTicket, smart grids/networks, online city services and smart living. In summary, this chapter looks at the key challenges faced by cities in the twenty-first century and proves that development of smart sustainable cities and villages can provide a solution to overcome all challenges posed by the rapid urbanization and sprawled cities.

Smart cities involve the use of ICT to address social, economic, environmental, logical and governmental problems of the city. However, "smart" is not limited to the use of new technologies. According to a study by Nam and Pardo (2011), "smart sustainable cities" require a complex approach. Having analyzed about 120 definitions from various sources, ITU (2016) proposed the following definition of smart city. Smart sustainable city is

> innovative city that uses ICT and other means to improve quality of life, efficiency of urban operation and services, and competitiveness, while ensuring that it meets the needs of present and future generations with respect to economic, social, environmental as well as cultural aspects. (ITU, 2016)

In addition, six primary indicators were identified for analysis: smart lifestyle, smart people, smart environment, smart management, smart mobility and smart economy (ITU, 2016).

Digital Agenda of Ukraine 2020 states that the concept of "smart city" is a model of the city based on a full-scale use of digital technology as a tool to address current problems of the city, its sustainable development and improving the quality of life of citizens (Ministry of Economic Development and Trade of Ukraine, 2016). The main pillars of *Ukraine Digital Agenda* include telecom & ICT infrastructure, digital skills, e-market digital governance, innovations and R&D, trust and cybersecurity society, and benefits from ICT which boosts the economy and the society.

Most researchers in their analysis cover four dimensions. These include: smart people, smart economy, smart environment, the so-called "Triple Criterion Model" (cf. Leydesdorff & Deakin, 2011). Smart management, that is, the fourth dimension, is an inseparable part of the previous dimensions and is necessary for social stability, justice and the citizens involvement, etc. The model of a smart sustainable city (Fig. 13.1) should also include ICT. In brief, it is challenging to provide a universal definition of a smart sustainable city (cf. Bibri & Krogstie, 2017), because it is an entity that has certain inherent characteristics that allow people to make their living and environment better.

Against this backdrop, one may argue that a smart sustainable city must meet the following four criteria:

- it should address the needs of the modern generation;
- it should provide opportunities for the development and growth of the potential inherent in each individual;

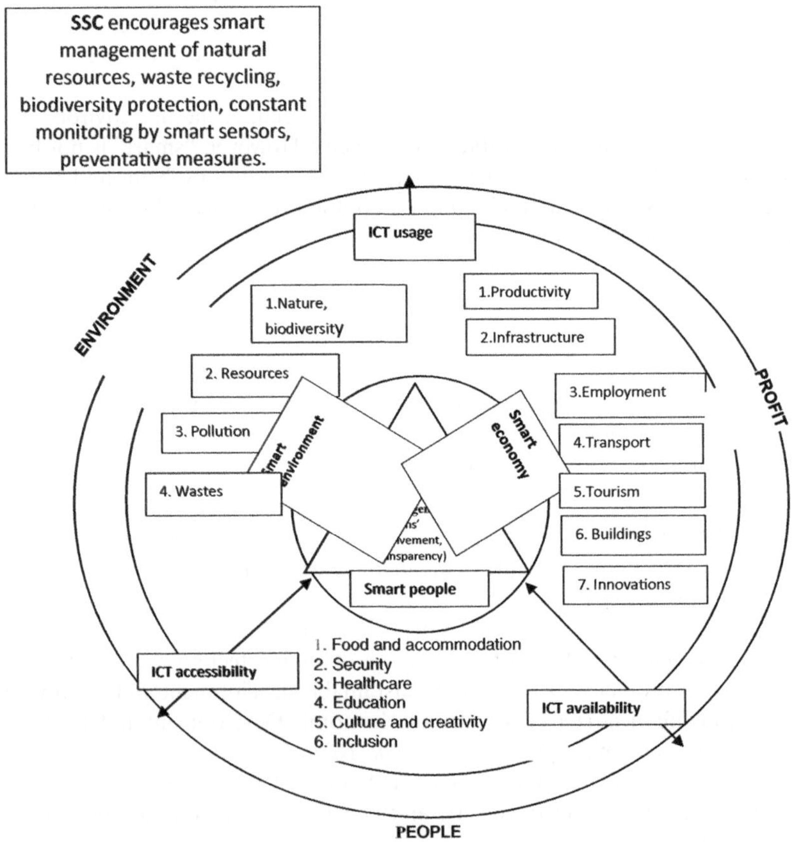

Fig. 13.1. Smart Sustainable City. *Source*: Authors.

- it should not jeopardize the possibilities of the future generations to meet their needs; and
- it should do so in a "smart way," that is, using first of all, ICT and other reasonable means, that is, means that are safe and do not violate the obvious environmental constraints of local and global scales.

3. Smart Cities Worldwide

According to various sources, there are about 88 smart cities and 250 smart projects which are being implemented in various cities around the world. Since 2017 the number of cities that have adopted official comprehensive concepts development of "Smart Cities" instead of simple implementation of smart solutions in certain sectors has significantly increased. In particular, the following ones should be mentioned: Smart City of London (official strategy v.1.0 was adopted in 2013), Smart City of Vienna (2014), the Smart City Stockholm (2017), Smart City Amsterdam (2009), built from scratch Songdo in Korea and Masdar (UAE), etc. (Lutsiv, 2020).

Data and networks are one of the tools of smart cities to address pressing urban problems. Fig. 13.2 shows ways of their applications worldwide.

The improvement of administrative services can be obtained through the transfer from offline to online, by giving citizens the opportunity to control online budgeting, as well as to influence the quality of services through feedback.

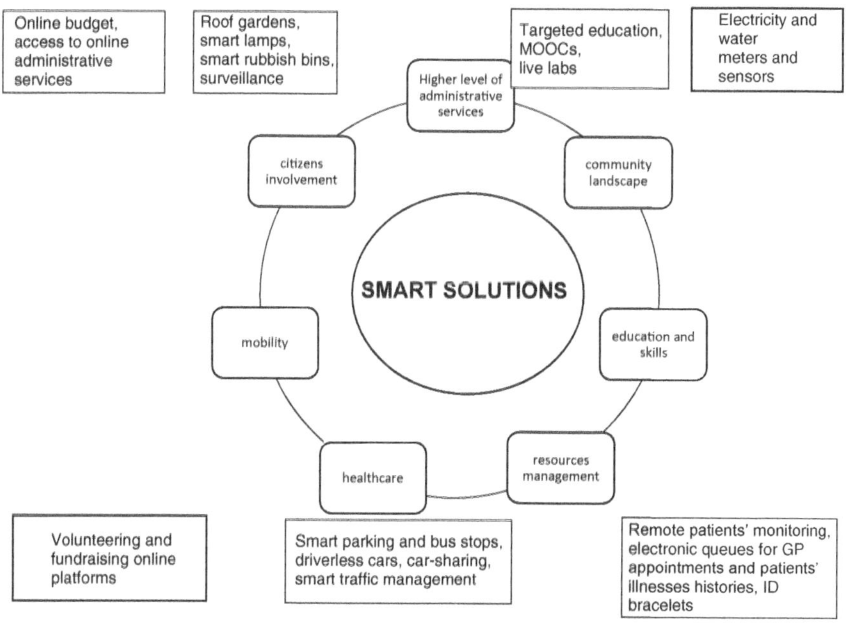

Fig. 13.2. Applications of Smart Solutions Worldwide. *Source*: Authors.

Public space can be based on the usage of open data from the public which can significantly improve the urban planning: equipment of schools, parks, shops, etc. This component also includes the creation of green gases in cities, WIFI access, smart lights that are controlled remotely, etc. Stockholm uses solar panel tanks which notify the achievement of the maximum coverage level. Greening projects have been implemented in Vienna and Stockholm. Training activities are about the enhancement of skills and the involvement of as many people as possible to study, including people with disabilities, lacking education and those who require retraining. Adaptive learning materials have been developed in Stockholm. They track reading problems in children using methods of artificial intelligence. Most universities offer mass online courses for anyone who has a computer and internet access. London has programs to increase digital competences of Londoners (cf. Zait, 2017).

The involvement of citizens is encouraged worldwide in smart cities through crowdfunding platforms, participatory budgets to obtain fundings for the most important public projects, online volunteer platforms (Speed Volunteering London), various hackathons (Climathon London) and competitions. For instance, Stockholm (*Make a suggestion* app) and Vienna (*Sag's Wien* app) launched publicly available applications designed to enable the citizens to make suggestions on how to improve the city.

As for mobility, the most common practices implemented in smart cities are data collection and analysis from drivers, for smart traffic management, and the use of special applications to track areas in need of roadworks. Moreover, cities worldwide are pushing toward the increase of the share of non-motorized transport. Resource management involves the collection of formations on the level of consumption by sensors that can also track resource losses in the event of infrastructure damage. It also comprises circular economy development and generation of more energy from non-traditional sources. In the field of smart health care, smart cities are starting projects to collect data and use ICT for the treatment of patients remotely, monitoring health indicators, the development of the e-health system for electronic accounting, etc.

4. Implementation Smart Cities Projects in Ukraine: The Cases of Kyiv and Kharkiv

Ukrainian cities are also broadly implementing smart cities projects because the prerequisites and the need for innovative solutions are crucial as well. Advanced cities to implement smart projects are Kyiv, Lviv, Kharkiv, Vinnytsia and Dnipro. The Kyiv Smart City Concept and Vision is designed to create opportunities for the growth of the Ukrainian capital by combining a strategic approach, technological advances and wide public engagement in the creation of a new quality of life. The Kyiv Smart City Concept lays the foundation for further infrastructural, technological and social development of the city and defines a new trajectory in the transformation of its urban space in accordance with the standards of the future. Kyiv Smart City Concept takes into account the interests of all residents, businesses and non-profit organizations and defines new roles and functions of city governance (Polese et al., 2021). The implementation of Kyiv Smart City Concept and its strategic objectives will contribute to the transformation of the Ukrainian capital into a technologically advanced, comfortable and socially responsible metropolis of Eastern Europe.

The Kyiv Smart City Concept envisages the development of the city in the following key areas:

- improving the quality of life for residents;
- upgrading the physical and developing the technological infrastructure of the city;
- using technologies for effective management of the city;
- assuring compliance with standards for environmental protection, sustainable economic development and social inclusion; and
- engaging the people (International Renaissance Foundation, 2020).

A number of services have already been created to improve the life of their residents: online maps of emergency works, electronic petitions, an application for assessing the motorways quality Navizor, a platform for providing online administrative services iGov, open budget and participatory budget, electronic queues to kindergartens and hospitals, etc. (Pozdniakova, 2017).

In addition, cities are launching pilot projects on the creation of closed areas for testing smart solutions, in particular smart streets, for example, the Melnikova Street in Kyiv. This is a platform for communication between the public, the authorities and technology developers. Another project "UNIT. City" (Kyiv) aims to create an innovative town within another city.

Kharkiv, the second largest city in Ukraine, has been the major scientific and technological hub of the country for decades. Today, the city is leveraging its technological talent to assert itself at the forefront of the movement to make Ukrainian cities more tech-savvy. Digital technologies were implemented for the first time in the city's management back in 1997. A year later, in 1998, inspired by the example of the French city of Lille, *City Information Centre of Kharkiv City Council,* started improving Kharkiv's connectivity by linking all the city services into a single system via the web. All the smart city projects developed in *Kharkiv* up to 90% were financed thanks to the reinvestment of funds earned by the utility.

As part of the data digitization project, information on municipal property, including the value of each of its objects, as well as the Information System of City Planning Cadaster has been made publicly accessible online. The approach helps increase the transparency and accountability of the city government. To enhance the dialog between the urban authorities and the city community, a monitoring service dubbed "1562" was launched in 2007. Since then, residents have been able to register any complaints or make suggestions with the city council via phone or email. To boost citizens engagement, a local IT company, *Artjoker*, upon the request of the city managers, has designed a mobile app dubbed "An Active Kharkiv Citizen." Kharkiv residents can send petitions, vote and provide feedback on any aspect of city life via the app. As part of the "Safe City" project (2016–2020), the main sightseeing attractions are equipped with a video surveillance system. Documented violations will be reported to law-enforcement authorities. Several schools throughout the city are equipped with such systems.

Connectivity is considered as one of the underpinning characteristics of a smart city (Troisi et al., 2021). To ensure consistent connectivity, a cloud service offered by local player *OnAir* has been introduced as the basis for a range of other services. Transforming Kharkiv into a smart city will involve optimizing internal city management processes. A number of companies located in Kharkiv harness their technological expertise to make city life better not only in Ukraine but also in abroad. *CodeIT*, a Kharkiv-based software development company with clients worldwide (32% of them come from North America), has developed two applications for Swiss municipalities. The first one is a local Swiss platform that helps municipalities to organize efficient disposal. Through the application, local municipalities solve the problem of how to effectively inform citizens about the upcoming recycling of various materials. The app also reminds users about the schedule of the next disposals via push notifications. Moreover, municipalities can send users custom messages, for example, local news bulletins. Launched and operating successfully in one of the Swiss municipalities, the platform has rapidly expanded to three other cities. The second one is called *Grippe*. It provides its users with the ability to check their health by undergoing an online test. It also allows users to manage a centralized "health calendar."

Another local company, *Itomych Studio* has designed a similar app to track public transport for a client from Delaware, USA. Dubbed "UD Shuttle," the app is available on App Store and Google Play for free. In cooperation with talented local developers, Kharkiv authorities are determined to help the city perform even better in future and become the next smart city.

5. Modeling The Smart City Algorithm

Based on the experience of several European cities, the following algorithm of construction of the model of smart cities in Ukraine can be offered (Fig. 13.3). The main idea is to involve all stakeholders in its development: municipalities, the business sector, academia and the public. The first stage envisages vision formation, strategy development and platform creation in each city. The next stage is the synchronization on the national level through a common platform to share experiences and communication.

6. Conclusions

The concept of smart sustainable cities and positive international experience of its implementation are of great interest to Ukraine. Several cities have already

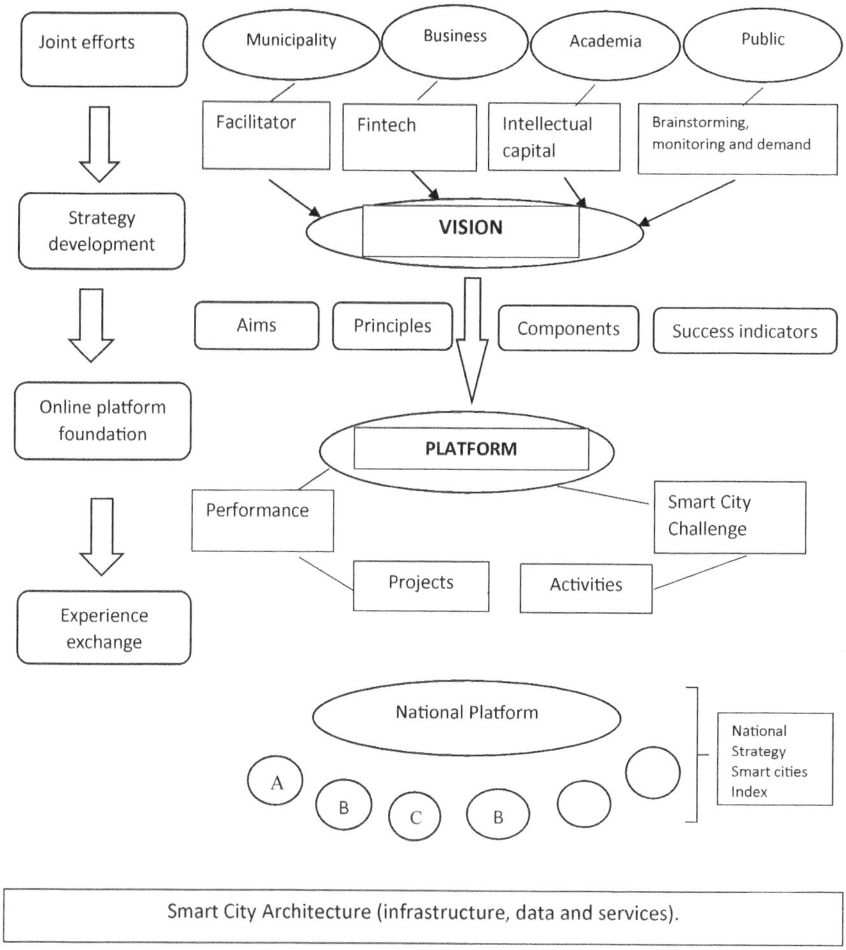

Fig. 13.3. Algorithm for Building a Model of Smart Cities in Ukraine. *Source*: Authors.

begun to actively implement certain elements of the concept (Kyiv, Lviv, Dnipro, Kharkiv, etc.), but the process is contingent due to the following issues:

- overall low level of digitalization of the society. Only 48.8% of the population use the Internet, most people in rural areas do not have access to the Internet and the necessary skills. According to the ICT Development Index, Ukraine ranks 79th place out of 176, with a score of 5.31 on the scale of 10 (ITU, 2017);
- lack of a holistic approach on the national and city levels. Smart City Strategy was adopted in Kyiv (2017), some other cities (Lviv, Dnipro and Kharkiv) have digitalization strategies for their cities, or isolated initiatives to implement smart decisions;

- lack of necessary skills and qualified staff at the management level; and
- lack of financial resources and research of the world's best practices.

At the same time, Ukrainian cities have a number of positive factors that, if successfully used, will make our cities more livable and smarter: (1) availability of creative class of volunteers; (2) great number of highly qualified IT specialists; (3) a high level of computer literacy among the population; (4) a society that seeks and is ready for change; and (5) generated demand for smart and more user-friendly cities.

To build the concept of Smart Sustainable Cities Ukraine needs a comprehensive approach that will include (1) state support for regional initiatives aimed at overcoming the "digital gap"; (2) measures to increase quality of services provided in the ICT sector, their compliance with national standards, which, in their turn, are in line with international standards; (3) conducting information campaigns in order to ensure public awareness about the available opportunities; (4) encouraging effective exchange of information and experience at national (between regions) and international levels through joint platforms, round tables, etc.; and (5) common vision and strategy at a national level, as well as in line with development of strategies at the local level.

References

Bibri, S. E., & Krogstie, J. (2017). Smart sustainable cities of the future: An extensive interdisciplinary literature review. *Sustainable Cities and Society*, *31*, 183–212. https://doi.org/10.1016/j.scs.2017.02.016

Giffinger, R., Fertner, C., Kramar, H., & Meijers, E. (2007). *Smart cities ranking of European medium-sized cities* (p. 11). Centre of Regional Science.

International Renaissance Foundation. (2020). Kyiv smart city concept. https://www.slideshare.net/KyivSmartCIty/kyiv-smart-city-concept

ITU. (2016). Shaping smarter and more sustainable cities. https://www.itu.int/wftp3/pub/epub_shared/TSB/ITUT-Tech-Report-Specs/2016/en/flipviewerxpress.html

ITU. (2017). Measuring the information society. https://www.itu.int/en/ITU-D/Statistics/Pages/publications/mis2017.aspx

Kashef, M., Visvizi, A., & Troisi, O. (2021, November). Smart city as a smart service system: Human–computer interaction and smart city surveillance systems. *Computers in Human Behavior*, *124*, 106923. https://doi.org/10.1016/j.chb.2021.106923

Kitchin, R., Lauriault, T. P., & McArdle, G. (2015). Knowing and governing cities through urban indicators, city benchmarking and real-time dashboards. *Regional Studies, Regional Science*, *2*(1), 6–28. https://doi.org/10.1080/21681376.2014.983149

Leydesdorff, L., & Deakin, M. (2011). The triple-helix model of smart cities: A neo-evolutionary perspective. *Journal of Urban Technology*, *18*(2), 53–63. https://doi.org/10.1080/10630732.2011.601111

Lutsiv, R. (2020). Smart cities: Economic dimensions of their evolution. *The Herald of Ternopil National Economic University*, *2*, 50–61. https://doi.org/10.35774/visnyk2020.01.050

Lytras, M. D., & Visvizi, A. (2021). Information management as a dual-purpose process in the smart city: Collecting, managing and utilizing information. *International Journal of Information Management*, *56*, 102224. https://doi.org/10.1016/j.ijinfomgt.2020.102224

Ministry of Economic Development and Trade of Ukraine. (2016). Digital Agenda of Ukraine – 2020. https://ucci.org.ua/uploads/files/58e78ee3c3922.pdf

Nam, T., & Pardo, T. A. (2011). Conceptualizing smart city with dimensions of technology, people, and institutions. https://inta-aivn.org/images/cc/Urbanism/background%20documents/dgo_2011_smartcity.pdf

Polese, F., Troisi, O., Grimaldi, M., & Loia, F. (2021). Reinterpreting governance in smart cities: An ecosystem-based view. In A. Visvizi & R. Perez del Hoyo (Eds.), *Smart cities and the UN SDGs* (pp. 71–89). Elsevier.

Pozdniakova, A. (2017). Digitalization process in Ukraine as a prerequisite for the smart city concept development. *Baltic Journal of Economic Studies*, *3*(4), 206–215. http://www.baltijapublishing.lv/index.php/issue/article/view/236/pdf

Troisi, O., Visvizi, A., & Grimaldi, M. (2021). The different shades of innovation emergence in smart service systems: The case of Italian cluster for aerospace technology. *Journal of Business & Industrial Marketing*. https://doi.org/10.1108/JBIM-02-2020-0091

UN Habitat. (2016). World cities report. http://wcr.unhabitat.org/

United Nations. (2015). Transforming our world: The 2030 Agenda for Sustainable Development. https://sdgs.un.org/publications/transforming-our-world-2030-agenda-sustainable-development-17981

Visvizi, A., & Lytras, M. D. (Eds.). (2019). *Smart cities: Issues and challenges: Mapping political, social and economic risks and threats*. Elsevier. ISBN: 9780128166390. https://www.elsevier.com/books/smart-cities-issues-and-challenges/lytras/978-0-12-816639-0

Visvizi, A., Mazzucelli, C. G., & Lytras, M. (2017). Irregular migratory flows: Towards an ICTs' enabled integrated framework for resilient urban systems. *Journal of Science and Technology Policy Management*, *8*(2), 227–242. https://doi.org/10.1108/JSTPM-05-2017-0020

Visvizi, A., & Perez del Hoyo, R. (Eds.). (2021). *Smart cities and the UN SDGs*. Elsevier. ISBN: 9780323851510. https://www.elsevier.com/books/smart-cities-and-the-un-sdgs/visvizi/978-0-323-85151-0

Visvizi, A., & Troisi, O. (Eds.). (2022). *Managing smart cities: Sustainability and resilience through effective management*. Springer. ISBN: 9783030935849.

Visvizi, A., Troisi, O., Grimaldi, M., & Loia, F. (2021). Think human, act digital: Activating data-driven orientation in innovative start-ups. *European Journal of Innovation Management*, *25*(6), 452–478.

Yigitcanlar, T., Kankanamge, N., & Vella, K. J. (2020). How are smart city concepts and technologies perceived and utilized? A systematic geo-twitter analysis of smart cities in Australia. *Journal of Urban Technology*, *28*, 135–154.

Zait, A. (2017). Exploring the role of civilizational competences for smart cities' development. *Transforming Government: People, Process and Policy*, *11*(3), 377–392. https://doi.org/10.1108/TG-07-2016-0044

Index